HOW'S YOUR DAD?

LIVING IN THE SHADOW OF A ROCK STAR PARENT

HOW'S YOUR DAD?

LIVING IN THE SHADOW OF A ROCK STAR PARENT

ZOË STREET HOWE

OMNIBUS PRESS

LONDON / NEW YORK / PARIS / SYDNEY / COPENHAGEN / BERLIN / MADRID / TOKYO

Contents

For Dylan

Acknowledgements

I'd like to send my heartfelt appreciation and love to everyone who contributed, encouraged, assisted, enabled and bravely bared their soul for this project. I hope it serves to shine a light on what's important and raises a few smiles in the process.

Special love in particular to Dylan Howe, my wonderful husband, the man who accidentally inspired the whole project and became the perfect advisor for it – I hope you like the result.

For contributing wit, wisdom, memories and insights: Charlie Harris, Cosmo Landesman, Aaron Horn, Baxter Dury, Calico Cooper, Pete Townshend, Callum Adamson, Celeste Bell, Christian Davies, Dylan Howe, Georgia Howe, Trev Lukather, Crosby Loggins, Eliza Carthy, Galen Ayers, Jack Gahan, Jazz Domino Holly, Julian Lennon, Lovella Ellis, Maria Gallagher, Natasha Eleanore, Keeley Bolger, Will Hunt, Zoë Clews, Harry Waters, Harleymoon Kemp, Chris Welch, Elizabeth Curran.

For linking me up (or at least trying to), coming up with ideas and generally being eggs of the good variety: the fabulous Street family and the marvellous Howe family; Jacqui Black, Charles R Cross, Steven Rosen, Steve Lukather, Gavin Martin and John Robb for encouragement, and giving me a platform to preview this book in its embryonic state at Talking Musical Revolutions 3, Ken Hunt, Johnny Sharp, Joel McIver and all on the NBT forum who shared their thoughts, Harriet at Glass

Ceiling PR, Dave Clarke at Planet Earth Publicity, Zoë Stainsby and Andrew Soar at Idea Generation, The Beatles Story (White Feather launch), Trish De Rosa at Roots Rockers, J. Thompson, Erika Thomas, Alice Harter, the perfervid Griff Mellhuish, Nigel Price, Tim Cooper, Nicola Joss, Scott Steele, Sarah Gillespie, Craig at Hootananny, Wilko Johnson, Tessa Pollitt, Damian Rafferty, Vincent Hazard, the Quietus … basically everyone who has taken an interest and helped where they can.

I'd also like to thank my very hard-working laptop for its faithful round the clock service on this intensive project. I have completely flat thighs and fingertips now, but it's worth it.

Appreciation to those who chose not to be interviewed but still took the time and courtesy to respond and let me know.

And of course, Chris Charlesworth and Omnibus Press for taking on this project with such enthusiasm.

Last but absolutely not least, thank you for picking up this book – I hope you enjoy it. (You *are* going to buy it, aren't you? Just checking.)

Introduction

Rock star kids, A-list offspring, celebrity brats – they've got it easy. Effortlessly turning their unblemished hands to whatever artistic pursuit they desire, cushioned from the hardships and realities of everyday life, and gorgeous, obviously, thanks to the fact that Rock Star Dad hooked up with a doe-eyed model (or Rock Star Mum had to look like a model to even make it to be a Rock Star Mum).

If the above paragraph sums up your general feeling about the children of famous musicians, then this book is here to prove you wrong in some cases, right in others and encourage you to at least try to view the likes of Stella, Jack and Pixie with a bit of compassion and understanding rather than writing them off as a bunch of spoilt wasters. While some of the children of our heroes might indeed be sunning themselves in reflected glory as they attempt once more to get into Boujis without having to pulling the old 'Don't you know who I am?' trick, there are many more still who do quite the opposite, striking out on their own and, get this, paying their own way.

Whether struggling to escape or basking in the shadow of a famous parent, the situation of a rock 'n' roll heir or heiress can be uniquely complex, and sometimes troublesome. (There is a book to be written about the parents of celebrities too of course – at the time of writing I happened to notice on Twitter that the ever PR-savvy Mitch Winehouse, Amy Winehouse's taxi driver dad for the few of you who have up to now been blissfully unaware, is 'finishing my album in January, number one priority'. Oh right. Well, I did think he was dragging his heels a bit.)

One of the issues with being the child of any well-known figure is the fact that whatever you do is automatically upstaged by the fact that your parent merely exists. They might not even be there, but a healthy percentage of people, say, at your own gig will be there just to corner you at the end to say, 'How's your dad?' in a slightly over-familiar way. (And the reason I am using 'dad' instead of 'mum' is that, if you'll forgive my generalising, this does seem to be a predominantly male thing – fans of male stars are keen to be matey with their idols and their families, proving that they know a bit about them. Fans of female stars tend to take a different approach and, apart from this, if a female celebrity becomes a mother, this often pulls them out of the public eye anyway.)

Indeed, the very question – 'How's your dad?' – provided the inspiration for this book: I have heard it posed by well-meaning fans to my husband, Dylan Howe, at his own gigs. These fans would not be Dylan's, specifically, but those of his father, Steve Howe, the virtuoso guitar hero from prog rock titans Yes.

There's a sense that, if the diehard fan's approach is anything to go by, they do in some way own a bit of your parent, they certainly feel their relationship with them predates yours, and whether it's an attempt to make you like them or subconsciously remind you of your place and that you'll never escape that legacy, not even at your own gig, wording one's opening gambit in this way doesn't always go down well.

No matter if your parent was a Stock, Aitken and Waterman pop confection and you are making your mark in the world of free jazz, after your blistering gig, the highlight of your career so far, you will see a group of people coming towards you. 'That's strange,' you'll say to yourself. 'They don't look like your average beatniks... Hang on, is that a Rick Astley T-shirt?' Your adoring audience is not your adoring audience at all. It's your parent's adoring audience. But this book is, among other things, an important opportunity to shine a light on what many of these figures are doing in their own individual rights, with respect earned as a result of their own gifts and hard work.

My intention is not just to provide an A-Z of every single famous musician's child in the entire world ever (that would be impossible; there are new ones popping up all the time anyway, and not just those fathered by Rod Stewart or Mick Jagger). It is more a study of a phenomenon, an attitude we have towards the children of rock stars, an opportunity to look at the preconceptions we have and why.

We'll be hearing their stories, which range from the amusing to the lurid to the eye-crossingly weird; we'll learn about their individual journeys, how they developed because of or despite their upbringing; their reflections on their birthright, their plans and hopes. It also doesn't matter whether these children continued in the family business or not; I am as interested in those that didn't as much as those that did. (The assumption that the child of a musician must surely be musical too is "so boring", Steve Howe's daughter Georgia tells me. "People always ask, 'What do *you* play?' But it's fair enough, I suppose.")

Spoken to and discussed within these pages are also the children of Joe Strummer, Poly Styrene, Ian Dury, Alice Cooper, Trevor Horn and Jill Sinclair, Jack Bruce, Jimmy Page, John Phillips, John Lennon, Alton Ellis, Quincy Jones, Martin Kemp, Dave Gahan, the Geldofs, Woods, Osbournes, Starkeys, Zappas, Wainwright/McGarrigle, Buckley, Waterson/Carthy, Jackson, Gainsbourg, Cash and Presley. All have their unique standpoint, all are connected in some ways, disparate in others. To paraphrase John Peel's description of The Fall, they are different and yet in many ways the same. There is definitely a thread running through every example. Sometimes it's a smooth, golden cord, sometimes it's tough like wire, or rough and frayed, chafing your fingers if you don't handle it with delicacy. But it's basically the same thread.

We are naturally interested in the children of our heroes, but while society may more readily accept the notion of an acting dynasty, often viewing a distinguished theatrical bloodline as a guarantee of quality, to a seemingly greater extent the rock royal will, no matter what they do or don't do, have every move scrutinised and judged with gluttonous enthusiasm by tabloid readers, gossip lovers and even contemporaries with varying levels of resentment. As Bob Geldof once observed: "Their mums and dads were famous people in a country where rock 'n' roll is the Hollywood. Britain doesn't have a Hollywood. So the glamour is in rock, rock stars are all over the tabloids, and those kids were born into that sort of atmosphere."

How many times have *Sun* readers gone online, become irresistibly drawn to a picture story – maybe of Kelly Osbourne, Nicole Richie or Peaches Geldof doing something exciting like talking on the phone or getting into a car – and commented thus: 'What a nobody! / wannabe! / spoilt brat! She'd be nowhere if it wasn't for (fill in blank with famous parent name).' This is irrespective of what the story might (not) be about. Maybe there really is nothing of interest about these well-groomed characters. So why click on the story?

What is of greater concern is that this bilious attitude spills over and affects those of a similar parentage who couldn't be more different from their tabloid darling contemporaries. In the main, people see the most immediately media-friendly examples, make their minds up (with a bit of help from the press) and that creates the blueprint for how they perceive all children of celebrated musicians across the board.

So are these preconceptions fair? Not always. Are they just lazy, resentful assumptions? Not always. But where sometimes being a second-generation rock aristo is fabulously beneficial – great schools, guaranteed popularity (when there's a gig coming up) and an intriguing menu when you come home for tea – you also might be well versed in the ways of touring or being in a studio because that's just how you grew up. Or you may be so used to seeing Pop smoke a doobie that drugs aren't too glamorous as far as you're concerned (or you have fantastic access to drugs, and again are, therefore, hugely popular). But there are other elements that create the sort of barriers that those of us from more conventional backgrounds never need consider.

The word 'nepotism' hangs like a cloud over every rock offspring, even if their chosen path is a million miles from mum or dad's career. The mythical and never-ending list of contacts that said child supposedly inherits isn't always the door-opening influence outsiders like to imagine it is. And the public's knowledge or idolatry of Rock Star Parent can overshadow a career to the extent that some people might just attend your gigs or buy your work because you are seen as a kind of rock 'n' roll souvenir (we're back to the 'How's your dad?' factor): these punters are more interested in the association with their real hero, and this might be the closest they get. They love Ronnie Wood, say, and as far as they're concerned, you're just another Wood to collect, another step closer to the REAL star. Jeff Buckley might have eclipsed his father, Tim's, success, but he still had plenty of people turning up at shows just to ask questions about Buckley senior, a man he never really knew and rarely wanted to discuss.

Of course, there *are* those who happily accept, as they whizz up the freeloading freeway, that the only reason they are famous or outwardly interesting is because of their connections, they are cool by association and are doing rather well out of it – whether simply getting stoned and watching Miss Marples all day, knowing that funny thing called rent (something to do with Monopoly?) is magically taken care of, or breezing into exclusive parties and TV work without ruffling an eyebrow. But how long can this last? What is the public's view of this? Should it even matter?

Peaches Geldof has, to date, been granted her own column, a TV show and the post of editor at a trendy magazine. Capability and personality aside, why wouldn't she snap these offers up when they're dangled in front of her face? The fact is these opportunities can come at a price – the givers are crossing their fingers that you make a blithering berk of yourself. They will then beam your monstrous clangers and tantrums (after some nifty editing) out on prime-time TV. We pillory the likes of Peaches for her ill-advised musings and posy soundbites, but who didn't sound stupid and pretentious when they were a teenager? The difference is, we of the non-famous variety were allowed to grow out of it without having everything we did recorded and exposed. (There was also less opportunity to come out with any pretentious insights because no one was shoving a microphone in front of us and making us believe our opinion was interesting or valid anyway.)

Whenever I told anyone I was writing this book, the first question they would ask invariably included the words 'Peaches Geldof'. Peaches wasn't the first person I thought of when I started working on this, but I do think the way we view people like her affects how we make snap judgements about others – they must be rich, it must be easy, they must be brattish and unapproachable, they're living off their parents. So yes, she is an important example, but there is a lot more to this subject, and the raison d'etre of the project is to try to add a bit of perspective to how we view it. It might even alter your perception of the 'rock stars' themselves. In some cases it might confirm what you already thought, of course…

Many of the interviewees and figures featured in this book don't get showered with TV shows, columns and the like – those are quite extreme cases. But most were brought up on the road, and some would experience the 'rock 'n' roll lifestyle' at first hand from an early age (Charlotte Gainsbourg was taken to nightclubs by Serge and her mother, Jane Birkin, as a baby in a basket, for example). Others had a determinedly down to earth upbringing, normal schools (perhaps with a flashy car picking them up at the gates), normal friends and encouragement to do their own thing, protected from the limelight. Some go down the same career path as their mum or dad and make a success of it in their own right. Although we won't pretend that the surname (Starkey, Bonham, Wakeman…) didn't help draw a little attention to them.

Happier examples contrast painfully with those whose unconventional childhoods caused them to go off the rails, or fight to escape a destructive relationship. What must it be like to be forever associated with someone who, in some cases, took away your childhood or has no real emotional connection with you? There are, of course, plenty of wonderful parents within these pages too, and while I have no wish to taint our perceptions of certain 'stars', I do believe many of us view celebrities in an often unrealistic way: we like to think Ian Dury or John Lennon were 'likeable' because their work excites us, we love what they stand for; if we identify with their music or concepts, it jars if we can't identify with them as people. But this book's intention is rather to take what is relevant in their characters, behaviour and legacies and look at how those things affected their children, positively or negatively.

This is an attempt to bring balance and fairness to this subject, with affection and humour, but also honesty. If nothing else, I hope it will break some of our conditioning and encourage us to look beyond the stigma and appreciate that the situation is not always as simplistic as it looks…

CHAPTER 1

The N-word

"There's nothing wrong with inherited wealth, if you melt the silver yourself..."

(The Upper Classes – The Auteurs)

If the average person, should there be such a thing, played a word association game commencing with the phrase 'rock star offspring', it wouldn't take long for the word 'nepotism' to come up. So what exactly does it mean? We should start our journey by looking this beast right in its N-shaped face if we're going to mutter it whenever we see a greater-spotted Geldof. We talk about it enough, particularly in this age in which rock 'royalty' seems to have replaced real royalty. Once, decorative aristocrats were ubiquitous in glossies like *Tatler* and *Hello!*, doing the Highland Fling with ruddy-cheeked young shavers. Now we're more likely to see pictures of Coco (Sumner) and Theodora (Richards) stalking up a red carpet or hanging out with society's elite.

They're not so different from each other when it comes down to it. Both examples are there, first and foremost, because of an inherited cachet, and this is what causes the rest of us to cry 'nepotism' when we see another opportunity seemingly being flung their way. But media saturation is such that even the more broad-minded among us can project these judgements onto those who don't always deserve it.

We should start by looking up the very word that brings most rock heirs out in hives, or at least a familiar sense of dread. I tapped it into my computer's dictionary and thesaurus, and this is what came up.

nepotism |,nep 'tiz m|
noun
the practice among those with power or influence of favoring relatives or friends, esp. by giving them jobs.
DERIVATIVES
nepotist noun
nepotistic |,nep 'tistik| adjective
ORIGIN mid 17th cent.: from French **népotisme**, from Italian **nepotismo**, from **nipote 'nephew'** (with reference to privileges bestowed on the "nephews" of popes, who were in many cases their illegitimate sons).

nepotism
noun
hiring my daughter was not nepotism—it was just good business favoritism, preferential treatment, the old boy network, looking after one's own, bias, partiality, partisanship. antonym impartiality.

As Steve Howe's son Dylan is the inspiration for this book, I shall hand over to him first for his take on the concept in how it, and assumptions of it, affect him: "If there's a family business and there are people in your orbit, you might hire them on trust and hopefully affection as well. (Producer) Trevor Horn would not have so readily known me as a drummer from an early age if I hadn't met him in a social situation through my dad. If you take that as a template people will think, 'He's going to be calling you all the time! You're going to be rich, doing sessions for him all the time.' No. He's always been very supportive, but I think he's really only called me for sessions a couple of times in the past 20 years. He recommends me for projects sometimes, and now maybe I'm good enough to be called by him, but there are other people out there.

"There's a small pool of the A-list players but how does everyone hear about them? It's word of mouth, it's association, it's somebody going, 'I know someone…' Not dissimilar to having a well-connected father in the furniture business or whatever. But even after you've been recommended, you have to be able to cut it. This made me work twice as hard to be twice as good."

Familial partiality is obviously everywhere, in every field, but in this case, whatever happens is to varying extents public fodder, and perceptions of it spread to the point that we assume every child of an iconic figure has got it made. Quincy Jones' rapper son QD3 (Quincy Delight Jones III) grew up in public housing in Sweden with his drug-addicted mother. Meanwhile his half sister Rashida grew up in luxury in Los Angeles with her father, who taught her how to orchestrate and arrange. The gulf between siblings was considerable, but when QD3 moved to LA himself as a young man, he was immediately presumed to be a super-brat, which couldn't have been further from the truth.

"Having grown up in Sweden where not a lot of weight is placed on famous or wealthy people, I always looked at (Dad) as a human being, not his persona," he said. "I don't think I really 'got it' until I was much older. It was harder to deal with the 'kid of a famous person/silver spoon' projections I got hit with once I moved to the US. It was a strange transition."

An entry on Wikipedia explains 'nepotism' as a favouritism granted 'without regard to merit'. It goes on to reference *The Kevin Bishop Show*, a satirical sketch show that spoofed Peaches Geldof in a mock perfume advert: 'Nepotism – the smell of Peaches Geldof', after a voiceover from 'Peaches' proclaimed: "I'm a fashion model, a TV presenter, and I'm a journalist as well… did I mention my dad's Bob Geldof?"

In 2008 Peaches became the editor of a magazine, the perhaps inauspiciously titled *Disappear Here*, and was filmed by MTV strutting about in chic clothes and being bossy to a collection of fresh-faced, trendy-haired writers who spent most of the time quivering, glancing nervously at each other, and occasionally crying. The whole shebang was produced by Ten Alps, a company owned by Bob Geldof, who had the final say in what was eventually broadcast. Although the amount of good that did Peaches was negligible – MTV content director Heather Jones openly called Peaches a "monster. Everything that comes out of her mouth is horrendous, and that will still show through." They said it…

The pervading feeling while watching this programme was that we were seeing a child pretending to be a grown up, and getting rather carried away. She'd been handed a big toy and was tossing it about like a psychopathic kitten. Aspiring journalists observed with rage, magazines and newspapers looked on with a mixture of amusement and intense irritation.

Not all famous parents dish out fabulous jobs to their kids. A lot of them deliberately do the opposite in order to get them used to the 'real world', whatever that is, but Geldof also ensured his eldest daughter, Fifi, bagged a sought-after place at MTV. (Fifi, who now works in PR, is the Geldof girl you might not be so immediately aware of, because she isn't skinny with blonde hair extensions, nor does she dress like the sugar plum fairy; prerequisites for media attention for one in her position.)

"She doesn't look like her sisters," an old friend of Fifi's tells me. "Sometimes magazines even cut her out of pictures with her sisters. But on the other hand she doesn't want to be in the photos. She holds those cards close to her chest, I don't think she'd want to talk about them. It must be difficult having siblings like that."

Whispering Bob Harris' husky-voiced (naturally) daughter Charlie, a music-publishing PR executive, sat next to Fifi during her time at MTV, and remembers the eldest Geldof had plenty in common with Sir Bob. "I've never known a girl swear as much as her, it cracked me up. Absolutely her father's daughter.

"There was an immediate edge as soon as she walked in because everybody knew she was there because of who her dad was, and a lot of people probably fought quite hard to get their job there," explains Charlie. "I know she was immediately judged because she was Geldof's daughter.

"She could come in late, she could do what the fuck she wanted. If you're an hour late and you're Bob Geldof's daughter, no one's going to have a go at you. Bob's so important to MTV, so she had that on her side, but I don't think she milked that.

"While we were at MTV a TV programme approached her to be the host. She just point blank said, 'No,'" continues Charlie. "Not what she's interested in at all. She wanted to work at MTV, she's obviously passionate about music, she keeps out of the limelight. I respect that, she's a proper, down to earth, really nice girl.

"When she started her own PR company, a lot of my contemporaries immediately judged her, 'Oh, so Geldof's starting up her own PR company, we'd all like to do that… isn't it easy for her?' which is sad, it goes against them basically."

Geldof senior often describes Fifi as most similar to him in many ways, having inherited his belligerently independent streak, so it makes sense that she made her own luck in the competitive world of PR before long, even if she was in more of a position to than most. But sometimes gigs of quite a staggering nature are pushed determinedly the way of the rock baby whether they want it or not. When you've got a mother like Sharon Osbourne, you don't always have much of a choice.

Kelly Osbourne (in the book *Ordinary People*): "In all honesty, I didn't want to do the awards show. My mum was the real force behind it. As smart as MTV is at creating new projects, my mother is smarter. Somewhere inside her conniving mind was a vision of using the success of the series to launch me into my own career."

It was the early Noughties, the MTV series *The Osbournes* had taken off (after everyone's favourite dysfunctional family proved a hit on *Cribs*), reality TV was born and so were the series' stars. (Black Sabbath casualty Ozzy was more reborn, admittedly.) The kids, Kelly and Jack, had become cult figures after charming the world with their whiny teen antics – they were ripe for exploitation. Before long Sharon had engineered a performance slot for Kelly to sing Madonna's 'Papa Don't Preach' (of course) at the MTV Awards, against the advice of even hard-bitten Sony tycoon Tommy Mottola.

"Tommy kept telling me… 'She's going to need a psychiatrist after this is all done,'" recalls Sharon. "So many people thought it was too much pressure to put on a child. But I knew she was going to love it."

The pressure was indeed gargantuan. But the performance went ahead and Brand Osbourne had served another ace. And Kelly? "I felt like sobbing. I wanted to sit in a chair and cry." She spent most of the time prior to the show shouting, 'Don't fucking touch me!' at stylists and make-up artists. See? Loved it.

To plonk the poor girl in front of a star-studded crowd and order her to sing is tough enough. But what is possibly even tougher is the choice of song, 'Papa Don't Preach', anchoring her profile ever more to Ozzy. Good gimmick and an easy reference point, but from her individual perspective, would it not have been more helpful to have been allowed to sing something a little less parentally focused? We all accept she's famous first and foremost for being the daughter of Ozzy, but had her burgeoning singing career really been a priority, it would have been kinder to allow her to make her own mark after being handed, nay, coerced into, this once-in-a-lifetime opportunity.

'Mystery' big sister Aimee has deliberately resisted any opportunities that may be linked to what she refers to as the 'Osbourne hysteria'. She refused to be part of the show in the first place (prompting a vicious battle with her own mother about it, resulting in Aimee having to leave home). Yes, she wants to make music, but without being labelled a 'wannabe' forever linked with her father.

"It's taken me a while," she explains in *Ordinary People*. "I think I've found the right people I want to work with who understand me and don't want to turn me into another money-maker off this reality madness."

However, so far, by trying to escape the Osbourne circus, she is still largely known for being the one that 'got away'. So she didn't really get away. And trying to carve a niche entirely away from your parents' celebrated name but in the same field can put one in a strange position. People like the association, it's an easy pigeonhole (people like pigeonholes too). She might keep her integrity and turn certain jobs down, but what next? Some would advise her to choose another path, but why should she? It's not a straightforward situation.

Alice Cooper's daughter Calico works directly with her father on his horror-themed vaudevillian 'Cooper Show' for most of the year, performing various gruesome skits with him to a baying audience of (mostly) men in leather jackets. She is also an actress, keen to break through on her own merit. PMA (that's Positive Mental Attitude for the… well, I was going to say miserabilists among us, but let's just say Brits) must always be readily galvanised for whatever the day may bring.

Luckily Calico, 28 at the time of writing, is practically bursting with positivity, or at least she certainly seems to be during our phone conversation. (I sincerely hope it wasn't all an act and that, once our cheery goodbyes had been said, she didn't slump into a chair and pour a bottle of gin over her head in desperation.)

Yes, she who has graced such movies as Rob Zombie's *Halloween* with her spirited presence, comes across as a seriously dynamic character. She's also banged her head against the fact that whatever she wants to do is viewed with a critical eye because of her background, and sometimes she is pushed aside because of that. But when she is allowed to shine, that's right, it's supposedly all down to daddy.

"I've been trying to put a tape together to audition for *Saturday Night Live*," Calico explains. "It's not like it was a whim; I worked really hard for it. If I get it, the average person is not going to look at me and say, 'Oh well, she worked really hard to get on there,' they'll say, 'Of course she's on *SNL*, she's Alice Cooper's daughter.' You know?

"Or if I don't get it, it will be like, 'Well, she wasn't talented enough!' So I lose either way. But you have to get past it. I've been talking to my younger sister about it. I say, 'People are never going to give you the benefit of the doubt.' I used to take it personally, but you have to let those comments go.

"My parents are so supportive but they also let me fall on my face, I wasn't coddled. Something is so much better and more worth it when you're standing in front of a wall and you've pounded your head into it a few times and gone, 'COME ON!'"

Striking out alone is tough when you're so rooted in Cooper-world most of the time. It's almost as if you have to make a firm decision – stay within the confines of the world in which you were born or make your escape in a big way.

Guitarist Trev Lukather, son of Toto guitarist Steve, has also found battling the issue of being taken seriously as an individual is particularly difficult in Los Angeles. "It's all about entertainment and everyone wants to make connections," he says. "Everyone wants to meet as many people who can somehow benefit them. I understand, it's hard out there – I know for a fact, I'm going through it – but just to find real people sometimes … it's really hard, you know?"

"Leave home!" suggests Callum Adamson, son of Big Country guitarist and singer Stuart. Callum left his native Scotland as a teenager to live with Stuart in Nashville for several years. "I had to leave home to do it – so should they. I'm going to impose all my hardships on everyone else. Get the fuck out of LA. I like Nashville. Every single person's mum or dad was a musician and no one gives a shit, all that counts in Nashville is talent.

"If you're ever on stage with your dad, wrong. There you go. Dissociate and you can be your own person. If you work with your famous dad then you will be forever known as the kid who works with his/her famous dad. If you're going to do that you have to take the breaks that come with it.

"When your dad's famous you have to go twice as far to do your own thing, their aura is huge. I couldn't do anything in Scotland – can you imagine the nightmare that would be? Although I didn't spend enough time in Scotland to be Scottish anyway, plus I never spoke to anyone, I stayed in my room and played guitar and listened to Muddy Waters."

Although rock photographer Scarlet Page, the daughter of Led Zeppelin's Jimmy Page, has taken a different path from her father, she still operates within the same world. She is proud she never used her name to get where she is, although in a way she didn't have to, starting her career assisting photographer Ross Halfin, famous for photographing, that's right, Led Zeppelin. She remained more or less in the sphere she was born into, and perhaps that is the most sensible route; she won't come up against as much judgement, and she won't be as much of a curio.

Her acclaimed exhibition 'Your Child', which opened at the Royal Albert Hall several years ago, featured celebrities and their children, including images of Shaun Ryder, Keith Allen and Sadie Frost. It's a subject she is undoubtedly wedded to, and while she doesn't 'use' her name, it can't be denied that many who attended that exhibition probably did so because the name 'Page' caught their eye. But once they were in, her work could only have spoken for itself.

"People want some kind of angle," says Dylan Howe. "What's the story on this person, what sets them apart? When that's included in your name, it's an advantage, or at least it's something… it could be a disadvantage. They might think you're a brat, that you're going to be crap, but it certainly puts your name up in bold font."

One exception to the love/hate fascination we have with the children of famous parents is surprisingly on The *X Factor* – contestants have to be seen to come from 'nothing' to be held in the public's affection. Any link to showbiz or previous professional experience seems to be met with outrage and a sense of betrayal. 2008 winner Alexandra Burke kept the fact that her mother, Melissa Bell, was in Soul II Soul quiet until several rounds in. Any criticism was allayed when it was revealed that Melissa was in poor health and on benefits. Lest we forget, the sob story is king on TV talent shows.

How To Win The X Factor author Keeley Bolger: "Alex didn't want people to focus on (Soul II Soul). But when it came out, people appreciated the fact that Melissa had to struggle, bringing up four children alone, people just shifted any thoughts of nepotism or musical privilege they might have had. And the papers liked the 'fallen star' thing."

Singer-songwriter Galen Ayers, daughter of Soft Machine's psychedelic maverick Kevin Ayers, has a theory about this. And it's a good one. "People love stories of struggle, so when that story seemingly isn't there because so and so is your dad or mum, it's like they're (deprived) of the feeling of 'I could do it too.'

"You don't have their parents or their genes, so you feel helpless. 'Don't even try.' With a rags to riches element, you get the feeling of, 'If he can do it then so can I.'" This definitely goes some way to explain our complicated feelings towards those who blossom forth from an already established family, regardless of their personal journey.

Let's for a moment step away from the arena of mainstream visibility and media scrutiny (you can stop holding your stomach in for a bit) and cast our eyes over a genre in which family connections are vital to the purity and authenticity of its future: folk music. Within folk, it is accepted without question that each generation will follow the last into that musical tradition. (Although folk hero Euan MacColl's daughter Kirsty made her musical foray initially as a punk backing singer for a band called the Drug Addix, under the name of Mandy Doubt. I'd store that one away in case it crops up in the pub quiz.)

Folk icons Martin Carthy and Norma Waterson didn't have to encourage their singer and multi-instrumentalist daughter Eliza into the family tradition – which, by the way, Eliza can trace back centuries.

According to the Carthys, the folk baton, being passed on down the years, is no burden. This is how it develops and evolves. However, it comes with its own complications when generations of folk music, represented by families like the Carthys and the Watersons, come up against the dilettantes of the scene.

"Traditional music is about continuity and pride," Eliza explained during our phone conversation (in which her baby daughter called for her for the first time – the next generation clearly in fine voice). "I was brought up in a vision of inclusivity, all people are equal, all musics are equal. I didn't feel like rebelling.

"I don't know how to say this without sounding incredibly arrogant, the thing about my family is that we are a living tradition, we actually are. It's different from people who have adopted the music for themselves.

"The people that want to work within the commercial folk scene seem to resent the family in some ways, but the folk scene isn't about tradition, funnily enough. It's a microcosm of the music industry; they're like, 'Why do these people get a leg up? Why are these people on the radio? Where's my turn?' I think we shouldn't be taking work away from those people either. We shouldn't be in the same ballpark, not that I'm saying we should be elevated above anybody – it's just different."

Another example of this living tradition is the Wainwright family – Loudon, Kate (McGarrigle), Rufus and Martha – also firmly rooted in folk, although Rufus in particular rebelled by throwing himself into opera and classical music, show tunes and the glittering genre that is Judy Garland.

There is a curious magnetism that forces the Wainwrights simultaneously together and apart, and it apparently stems from Loudon, already one of the few famous parents to have been superseded by their offspring. He is nowadays referred to frequently as 'Father of Rufus and Martha, Loudon Wainwright III', and unfortunately he doesn't always handle this with grace. This is made particularly painful for his family because whenever he gets angry or bitter, which seems to be quite a lot, he writes a song about it. And, forget metaphors, the lyrics are wincingly literal.

His jealousy of Rufus started, famously, when his firstborn was barely out of the womb. Loudon went into an enormous sulk when he realised his baby son had first dibs on Kate's breasts, and while some songwriters would be moved to eulogise, damp eyed, about the wonder and magic of their newborn child, he spat out the envious and fairly revolting 'Rufus Is A Tit Man' instead. Loudon, who was not about to win any 'Best Dad' or indeed 'Best Husband' awards, felt usurped, and would forever feel like a rival. Kate would always have Rufus' back, but any chance of being handed opportunities by his dad seemed unlikely after this rather ill-fated start to the relationship. (Rufus apparently used to shout out a request for this song at Loudon's gigs before he was old enough to know what it meant. He now shrugs it off, joking that Loudon clearly just read too much Freud.)

In later years there was a rather cruel suggestion at a reversal of the well-trodden path of parent-child nepotism. Throughout the late nineties, Rufus was reaching new heights as a performer, and he would boast that he was playing venues his father had never been asked to appear at himself. He knew it was tough on Loudon to see him doing well, and their brittle power struggle finally came to a head when eating together after a shoot with *Rolling Stone* magazine. Rufus challenged that the only way his dad could muster any interest in the hallowed rock monthly himself was if it was in some way connected to Rufus. Loudon exploded and ran him out of the house. Rufus later wrote 'Dinner At Eight' about this unfortunate incident, which was the prelude to months of silence between the pair.

Rufus knew his dad's connections would help him in his early years as a songwriter, and he pushed himself forward whenever he could. Maybe the sense of paternal abandonment he felt from babyhood meant he knew opportunities wouldn't fall into his lap, even if they weren't too far away. He'd have to be responsible for finding and exploiting them. He'd been told his music sounded like psych-Americana icon Van Dyke Parks, so when he realised Loudon was going to dinner with Parks, he pressed his father to pass on his demo, which he did.

According to Kirk Lake's fascinating Rufus Wainwright biography, *There Will Be Rainbows*, "Parks adored it, sending them on to Lenny Waronker, who had just started the Dreamworks record label (the musical arm of Spielberg's movie behemoth). Parks: 'It was a cut above anything I'd heard at that time, in its individual nature, its intimate interpretations of small, personal events... I decided to try and effect a contract for Loudon's son.'"

Loudon's status never did Rufus any harm as he started establishing himself, and fortunately for him, many of Loudon's fans were seriously powerful. Elton John invited Rufus to singing backing vocals on his album *Songs From The West Coast,* on the track 'American Triangle'. Elton would later inform Rufus that he used to have 'a terrible crush on Loudon', flying in by helicopter to catch his gigs. At least, gigs that had helipads or large fields nearby, anyway.

You can never say never, but one megastar muso parent who is unlikely to be eclipsed no matter how brilliant his brood is Sir Paul McCartney. It may be tough to muster up sympathy for people who have grown up into the ultimate lifestyle of privilege with responsible and loving parents (and this is not always a given – more on that later), but Stella McCartney has been relentlessly judged. Although imagine what it would have been like if she'd decided to go into music herself? (Watch this space though – she recently proclaimed that she's "got the gift" and is a frustrated musician.)

It's tricky – you want to play the card you've been dealt to the max, but discretion is needed when it appears you've been dealt a hand of solid gold aces.

Stella applied to Central St. Martin's College without telling her parents in case it was assumed they had used their influence to help her get in. However, people found it hard to know what to think when, for her student show, while her classmates used unknown models, Stella had Kate Moss and Naomi Campbell. Even the music she had playing on her runway show was a track called 'Stella Mayday', which her dad had written especially for the event. I suppose it would have been difficult to turn it down… And if these are the people you grow up surrounded by, why should you go out of your way to 'normalise' your behaviour in order to keep the status quo? The thing is, England is the sort of place that respects you if you play things down, if you do yourself down, even. This behaviour doesn't fit into that, and therefore: instant outrage. The press buzzed around the show, keen to portray her as 'playing at fashion'.

One thing that can be a considerable benefit when it comes to being the child of a rock or pop star is that you tend to know what you want to do a lot earlier, you're surrounded by inspiration, by interesting adults, maybe you're encouraged to be a bit independent and more questioning.

. This, tempered maybe paradoxically with a sense that there 'isn't a rush' (a phrase I've heard in most of my interviews for this book, interestingly), makes for a healthy combination of focus without panic about advancing years. This possibly also has something to do with, in some people's cases at least, the fact that there is often a financial cushion. But not always.

Zak Starkey is a case in point – his father, Ringo's, influence loomed large over his life (as it did most people's during the Sixties) and, from an early age, a future playing drums seemed inevitable. Zak has rather bitterly claimed that his father did nothing to help him further himself as a musician, Ringo admitting once that he'd have preferred it if his firstborn had become a doctor or a lawyer. But Starr did introduce Zak to his real drum idol – Keith Moon.

Moon rather sweetly acknowledged Zak's obsession with him by giving him an expensive drum kit in one of his many spontaneous moments of generosity. He apparently had no memory of this act of kindness when it was later mentioned to him but that didn't matter. Zak might not have been interested in becoming his dad, the way people might have expected him to, but he was damn well going to turn into Keith.

Zak, according to Alan Clayson's book about his Beatle father, was disappointed that Ringo was wary of his son embracing the often inconsistent life of a musician, his own experience being somewhat exceptional, but this was interpreted by Zak as mere lack of support. Add to this the persistence of people "only talking to me because of who my dad is", and you've got one angry young man.

In his early twenties he started drumming for punk band The Next. Zak would then announce, as I suppose he felt he should (particularly seeing as he was a punk now): "I don't want any help from my dad, he hasn't done a thing to help me, and I don't want him to." Ringo let them use the studio at his lavish Tittenhurst home, where Zak lived in the lodge house, but that was probably taken a bit for granted, like being allowed to practise in your parents' garage. It's all relative (no pun intended).

He was careful to ensure no one assumed he was getting any handouts or special treatment from his father too, insisting, "I'm every bit as hard up as the rest of the band. I have to get a train from the station (like everyone else)."

If Zak felt he wasn't encouraged by Ringo, 'Uncle' Keith Moon made up for it. Starr's wild drinking buddy would ensure that his PA Pete 'Dougal' Butler acted as manager for Zak's post-Next band Monopacific, according to Clayson, and he also brought the young musician to the attention of the rest of The Who. Bassist John Entwistle in particular took him under his wing.

Alan Clayson: "Through Entwistle, Zak was employed for what he did rather than what he was on many lucrative sessions... Zak soon felt ready to record his debut album, a musical version of *Wind In The Willows*. For all Zak's desires to be accepted on his own merits, pragmatism ruled and he'd acceded to his father's trick of giving the record more than an even break by garnering a shoal of whatever well-known names could be trawled to sing on it, Donovan, Entwistle and Joe Fagin...."

Clayson's book swipes at Julian Lennon being a "howling example" of how a famous name can open doors (and in Lennon's case, secure him a Top 10 hit), but it didn't seem to matter how many names were thrown at this particular project – it was not a commercial success.

Zak's trump card, however, turned out to be his passion for his beloved Keith Moon, whose picture apparently adorned the walls of his lodge house. He taught himself to play by listening to records, on his father's advice (this is how Ringo learnt), Who records mainly. His concentrated study of Moon's style and technique since childhood meant he was morphing into a mini-Moon himself, which turned out to be quite useful when The Who employed his services in 1996 and on a regular basis thereafter. Pete Townshend himself hailed Zak's playing as "the most accurate emulation of Keith's style... many have been moved when listening to his explosive solos to say, 'My God, it's him'." Maybe it's just as well Ringo encouraged him to go his own way at such a formative age.

Continuing the theme of the early developer/overachiever, Trev Lukather became the musical director of perky American actress/ pop princess/tabloid superstar Lindsay Lohan's show at the age of 17. Seventeen! True, he was preternaturally gifted and had a great attitude, but his dad had also brought a friend down to his show who was capable of making something major happen for him. (Trev, a lovely guy, complete with LA rock god hair and eye make-up, has a good pedigree in rock 'n' roll – not only from his father's side, but his aunt is Runaways bombshell Cherie Currie, now a chainsaw artist…Was this young man not born to rock?)

Trev tells the story of how he went from teenage rock dude to being thrown headlong into the shiny pop world of la Lohan: "We were about to play the Roxy, and my dad's friend Tom Fletcher turned up. He was flipping out over us, he was like, 'Dude, I have to work something out with you, let me make some phone calls…' I was like, 'Great.' I never wanted to ask my dad for any help, you know?

"We get a call from Universal saying, 'We have this actress Lindsay Lohan, have you heard of her?' And I was like, 'Yes…that song I keep hearing on the radio… but it's a dance track?' and they said, 'We want you to rock it up a bit.'

"We rehearsed and then played for the record company, and they said, 'Let's get you guys some experience on the road working with her, and let's talk about you guys afterwards.' I was like, 'What?! Man, we're going to live and play music, all right!'"

Crucially, once Trev became ensconced with Universal, he deliberately never mentioned his family connection, and if anyone was aware of his background, they didn't let on. It was only brought up halfway through by one of her managers. "He was blown away that I didn't throw it out there, I earned respect on my own," he says.

There was a sense of history repeating itself, as far as Trev was concerned, and this validated the experience even more: his father, Steve, had begun his professional journey in the same way, playing in Boz Scaggs' group, paying his dues on the road before he and his bandmates developed into the Eighties pop rock band Toto. A good way to start, not only to grow up fast on the road and seriously learn your craft, but also to learn how to work in close contact with others, travelling with them, supporting each other if need be and, most importantly, dealing with other people's egos. And it's rumoured that there are at least one or two quite big ones bobbing about in the music industry… This may be why Trev and Steve both ended up becoming two of the loveliest guys one might meet in the tangled, dark, sticky and sometimes poisonous forest of pop.

Trev continues: "We worked with Lindsay for about a year. You know, I'm not going to get into it, but I stopped with her after a while. I'm not going to say anything but she… we had our time and that was that." We read you, Trev.

One of the unfortunate results of this stint on the road with Lohan was the way the band itself was affected. Basically it fell apart. But Trev sees the whole experience as a necessary rite of passage, better that it happened sooner rather than later, a period that has armed him with a vital shield of knowledge about human beings, let alone the music industry.

"When money is involved you see people's true characters," Trev explains. "The deal that could have happened after Lindsay didn't happen because we just couldn't do it any more. And damn, the craziness with her, and the people surrounding her and the famous friends I made in that pop circle, there were so many people using and abusing each other. It's a scary world. My dad still goes through it now, he always says, 'You lose a pall-bearer every year', people you think are your friends and then they turn on you over the littlest things. Stuff like that gets to me. Everyone's just people! Let's just treat everyone the same, with respect. Everyone's trying to live a normal life, even the most famous person is still trying to live a normal life.

"Great experience to have though, I wasn't even 18 and I was musically directing this massive pop star chick, I was the one getting a mouthful if my band messed up, I was the one dealing with Lindsay… you know, I held my own. I matured really quick! Playing stadiums, Times Square in New York on New Year's Eve for MTV, it was a nutty experience, but it only made me want to be my own artist more. 'OK, so this is what it's like. I've played live TV now, I've played in front of a lot of people, I know what it takes, I'm ready to make the step for myself.'"

The career of Mackenzie Phillips, the rather haunted actress daughter of charismatic Mamas & Papas star John Phillips ("like Jesus in tie-dye" in her words), sprang into life in much the same way. She formed a band with school friends called Class, performing at open mic nights at the Troubadour club in LA at the age of 12. "We wrote songs about being in prison, eating cold soup and drinking beer," she recalls in her autobiography, *High On Arrival*. "No one had yet told us, 'Write what you know'."

The group's live debut was a major landmark for Mackenzie. When most school bands would be playing to their families and the odd supportive teacher... well, Class played to their families too, which included Mackenzie's pop star dad, a major executive from Elektra Records and a Hollywood film producer and colleague of Francis Ford Coppola.

"There was rampant nepotism among us hipster kids of power-hippie parents," admits Mackenzie, "so nobody was surprised that Fred Roos, the producer, was in the audience. He would later ask me if I would like to be in a movie. I was a total Valley girl, I said, 'That would be so cool!'"

Mackenzie ended up landing the role of Carol in George Lucas' breakthrough 1973 movie *American Graffiti*, produced by Coppola. Mackenzie was 13, and would star alongside Richard Dreyfuss and the then relatively unknown Harrison Ford. She bonded with the older cast by entertaining them with lurid anecdotes of the hedonistic narcotic wonderland she called home. This was a period when the stories she would relish telling were not quite as disturbing as they would later become.

An entire chapter of this book is later devoted to the connection between drugs and the children of our idols. In many cases, tired assumptions that the little darlings grew up on spiked milk and cannabis cookies are satisfyingly crumbled. But in this case, when the barely pubescent Mackenzie was taken to the cast and crew screening of *American Graffiti*, her dad gave her a handful of Quaaludes (downers), and then administered regular doses of cocaine to keep her awake throughout her big night. If British mainstream cinemas are anything to go by, these 'treats' were probably still cheaper than the usual tea chest of popcorn and bucket of lemonade combo.

One issue that gets shoved in with nepotism, and certainly has a similar effect, is that of reflected glory and the benefits and drawbacks of it. It can be even more useful than nepotism in a way. It's certainly broader. Even if your starry folks cut you off, your glittering association and inherited cool thanks to that surname, and often first name – Rolan, Rocco, Bijou or Boysenberry (OK, the last one's fake) – usually ensures you are never short of attention.

CHAPTER 2

The Power Of Reflected Glory

"He wasn't looking for fanfares or fame, but it all came around just the same…"

'Coattails Of A Dead Man', Primus

To me, the following quote from the then 15-year-old Frances Bean Cobain, daughter of Kurt Cobain and Courtney Love, says it all about the chapter you are about to read. "People are fascinated by me, but I haven't done anything. I'm not my parents. People need to wait until I've done something valid with my life."

Yes, a glistening tributary of nepotism is undoubtedly the way our starry-eyed society favours the children of famous figures, simply because they *are* those children. MTV fed our drooling fascination with the series *Rock The Cradle,* in which the kids of rock, pop, metal and rap stars threw their hands up in resignation (or jumped at the opportunity of a bit of attention) and pitted their musical prowess against each other.

Californian recording artist Crosby Loggins, son of Kenny, won the contest. The result? A life of being questioned about the 1984 movie *Footloose,* soundtracked by Loggins senior, has now become a life of being questioned about *Footloose* and *Rock The Cradle…*

"That show was like an exposé in terrible parenting," says Crosby, who is refreshingly frank (I was expecting a magnolia, media-trained reply on this). "It was the most stressful and bizarre experience of my life. I'm glad I did it, but I would *never* do it again. I still can't believe I won. I know I'm supposed to say, 'I always knew I'd win', but that couldn't be further from the truth. I guess if I possessed a more egocentric personality I'd be a lot further along in this business, but that's just who I am. It's never been about me. Not until all this *Rock The Cradle* stuff."

The hothouse backstage atmosphere, with celebrity parents and contestants bitching at each other and singing intimidatingly, was part of what made this experience a less than joyful one. MC Hammer was apparently the only parent who was vaguely down to earth (Loggins Jr puts this down to his recent bankruptcy). Come on, Crosby, let it all out…

"There were the young, innocent contestants who I couldn't possibly say anything about – how could you know where you fit into this crazy progeny game at 16? But there were decidedly less innocent folks. Landon Brown (son of Bobby) and 'Lil' B Sure (singer and producer Al B Sure's son) were intensely aggravating, constantly providing unsolicited a cappella renditions of the Backstreet Boys and O Town (a US reality TV boy band).

"The overwhelming sense was that everyone had been raised to focus on themselves above all others. Entitlement ran rampant. When Jessie Money (daughter of rock'n'roller Eddie Money) lost in Episode 1, she ran to her dressing room and threw her fruit bowl through her dressing room mirror. Some even more distasteful personalities, a la Lucy Walsh, daughter of The Eagles' Joe, were old enough to recognise that revealing one's self-centered nature could cost them votes, and made sure to keep their egotistical chatter off the air." Sounds like he deserved an award for just being able to stick out the company…

Infatuated as we are, young rock scions in the spotlight, or even on the periphery of it, can be as stigmatised as they are celebrated. *OK!* journalist Elizabeth Curran suggests that while A-list sons and daughters have the right to do as they please, they may be lacking the feet-on-the-ground advice a 'normal' parent could provide.

"When I interviewed Peaches Geldof, I said, 'People's perceptions of you are skewed because they see you do all these things, 'I'm going to edit a magazine...' but you have no experience.' She said, 'I've been presented with so many opportunities, why shouldn't I take them?' I think she's missing that advice which says you don't have to do everything life presents to you, you might benefit from taking a step back."

However, as it stands, these babies born during Thatcher's reign appear to have absorbed the 'much gets more' mentality. It is the 'me' generation, and they are not alone in wanting to push their profiles and grab whatever attention they can – there are plenty of regular people untouched by fame who pose like *Big Brother* finalists on their Facebook page, know exactly how to present the right information about themselves in a bid to create an appealing image, and more importantly, know how to stand in order to make their calves look smaller in photographs. I remember when it was OK to just wave and grin at the camera, or even, God forbid, pull a silly face. Not any more. Life is one big virtual advertisement, and it's the survival of the sexiest.

Eighteen-year-old Pixie Geldof, Peaches' sister, is already benefiting from her status, having recently been gifted the post of 'teen correspondent' by the trendy quarterly *Love*. She is perfectly qualified as she *is* a teen, but more importantly a very famous one.

We are apparently more interested in what a famous teen can tell us than a regular one, even if we have little in common. And it is much easier to find famous teens by looking at the kids of famous people, rather than hunt for a teenager who is, say, just good at writing and interviewing and has a winning personality. We don't have the time or the attention span, and of course, we are obsessed with celebrities. This explains why, even on specialist radio stations, or programmes about art or classical music, we are served up 'personalities' rather than straight-up good broadcasters or experts in their fields. Although I don't doubt that Pixie is an expert at being a teenager.

Calico Cooper, on the other hand, finds breaking into acting can be a struggle as well as a moral minefield. It's not like the jobs aren't there. They are – on one condition: that her dad can be in the production too.

"People have the preconceived notion that if you're 'rock aristocracy' then everyone is just going to die to have you in their movie," she says. "What they're dying for is for you to be in their movie and then your dad to do a walk-on. I get calls for these movies and I go, 'That's awfully nice that they thought of me!' And then they say, 'So, is there any way we could get your dad to be the janitor?'

"The depressing part is I am well schooled, I don't do anything half-arsed. And you train that hard and for somebody to call you up and be like, 'We're going to do a horror movie…Is there any way your dad could maybe just poke his head in for two seconds and be like, you know, the cranky bus driver…'

"We laugh about it. Dad's like, 'Let me guess, they're only going to make this movie if I'm in there as a tap-dancing nun or something…'"

The reality is rather frustrating for those determined to keep their integrity and move forward on their own when potential employers won't let them. Add to that the outside view that you are coasting along on your parent's coat-tails, and you have a demoralising result.

When it comes to the ultra-visible, uber-cool descendants, artists striving to progress in the conventional way could be forgiven for thinking that there is a certain amount of the following: 'Hm, my nails are dry. What shall I do now? I know, I'll put out a record… maybe I'll 'do' a fashion range.' There'll be some level of interest, and it passes the time between hairdresser appointments. But it's hard to focus, let alone 'try, try and try again' when you know you have the resources to potentially try anything.

Rod Stewart's daughter Ruby, apparently less wild than Kimberly, sums up her big sister's experience. "She's realising she has to work," she told *The Times*. "She had a clothing company which didn't do so well, and when it collapsed she made an album, but it didn't come out right. She didn't know what she wanted to be, and I think she gave up for a while. But she's gotten over that stage."

A strange kind of partiality could be seen between the Stewart ladies and lingerie brand Ultimo. Penny Lancaster, Rod's partner, became the face (and the rest) of the brand, before being controversially replaced by Rod's ex, Rachel Hunter. Kimberly then modelled for the company, followed by, most recently, Ruby. Rod had better get busy again otherwise they'll run out of Stewarts.

(I checked a tabloid website and behold! Not only have plenty of blokes clicked on the most recent story about this, complete with slideshow of Ruby in her bra and pants, there is the usual comedy list of harrumphing comments from self-loathers along the lines of 'I've seen better-looking girls on the checkout down Sainsbury's...' Should a woman post up something even approaching this, however, she will be shouted down by her fellow polemicists for being "jealous".)

With the greatest respect, however, one can't ignore the question: would they, or the likes of Leah Wood and Peaches Geldof, be accepted by modelling agencies, record companies or design brands if it wasn't for their heritage? And the boys are just as sought after: Nick Cave's son Jethro, a fairly ordinary-looking chap before being styled at least, is also a model, as is James Jagger. (He would have been an astronaut, but he was put off when he realised he'd have to have spinal taps.)

Daisy Lowe, daughter of Pearl Lowe (the sort of singer the red tops once referred to as 'troubled') and Bush singer Gavin Rossdale, presented the following argument: "If my parents weren't famous I probably wouldn't be doing this," she told *The Times*. "But it's also how I've managed to have a platform to be able to model with boobs and arse and some thighs..." However, this is surely a perfect example of the fashion industry on the whole making an exception, because even though they can't see her hip bones poking out, she offers something of even greater value.

The louche, faintly dangerous rock 'n' roll pedigree is magnetic as far as the fashion industry is concerned, overriding any elements that would otherwise be less acceptable to them. They're happy to overlook such glaring faults, like being shaped like a woman, or being below a certain height. When it comes to that special rock fairy dust, the rules can always be bent. Every drop of that dirtily glamorous DNA is too weird and wonderful to waste.

"Having famous muso parents does seem to help most people's careers," says Georgia Howe, daughter of Yes guitarist Steve. "Journalists are looking for a point of reference so they get more attention. It's so British as well, the aristocracy parallel. And people love it when you live up to a stereotype or their expectations: 'Yes, we had a yoga teacher, followed macrobiotics and ate flowers ...'"

Charlie Harris, daughter of Whispering Bob, grew up in the celebrity kid community, playing on the beach in Ibiza as adults boozed the day away, and she watched some of her earthy "raver" friends suddenly transform into elegant swans… "I remember seeing India Waters (Pink Floyd Roger's daughter) on the cover of *ES Magazine*, my jaw dropped," she says. "When we hung out she used to have dreadlocks in bunches, beads, wearing hippy clothes, face paint…

"We all blossom, but talk about a metamorphosis, that was a big one. Nice girl. She probably found it quite easy to get into modelling because she's Roger Waters' daughter. These kids may have worked in McDonald's when they were 15 but no one's going to know about that. When people discover them is when they're looking size eight in amazing clothes being photographed."

Sting's daughter Coco, a teenager at the time of writing, was modelling for Burberry one minute and signing up with Island Records the next, being sent out to Jamaica to record her debut album with her band, I Blame Coco. She has ambitious, clever, talented parents who are also nice and symmetrical, so these gifts indeed have been inherited. Apart from anything else, her voice is staggeringly Sting-like, in a good way, right down to the pitch. Things happened quickly for Coco, definitely quicker than if she'd had to spend her week working in Dixons in order to afford a bedsit in Penge, or leafleting while dressed as a Womble to pay for publicity shots. Although we might not recognise Coco if she was dressed as a Womble anyway.

Because these high-profile, high-cheekboned examples are deemed so fascinating, we bristle at the apparent gulf between them and us. It's as if there is no discernible grey area, because in the main we don't hear about the grey area.

Leah Wood's group may have supported David Bowie on his 2004 'A Reality' tour (the knowledge of which might make struggling bands shake their fists at the sky) but stifle your rage, there is an alternative view: if it's tricky for regular oiks like you and me to launch projects, it's equally difficult, Calico Cooper claims, for the celebs who grab opportunities as if they were dishes on a sushi conveyer belt and then bugger them up.

Expectations are high when you're famous, more so when you've fame by proxy. "If I woke up one morning as Anne Smith and thought, 'I want to do a line of bags,' you know how hard I would have to work to get that off the ground? It's hard in a different way for celebrities or celebrities' kids; if you put out something crap, for the rest of your life that is stuck on you." Fair point, and in Britain especially, we tend to have gleefully long memories for such disasters, particularly when administered by those who haven't 'earned' their success in the first place.

No line of handbags has yet been designed by Celeste Bell, daughter of X Ray Spex singer Poly Styrene, but when it comes to breaking through musically, coming from iconic stock can be advantageous if you have the ability to prove yourself thereafter. "Imagine you send in your CV to a job, and they get millions of CVs and half of them end up in the bin, there's got to be something that makes it stand out. It's the same with new bands, sadly – if you have a connection it will prick people's ears up and they may pay you a bit more attention. But if you are crap, you're not going to get anywhere.

"I've been in Spain for the last four years, and I started a group with a friend of mine from the UK about a year ago, we're called Debutante Disco. We had our first show in the UK supporting my mum, she had a show at the Roundhouse in September 2008 (the X Ray Spex 30-year anniversary show). That was a good opportunity for us, we got a lot of offers."

Naturally most descendants of the famous are sensitive about possible accusations of using the family name for advancement, particularly if they have chosen the same field, but there is a splendidly blatant example of one enterprising soul doing exactly that. At this early stage of his nascent musical career it also made perfect sense.

Will Hunt is the son of ELO and Wizzard sideman Bill Hunt (and cousin of Wonderstuff singer Miles Hunt. A double threat). I met him just weeks after he'd signed with his group, Dansette Junior, to Columbia, but even at 13, he understood how he should be marketed. "I was doing my first gig, selling tickets at school and stuff. Because my cousin Miles and my dad were there it got into the local papers. Everyone was there, there were riot vans, people smashing windows trying to get in."

Blimey...

"Well, it's such a little town (Bromsgrove) it was like the only big thing going on. It made the front pages of the *Mirror* and stuff, went national. All the local papers covered it and interviewed us afterwards. It was chaos. Absolute chaos. After that, whenever I did a gig, I would get in touch with the papers, and you'd get articles starting thus: 'Son of…' for three paragraphs, 'Cousin of…' another three paragraphs. Then finally, 'Will Hunt plays this Saturday!' One sentence! But it gets you in.

"Starting out, it's a real foot in the door. When I was really young, without my background, people wouldn't be ringing me from local papers. All press is good press, it can help in a way, but at the end of the day I've been gigging my arse off to get to where I am now, that should speak for itself."

As a youngster, Will was encouraged to send a demo to his dad's old manager, the notorious Don Arden, father of Sharon Osbourne, famed for having people dangled out of windows if he didn't get his way. Good person to have onside, potentially. But if you're already gnashing your teeth at the thought that kids such as Will had instant access to vital figures in the music industry just waiting to push them into the limelight, then gnash no more. "I didn't get any feedback," says Will.

After his first foray into playing live, Will joined a group called Grin And Bear It, an interesting name choice given that most rock progeny bear what can be the burden of a hefty legacy on their backs. At this early stage, his dad's name was a nifty way of pushing himself forward but he also knew when to stop. The fact his current group have been snapped up by Columbia has nothing to do with his dad at all. (Bill apparently responded to Will's excited news that he'd signed the contract by retorting: 'Wicked. And I've just won two tickets for Womad…')

There were no phone calls to old contacts, no pearls of wisdom even, just Will and his bandmates' determination, hard work and ability. And, importantly, belief. What can be a beneficial by-product of such a background is the fact that you are instilled with a belief that you can make a success as a musician or an artist of any kind – your parents did it, after all. Adolescent fantasies of standing on a stage wielding a guitar are less likely to be dismissed with a shout of derisive laughter from dad before he flaps open his newspaper, shaking his head, or the rumple of the matriarchal brow accompanied by the words: 'Very nice, dear. Now what about a proper job?' The right mindset can be the most useful gift your parents can pass on.

Hunt continues: "Now I've got to this stage I want to keep the family link quiet. My friends and even people in the industry are like, 'Oh, your dad can probably help,' or 'You've got to where you are because of your dad.' And that's bollocks, absolute bollocks. My dad doesn't know anything about the industry today. He doesn't know you need press officers, radio pluggers, lawyers, PR people, it's a different ball game, it's a business now, rather than just, 'There's loads of money, go and tour.'

"Signing with Columbia was like putting a flag on the top of this mountain which I've never seen the top of. Then you see this bigger mountain, which I'm now at the bottom of! At least I can rip up my Wetherspoon's application for a couple of years... hopefully."

Outside of the music industry, Will's parentage is less known and therefore likely to be less of an issue for him. Sharing one of the more widely recognised names in pop does not always guarantee a warm reception. It is always assumed that either daddy has engineered everything nicely for you to step right into, or that you simply expect doors to fly open because of who you happen to be.

One of Stella's early employers, Betty Jackson: "The name McCartney closes as many doors as it opens. I was very severe when I interviewed her, poor thing, because I didn't really want a pop star's daughter working for me. I thought it would be too disruptive. Of course, when she came, she couldn't have been any more diligent and less grand, arriving at 9.30am sharp every day, making tea and coffee, always asking the machinists how their weekends were and not saying a word about her own, despite the fact her weekend bag might have had a Concorde sticker on it."

Stella was particularly under scrutiny when in 1997 she was taken on by fashion house Chloé to revamp the brand, but when the label's boss, Monsieur Mounir Moufarrige, was asked whether her name, pulsing with celebrity cachet, had affected his decision to hire her, he said no – he thought her name was Stella McCarthy. I really want that to be true. At interview, when asked about her family, she had evasively replied, "My mother is in food and my father is in music."

Stella was replacing the perpetually leather-clad Karl Lagerfeld (it's hard to imagine him and vegan Stella getting on) at the label. On being ousted for someone younger and cooler, the pompadoured German couldn't resist getting his tailoring pins out and having a little jab: "They should have taken a big name... they did, but in music, not fashion." Stella might be known as Stella Steel for her implacable persona, but

Lagerfeld's words stung. She retorted: "I don't think Chloé would be stupid enough to ride a whole company on me because of who my father is."

This must have been a tiresome issue for Stella of all people, and one might have hoped someone like Lagerfeld would have been old enough to know better than to sink to such an obvious low. Two years into her contract with Chloé, Stella would lament: "I'm so sick of this 'my parents' thing. It's not my fault. It's been this way my whole life. When I would make a good drawing at school, it was because my dad was a Beatle. Or if I got a part in the school play, it was because dad was a Beatle. What do I do? Do I become a smackhead and live off my parents' fortune, or do I have my own life?"

Joining Chloé was, of course, a time of great triumph and celebration for her, but it was also one of tension and even Paul had to wade in and defend her after the sniping showed no sign of relenting. He told the *New Yorker*, "When she started (at Chloé) people said, 'She's a bit young, it's a big job, she's 25.' I said, 'Yeah, well the Beatles made *Sergeant Pepper* at 25 and we weren't too young for that.'" Go dad!

Stella won through with her determination and talent for designing contemporary, pared-down, feminine but unfrilly clothes, which were inspired, she says, by her mother's eclectic wardrobe. She even ended up designing Madonna's wedding dress. (I can't imagine the pop dominatrix not being impressed by the name though.)

George Harrison's musician son Dhani remains perhaps understandably below radar, but he was clearly also brought up in a loving, stable environment, and he is blessed and cursed with looking eerily like his dad (resulting in him having had to practically dress up as George in certain fashion shoots, which seems a little macabre). But the relative spotlight on him, the Starkeys and even the McCartneys put together cannot match the glare of publicity in which Julian Lennon especially has grown up, and the often harsh reality of life with – and without – his dad.

John Lennon has long been known to many as the 'cool' Beatle, certainly in comparison with how Macca and Ringo are generally seen – how exciting must it have been to have a dad perceived to be so hip that, even during the Ground Zero era of punk, when even the recent past was supposedly irrelevant, the lyrics to The Clash song '1977' began 'No Elvis, no Beatles, no Rolling Stones' after which Joe Strummer would often add live 'Except John Lennon!' after 'No Beatles'. A trendy proto-hippy icon of peace and love he might have been, but life with Lennon could lack both of those qualities, as Julian in particular has admitted.

Despite how it may have appeared on the surface, musically Julian did have his work cut out for him. No disrespect to his obvious talents and individual success, but a lot of the buzz around him when he broke through in the Eightiess after his father's death can't not have had something to do with his striking resemblance to John, and many critics found this hard to get past.

In later years, when his half-brother Sean put himself out there musically, something odd appeared to be afoot – Julian's album *Photograph Smile* was to come out on May 18 1998, and funnily enough Sean's own album came out on the same day.

To make matters worse, Sean then announced he believed his father's death was part of a conspiracy, which ensured that every time Julian was interviewed, the press only wanted to ask him what he thought of Sean's controversial statement. It's been hinted at that Yoko was behind this, and Julian didn't hold back in interviews, telling one journalist, "Yoko is very insecure. Any success that I have is a bane in her life and a thorn in her side, because I'm John Lennon's blood."

The perceived silver spoon in the mouths of musicians' babies can take different forms. Its results can manifest in that, like Eliza Carthy, you are never short of the sort of gigs others would love to get – the downside of this, she says, is that "while I'm very lucky in that respect, there was a novelty factor to them booking me, which I didn't like". It hard to be seen as an individual in this context, but at least you're given a chance to prove your own worth; it's your opportunity to create your persona from that point onwards. And, while punters might initially come to you as a fan of your mum or dad, they might leave your gig converted to something a little more niche, benefiting a less populist genre in the process. It has been known to happen...

Harry Waters, son of Roger, used to play keyboards in his dad's solo group, and is now a "relatively unknown" (his words) jazz pianist in his early thirties based in Ladbroke Grove, West London. (Apropos of nothing, he is, so far, the only jazz pianist I've met with waist-length ginger dreadlocks and a bushy red beard, but then he did also used to tour with space-hippy rockers Ozric Tentacles.) Jazz is a notoriously hard business to make any money in, but he reveals his album is "selling well, for an unknown quantity jazz album.

"I made the record myself and I got really lucky, I got a distribution deal, they're called Alliance Entertainment Limited in America. They're one of the biggest distributors in the States.

"The VP came and saw one of the *Dark Side of the Moon* gigs in Florida or somewhere like that, and was doing some background checks on the various band members, and he came across my site and listened to some of the songs – and he's a jazz fan, just by the by – so he listened to some of my music and really liked it. He emailed me, it was like a cold call, and said, 'Do you need help? I'm a distributor, do you want distribution?' It was just handed to me on a plate.

"It was amazing. At that time I was just selling them on my website and I was getting a low hit rate, I was not selling very many, then he offered me this and I've sold close to 1,000, 750 or something, which is, as I understand it, really great, a) for jazz and b) for being an unknown in the jazz world,." If you look at the bigger picture, beyond the absolute heaven-sent jamminess of this deal, this is also fantastic for the profiles of those who played on his album, and is a strike for British jazz. It is, literally, all good.

North London-based singer-songwriter Natascha Eleanore, the daughter of the iconic bass player and Cream singer Jack Bruce, is proud of her heritage, but she understandably chose to drop her last name in order to be viewed in her own right. It seems to be working. Natascha, who also performs under the piratical name Aruba Red, is a very contemporary kind of protest singer, fusing reggae, soul and Eastern music with politically motivated lyrics. She won the chance to record with Nitin Sawhney after taking part in a project at the South Bank for young artists. The success was sweeter still that she'd managed to keep herself anonymous. For a while at least.

"Nitin didn't find out until it was the last day of the project," explains Natascha. "I liked that no one knew and I'd been chosen on the basis of what I'd done. But then when the press release came out for the album, obviously his people decided that that was a focal point, Jack Bruce's daughter. I was a bit upset but I guess they have to find things for the press to pick up on.

"I'm hugely proud of who my dad is, I just didn't want it to define who I am before I get a chance to do it. It's more for my own state of mind, to know I gave it a natural chance and whatever happened happened because it should have, not because there's someone at a record label thinking, 'Jack Bruce's daughter might sell some CDs!'"

Similarly, when Norah Jones first started making waves with her laid-back dinner jazz, she had to insist that her press pack did not contain references to her father, Ravi Shankar. Shankar, who has another daughter, Anoushka, who often plays sitar with him live, had no real relationship with Norah until several years ago. Her birth was not even mentioned in his autobiography *Raga Mala*.

It's accepted that gifts, looks and attitudes are often passed down whether the well-known parent is present or not. But there is another birthright that is rather cushy, depending on the level of your parents' status, or your own by proxy. Basically, even if you are a powder keg waiting to explode in the face of the nearest nightclub bouncer/ social worker/policeman, blind eyes may well be turned to your wild behaviour.

"My wayward years were between 11 and 30," laughs Maria Gallagher, daughter of Blockheads, Animals and Clash organist Mickey Gallagher, slightly ruefully. She isn't going into details. "I just remember that what was perceived as 'rock 'n' roll behaviour' would get a pat on the back. It was rewarded even if it was unbearably embarrassing. Who was around to look to?"

This kind of lenience is not really a benefit, rather just another construct to prevent people from living in the real world. Particularly in the following case, they eventually have to assimilate themselves into it at some point and when they do it is generally unpretty, involving the consumption of more than a few portions of humble pie (which they have to try not to throw back up in rehab).

Mamas & Papas star John Phillips' daughter Mackenzie would get drunk underage in bars all over Hollywood and no one would, or could, stop her. Not allowing kids into clubs obviously comes from trying to protect them, but Mackenzie was 'protected' in a different way. "Everyone knew I was Papa John's daughter so the people who worked there and the musicians around made it clear they had my back," she remembers. "There was an invisible barrier around me, nobody messed with me. I was living it."

It sounds familiar, but she'd be allowed to get away with myriad offences for which others would be penalised. She drove for a decade without a licence. Once, when going through customs, an officer found a block of hash in her purse – he silently put it back and sent her on her way. But complacency landed her behind bars in 2008. Mackenzie, now a mother in her forties, was busted with a bag of heroin and cocaine at LAX. She wasn't bothered until she realised her name was not going to make any difference.

"The overprivileged celebrity brat in me hoped I would get away with it," she admits. "After all those free passes, all those blind eyes, I felt immune. One time when Tatum O'Neal and I were coming home from a party, she was driving behind me on the Pacific Coast Highway at four in the morning, I got pulled over and Tatum pulled up behind me. The cop informed me I had been driving too slowly. I had a two-gram vial of coke burning a hole in my jeans pocket. I said, 'I'm sorry officer, I'm on my way to Tatum's house, she's in the car behind me.'

"It was not long after I had been arrested with enough Quaaludes in my system to kill a horse. He glanced back at her car and said, 'You've had enough trouble. I'm not going to add to it. Go a little faster but not too fast.' I must have been let off the hook like that a dozen times in my youth."

Blame the parents? Well you might. We'd better take a look at how all this started and see what childhood meant for a Zappa, a Lennon, a Wilson or a Dury. But be warned – life-sized Barbies will be thrown, Daimlers graffitied, macrobiotic baby sick barfed in your direction, toddlers with backstage passes will push past in party outfits and mini Harleys might run over your feet. There might also be some naked hippies wandering around and 'nannies' the like of which you have never seen. Brace yourselves, we're going in...

CHAPTER 3

Growing up

"If you ever have another baby, I'll shoot my dick off."
Bob Geldof to Paula Yates

"What was your childhood like?" This is almost without fail the question most frequently asked to those discussed in this book. This tends to be followed by, "What's it like having (fill in the blank) as a father/mother?" Which is an odd enquiry, because it isn't as if they have any other points of reference to compare mum or dad with. They didn't win a reality TV competition to spend a chunk of their childhood with a rock star before returning to their own 'normal' lives.

To the rest of us these rather nebulous questions seem quite fair, and they promise potentially intriguing answers. The response tends to be: "My childhood was normal!" Don't always believe everything you hear... One of the issues with this situation is that you can feel awkward about your background if you feel it was supposedly more privileged, than anyone else's. It takes time to be honest even with oneself.

"Now I'm older I can at least attempt this," admits Crosby Loggins. "I've come to believe my upbringing, however much I downplayed it over the years as 'just like yours, basically', was a total trip! We did *not* have a 'normal' upbringing. And what have I learned? Money can't buy me love, but being poor sucks too. Don't believe anything you see on TV. Michael Jackson is not a robot and Paula Abdul is from outer space."

We all know normality is a relative concept. Some people's upbringings really *were* normal, while others' were completely peculiar. But families are still families and it shouldn't astonish us when rock stars behave like parents just because that doesn't fit in with our two-dimensional image of them. Keith Richards, the consummate rock pirate, always insisted on tucking his son Marlon in and reading him a story regardless of what carnage was occurring beyond the bedroom door. Courtney Love and Kurt Cobain loved nothing more than bathing their baby girl, Frances Bean, while Kurt talked in a Donald Duck voice and dive-bombed rubber duckies. Elvis Presley was a kindly, fun-loving dad, performing puppet shows for Lisa Marie and singing her to sleep. (He became rather grumpy, though, when his daughter asked for Elton John records for Christmas, as opposed to one of his own.)

Because the first question is such a sprawling one, it's going to take a few chapters to really cover the answers. This chapter will serve as a starting point. There are many components (apologies if they sound like a bill of 'reefer madness' style B-movies): crazy nannies, awkward school days, tour-bus tribulations, music by osmosis, drug-related disasters, mad roadie mentors and … the last thing you would expect, growing up quietly in the suburbs, doing jigsaws and walking the dogs.

"But you don't want to hear about that… you want some rock," smirks Callum Adamson. Yes, Callum, we're not ashamed to admit it. That's why people ask in the first place. They want to hear about a life that's totally different from theirs. The truth is sometimes less spectacular and bizarre than what we assume, but not always. (Legend has it that the only time Grateful Dead drummer Bill Kreutzmann came close to throwing a TV out of a window was when his son Justin refused to come to the dinner table until the *Generation Game* had finished.)

Ronnie Wood's son Jesse was literally born into a party. It was Hallowe'en, it was 1976, it was Malibu, and there were some serious festivities going on chez Wood. What's that screaming noise? Probably just some crazy trick or treaters. Or, of course, it might be my wife in labour with my first child. Anyway, who's for apple bobbing?

"I said to her, 'I'll be downstairs with our guests, just yell when it gets really bad,'" said Ronnie to his first wife, Krissie, as she shrieked in agony upstairs. Thanks dear. Have I told you lately what a wonderful husband you are? Oh, you're already downstairs doing the conga with Diana Ross.

"She stayed upstairs to deal with the pain," he continues in his autobiography, *Ronnie*, "I kept partying because I didn't want to be rude to a house full of people. I could hear Krissie moaning louder and louder. Someone knocked on the door. She shouted, 'I'm gonna have the baby!' I said, 'Hang on a minute,' and opened the door."

Fortunately the guest at the door was Neil Young's roadie Sandy Castle. He drove a white ambulance for fun, but now it was going to be used for its original purpose. Not before they'd dropped off some pals at various locations first of course. The contractions might have been increasing in regularity, but that didn't change the fact that there were some celebs on board needing lifts to other parties at other beach houses. Mick Jagger at least came along to give them some support.

"The whole party came out to see Krissie get into Sandy's ambulance and then someone asked if we could drop him off at someone's house down the beach. I said, sure. Then Jerry Hall and Linda Ronstadt asked if we could drop them off too. Sandy turned on the ignition and drove us along Malibu Colony, stopping wherever anyone wanted to jump out," says Ronnie. Krissie must have been thrilled with this. I wonder why they split up?

After being told off by nurses for announcing the resulting baby boy would be henceforth known as 'Boy', he decided to call his son Jesse James Wood. An opportune choice too: the original Jesse James' middle name was, Ronnie later discovered, Woodson.

As Krissie crashed out, exhausted, after her ordeal, Ronnie decided to head back home to continue celebrating. Diana Ross asked Ronnie to show her the baby room they'd prepared for their new arrival. This was quite fortunate: Ross was the only person who had noticed there wasn't a cradle. Or a table for changing nappies. Or toys or indeed any of the usual paraphernalia one might assume appropriate for a baby. She decided to take Ronnie, presumably still scratching his head, shopping for baby essentials as soon as possible.

"I had no idea why we needed all of that stuff," writes Ronnie. Quite. Mere fripperies really.

After they divorced in 1978, Ronnie claims Krissie attempted to keep Jesse away from him, but father and son are evidently closer than ever now. Jesse is a model and a musician with his own group, The Black Swan Effect, who are signed to Peter Gabriel's Realworld label. But he's better known, at the moment at least, for having to have "crisis talks" with his wayward pops, trying to look out for the latter after he slumped back into alcoholism and left his long-suffering second wife, Jo, for Ekaterina Ivanova, a Russian teenager. Although within months Ronnie appeared to have left Ekaterina for another nubile companion. "He told me he's got a new girl," said photographer and fellow rake David Bailey, "But they're all new. Well, none of them are old anyway . . . "

Back in the eighties home life at the Woods' could be extreme, not least because of the abundance of class A drugs and strung-out people in the house most of the time. Jamie and Leah, Ronnie's children with Jo, once dashed into the living room to see a handsome, familiar-looking man lying in a wasted heap on the sofa. They stared for a while trying to work out who it was. And then they realised. It was Christopher Reeve, "out of his brain", chortles Ronnie. "(Jamie) came running to us, crying, 'You destroyed Superman!'"

Life at home for the family of the late Stuart Adamson, the photogenic star of Scottish bands Big Country and The Skids, was more sedate. The Eighties was an intense time for Stuart (who was tragically found dead in 2001, from self-strangulation). During the period that saw him ruling the UK pop charts with hits like 'In A Big Country' and 'Fields of Fire', packing out stadiums, however, he was at his most grounded. It's a time his son Callum remembers with fondness. "My mum (Sandra) made my dad really centred and focused," says Callum, a singer-songwriter and frontman of his own group, Ahab.

It's hard to know at first how to broach the subject of his dad at all, but Callum seems happy talking about him. One wonders whether when a famous figure dies, the media circus that surrounds the family is such that the children become strangely accustomed to talking about him or her in a slightly detached way, simply because they're asked to do so much at the most sensitive time, just after the news of the death is broken. Stuart had struggled with alcoholism throughout his life; he had managed to beat his addiction when Callum was born, but after the break-up of his family when his children were teenagers, he moved to Nashville and, it appears, started drinking again.

While living in Scotland with his young family, however, he wanted nothing more than just to come home, forget about touring for a while, tinker with his car, maybe make a model aeroplane… "He was not open to those sort of stereotypical rock 'n' roll distractions," explains Callum. "He'd come home to a perfect, cosy, non-crazy environment, mum would wake him up at 9am and say, 'Right, you've got to walk the dogs.' He loved that.

"He wasn't really that rock-starry, he could play the part when he needed to, he was articulate, intelligent, looked good, bought weird shirts, played well, sang well. But outside what he must have grown to think of as his day job he just liked being at home, playing football or watching TV, reading. And he was a big hobbyist. Building little models. And then he'd be onstage, silk shirt open to the waist, leather trousers on, playing guitar."

Frank Zappa was certainly at home a fair amount. And he didn't take drugs, which might come as a surprise to some. But that didn't mean that life chez Zappa wasn't a big bowl of weird.

"Dinner might be pancakes, breakfast might be stroganoff…" Ahmet Zappa, writer and third child of Frank, reminisced in an interview with *The Guardian*. This wasn't purely an attempt at being continually subversive on Mummy and Daddy Zappa's part (actually the Zappas insisted their kids call them 'Frank' and 'Gail'). It was more that the parents would work all night, and so dinner would be breakfast and vice versa. Gail, according to Frank, didn't put much importance on cooking, which meant Frank might be seen serving up fried spaghetti for breakfast, or nibbling empty hot dog buns for dinner whenever he emerged, blinking like a mole, from his studio.

The most important thing in this household was to respect the fact that everything had to revolve around the patriarch. For all of his unconventional, freethinking conduct, he ran his house with full-blown Italian machismo and he had to have his way. This only shifted slightly when his kids became older and more independent.

"It's like a dude ranch," Frank would grumble. "The house is like a teenage hotel, featuring our four kids and all their friends. If any groceries are brought in, I can never get to the stuff fast enough before it is inhaled. I work in the middle of the night so, when I get hungry, I wind up digging in drawers to find something a teenager would refuse to eat." (Elvis Presley had similar issues as he would also be up all night with insomnia. Fortunately he avoided the culinary issues suffered by Zappa because he had a full staff of day and night chefs on tenterhooks for whenever he might demand a pound of bacon or some deep-fried banana sandwiches.)

I wouldn't feel *too* sorry for Zappa. This is a man who refused to join his brood for family meals – even at Christmas and Thanksgiving – because he deemed such activities as symptomatic of "the worst aspects of typical familyism. It glorifies involuntary homogenisation." I think this can roughly be translated as: 'I have better things to do than pretend to enjoy talking to my kids.'

"I hate sitting around acting traditional to amuse the 'little folks who happen to be genetically derived from larger folks who buy them sportswear' enduring a family meal," writes Frank, "during which I might be required to participate in some mind-numbing family discussion. I eat, and get the fuck out of there as fast as I can." Love you too, daddy! Oops, I mean Frank.

His tongue was often in his cheek, but this doesn't change the reality that his eldest daughter, Moon, then 13, put a note under his studio door, introducing herself – 'I'm 13 years old. My name is Moon. Up until now I have been trying to stay out of your way...' – before asking if she could sing on his next album in an attempt to get his attention. (This culminated – eventually – in the production of Zappa's hit 'Valley Girl'.)

While Frank might not have been very present during their childhood, his kids certainly remember plenty of other people being around. Aside from the 'nannies' who we meet in a later chapter, there are tales of pungent old hippies staggering around naked among the children's toys, and melting their crayons to make candles. According to Barry Miles' Frank Zappa biography, Moon remembers a visitor who had drilled a hole through his nose in order to whistle through it. Simple pleasures.

As with the Zappas, the treatment of one's children as 'little adults' was also employed by Joe Strummer with his daughters, Jazz Domino Holly and Lola Maybellene.

As a child, to be approached as if one is simply a person who happens to be short can be a fun way to grow up, but in some cases, it can be an excuse to get the children out of the way. "He always had this thing,

'Every man for himself.' That's what he always used to say," remembers Jazz of Joe. "We'd go to Glastonbury and I'd be about 13, and he'd say, 'Right, it's every man for himself now, do you realise that?' So I'd have to look after myself. He'd slip me £20 and I'd go off, and usually I'd find my grandmother who was a hippie, she was always there.

"He'd invite weird crusties to come and sleep in my tent, things like that. That was him being his own freewheeling personality but it used to frustrate me, you know, 'Be a dad!' But he wasn't and that was something I had to realise.

"Dad had a lot of hangers on. He obviously enjoyed hanging out with them but I didn't want to hang out with them. He surrounded himself with these big characters, like Keith Allen. He's really nice but growing up I found it hard. I was already at that stage where I was a bit pissed off with my dad, the teenage thing, 'I don't give a shit, I just want to step out of your shadow a bit'.

"I remember getting frustrated with dad sometimes because he was like an overgrown child, he was all about having fun all the time! There were definitely times I felt I was looking after my dad in a way. I wonder if that's why now I like having order. I find chaos a bit stressful."

The other side of this, however, is that now Jazz doesn't feel compelled to stick up for him quite as much as she might have done. "That 'every man for himself' thing, I picked up on that too," she grins. "People are going to say that he did stupid things, which I'm sure he has, and that's his problem! My sister is more protective over his image but she was the baby, she had a different experience."

One person who fiercely defends her late father is Rosanne Cash. Rosanne, herself a Grammy-winning singer-songwriter, has understandably nominated herself as the guardian of the memory of the Man in Black. She was inevitably wary of the Johnny Cash biopic *Walk The Line* ("I just don't have a need to see the Hollywood version of my father's drug addiction and my parents' break-up"), but she was furious, with justification, to discover that the Republican party had chosen Johnny as a mascot, using his reputation and standing to "further their own agendas", she wrote.

Country star John Rich had appeared at a rally for the Republican presidential candidate John McCain in 2008, reportedly declaring,

"Somebody's got to walk the line in the country. They've got to walk it unapologetically. And I'm sure Johnny Cash would have been a John McCain supporter if he was still around."

Rosanne Cash responded on her website: "It is appalling that people still want to invoke my father's name, five years after his death, to ascribe beliefs, ideals, values and loyalties to him that cannot possibly be determined... It is unfair and presumptuous to use him to bolster any platform." Rich should have known better than to cheekily namecheck Cash while the similarly tough, protective Rosanne is around.

A protective stance does seem to be common particularly amid the daughters of rock stars. Even when Stella McCartney was a small child she flew into a rage when she spotted a paparazzi photographer lurking on the beach when the McCartneys were on holiday. "I remember in Barbados, this photographer was taking pictures on the beach, and I got so annoyed that I ran up to him and threw sand in his lens. We had to leave the country the next day because of what I'd done. My dad didn't really notice things like that because he'd grown up with it."

Elder sister, Mary, was the subject of tabloid interest when she joined Music Sales in 1989 as photo researcher for their Omnibus Press imprint. "On the day she started there were a couple of photographers hanging around on the street outside our offices," recalls Omnibus editor Chris Charlesworth. "They were obviously waiting for her but they were holding a copy of *Today* newspaper, which had published a story about Mary starting work but used the wrong picture, one of Heather, Linda's daughter from her first marriage. Heather is blonde and Mary is dark, of course. I offered to accompany Mary when she left the office in case there was any bother, but the photographers ignored her because she didn't look like the picture in *Today*. We both thought it was incredibly funny."

Often the party under scrutiny or attack is so accustomed to the questionable attention fame can bring that they are rather less bothered about it than their loved ones. When *The Osbournes* became a hit for MTV in the Nineties, Ozzy's children were furious with how their father was being perceived, thanks to careful editing and, well, Ozzy being Ozzy.

"He's like a laughing stock," fumed Aimee. "After all his years of hard work and touring, this is how he's being remembered and appreciated." Jack added: "They didn't show my dad for who he really is. You only saw him stumbling around, mumbling."

And Ozzy's take? "I'm in show business, man. What's the fucking problem?"

If one is a naturally unassuming, private character, it can be hard to retreat when you are born into a family in which anything goes. You are perhaps aware of certain things before you should be, and you are expected to be as much of a libertine as your parents before you. Expectations are particularly high when you have one of those legendarily unusual first names. Whenever the subject of almost self-consciously strange names arises, a reference to a Zappa is rarely far away. We are all aware Frank's daughter is Moon Unit (she dropped the less romantic 'Unit' as soon as she could. It could have been worse though; had she been a boy, she would have been called 'Motorhead' after Mothers of Invention saxophonist Euclid James 'Motorhead' Sherwood), Frank's youngest son is Ahmet, after Atlantic Records' boss Ahmet Ertegun, and Diva was so named because she displayed operative tendencies as a baby.

Zappa's eldest son, as most of us know, was named Dweezil, after the pet name Gail had for her oddly shaped toe. But this was apparently so infuriating to hospital staff that, to shut everyone up, they had to put a different name on the birth certificate, which ended up as an assortment of first names of various friends. For the first few years of his life Dweezil's name was officially Ian Donald Calvin Euclid Zappa (the Donald after Don Van Vliet – Captain Beefheart). At the age of five, Dweezil, who was always known as Dweezil, discovered this and had a monumental tantrum, prompting Frank and Gail to have his name legally changed to Dweezil. "Fuck the nurse if she didn't like it," sniffed Frank.

Dweezil is a guitarist himself, and has been touring with a show entitled 'Zappa Plays Zappa', celebrating his father's music. When you have a legacy you can't escape, you may as well embrace it. Frank Zappa believed kids would grow up in their own way regardless of their home life, but this sounds either naïve or like an excuse. As Dylan Howe says, "Anyone that isn't influenced by what their parents do or what they grow up with must be numb."

Rufus Wainwright's destiny for a life in music was sealed within weeks of his birth in New York in July 1973. The family travelled to Nashville where Loudon would work on the album *Attempted Mustache*. Baby Rufus would slumber in a guitar case as his father recorded nearby.

As he grew older, Rufus became a confident little prince of a child despite his father's corrosive jealousy of him since his infanthood, and he quickly became accustomed to the family's peripatetic, bohemian lifestyle. He relished the superior position of older sibling when his sister Martha came along in 1976, teasing her that she was an alien and that Kate was not her mother and challenging her to singing competitions she could never win. Well, not at the time at least.

One could view the ever-evolving careers of the individual Wainwrights as one long singing competition, with Rufus' accomplishments sitting awkwardly with Loudon and Martha's own breakthrough proving intermittently prickly with both men in the family. Before Rufus and Martha were born, when Kate's singing career with her sister Anna McGarrigle started to flourish, the positive reviews flooded in, but any pride Loudon felt was eclipsed by his simmering resentment, displayed in the song he wrote: 'Saw Your Name In The Paper'.

Rufus realised he was gay in 1986, when he was 13 years old. He felt at ease despite being surrounded by the AIDS fear-mongering of the time. But unlike the Zappas, who actively encouraged their children to explore their own sexual natures as soon as they feasibly could, the Wainwrights were unsure how to deal with Rufus' homosexuality. Kate went into denial, Loudon was bluff and insensitive. Rufus believes in hindsight that it was the emotional distance between himself and his father that led him to crave older male company.

Martha too felt the sense of paternal abandonment keenly, and antipathy between father and daughter seemed to strengthen over time, developing ever more tangled roots. She would brave a year with Loudon in New York when she was 15. They fought endlessly. While Kate McGarrigle has always remained a constant support to her children, Loudon was and still is a contentious figure in their lives.

Right. It's time to mop up the Wainwright bile and any Zappa-esque substances that might still be hanging around with something nice, wholesome and preferably vegetarian. Namely, Sir Paul McCartney. Whatever your feelings on the Beatle, he and his soul-mate Linda, who passed away in 1998 aged 56, were protective, supportive and unlikely to herald their kids' arrival with a song about how there's now some sprog in the way.

I imagine it also helped to strengthen the foundations of this family that Paul was so keen to keep Linda by his side. Rumours abound that the reason they spent barely a night apart was because Linda didn't trust him, but I like to think he'd moved on from the philandering stage of his life. It was his idea for Linda to plonk away on a keyboard in Wings. She refused but he insisted. The babies would often go on tour with them. It was a beautiful thing.

Within their unique situation, Paul and Linda went to great pains to ensure their kids were polite, hard working and didn't take advantage of their unusual status. In fact, it's hard to know when they even became aware of their unusual status. Stella admits it took her a while to even realise her dad was a Beatle. As a little girl she once said, 'Daddy? Are you Paul McCartney?' to which he replied, 'Yes. But I'm just daddy really.' There was no question as to where his priorities lay. He was daddy *really*.

The McCartneys were concerned about how their obvious wealth would affect the young Mary, Stella, James and Heather (no, not that one, rather Linda's daughter from her previous relationship), so they kept life at their Sussex home basic and rustic. The kids slept in the same room, helped around the farm on which they lived and were urged to earn their pocket money. Seeing the Macca children receive handouts was apparently as likely as Linda offering you a bacon butty.

Ringo and his first wife, Maureen, were also a basically down to earth couple but he admitted he was more likely to be the kind of dad that spoiled his kids, leaving the disciplining to 'Mo'. His kids – Zak, Jason and Lee – would indeed be born into a world that was filled with fun, toys and silliness. Although the toys were mainly Ringo's.

When the Starkeys moved to Sunny Heights in Weybridge, Surrey, in 1966, near John and Cynthia Lennon, Zak was one and Jason would be born the following summer. Ringo adored playing with his kids, but if they wanted bedtime stories, they'd have to be satisfied with Ringo's own succinct brand of storytelling, according to biographer Alan Clayson. 'There was Father Bear, Mother Bear and Baby Bear, and Mother Bear made some porridge but a thief broke in and stole it.' The End. (Where's Keith Richards when you need him?)

Ringo had go-karting tracks built into the grounds of the mansion and into the surrounding forest as well, not to mention a telly in each room, including the toilet. You could find any toy or gadget you could think of – for a while, though, there was no sign of a drum kit, apparently. This might have had something to do with the fact that Ringo was wary of any of his children wanting to carve out a life as a drummer, as we now know. So much for that...

This Sixties boho-power couple were, according to Cynthia Lennon, like a comedy double act, and it took parenthood to temporarily quell their lively nightlife. When Zak and Jason were small, Ringo certainly made sure he was around as much as he could be. The Beatles had stopped touring, and even though Ringo did briefly embrace his spiritual side and travel to Rishikesh, he and Maureen couldn't wait to get back to their sons. He'd pulled back on his copious drinking and revealed that his few vices now included coffee, cigarettes and indulging his children.

Despite his good intentions, however, it was only a few years until Ringo slipped back into boozing and partying, hanging out with Keith Moon (never wise if you want to stay sober), and he became increasingly absent, although his shadow loomed over his children immovably and infuriatingly.

Jason teetered off the rails in his teens, and it wasn't as if Starkey senior could say much to reprimand him or keep his kids on the right track – when Jason was arrested on drugs charges, Ringo's drinking was out of control. At least in his children's early years, life had been quite rosy. While there initially was no real need or encouragement for the Starkey kids to grow up too fast, conversely Julian Lennon became like a miniature adult before he'd even reached double figures, acting as protector to his mum in the freezing absence, and presence, of John.

Lennon's first son was born in Liverpool in April 1963, a few months before Beatlemania exploded in the UK. At the time, his mother, Cynthia, was not particularly recognisable as John's wife, because, for publicity reasons, she was supposed to be a secret. (This was Beatles manager Brian Epstein's idea, in case the group's quivering female fans felt betrayed if it turned out 'their one' had a partner.) John was away while Cynthia was in hospital expecting the baby, but when he arrived three days after Julian's birth, they had to be moved to a private room, and patients and staff alike would press their noses up against the windows. John held Julian's tiny hands and said, 'Who's going to be a famous little rocker like his dad, then?' Or because of his dad, perhaps?

As if this child wasn't already born into enough of a shadow, it was also decided his first name should be John. (Julian is his middle name.) This is also presciently symbolic of the all-pervading John-ness with which Cynthia and Julian, and Yoko and Sean, would have to live for the rest of their lives, albeit in very distinct ways. Everything was John, and everything would always be John, for better or for worse.

As thrilled as he was to meet his son, it was barely a fortnight after Julian's debut that John disappeared on that oft-discussed ten-day holiday with Brian Epstein that continues to raise eyebrows to this day. It was a period The Beatles had set aside for some much-needed time out, but instead of using the time to be with his wife and child, John still insisted on going away with Brian, who had a well-publicised crush on him. John later said, "I wasn't going to break the holiday for a baby. I just thought what a bastard I was, and went."

Cynthia coped with the baby on her own, and not for the last time. Being a lone mother is tough, but Cynthia experienced an extra level of strain as curious fans trailed her every time she went out with Julian in his pram, trying to work out if she was indeed John's fabled wife. When John decided to move his young family to London, the situation became even more ludicrous. Fans stuffed chewing gum in the keyhole of their flat to stop them getting in so they could swarm round them, begging for a chance to hold baby Julian. A little scary perhaps, but on the upside this transferred worship did at least mean that the Beatle bairns received mountains of birthday gifts every year from their dads' admirers.

Absence became a defining theme, as it does, in different ways, for many people in this book. As a result I felt 'absence' deserved a chapter of its own, but it's hard to describe the fundamentals of Julian's upbringing without discussing it now, because John's distance from his first child was emotional as well as physical.

On the rare occasions he would be at home, John would swing between rage and indifference, with occasional warm fronts. When Julian was tiny, a friend of Lennon's who had come to visit their Surrey house, Kenwood, remembers hearing John say to the youngster, 'No, I won't fix your fucking bike.' And this coming from a man deeply bitter that his own dad wasn't around when he was growing up. In fact this may explain it. At the beginning of the recent Lennon biography by Philip Norman, there is a quote from John himself: 'I was never really wanted,' and it is no secret that he had deep-seated abandonment issues with his own father, Alf, and his mother, Julia. One wonders whether, if he truly believed he wasn't wanted, he felt it redressed the balance to treat his own son periodically in the same manner.

Lennon clearly had his issues and was dealing with them in his own damaged way; he needed help but his spiralling drug use throughout the Sixties exacerbated some of the darker elements of his character. The principles he tried to instil in the world, peace and love, and obviously his musical legacy are beautiful and we are right to celebrate and treasure them. But Julian and Cynthia are often dismissed as they, and their experiences, just don't fit snugly into the glorious legend of St John.

John had a complex relationship with the notion of fatherhood and family as a result of his own confusing upbringing. He would have sudden rushes of love, documented in apologetic letters to Cynthia, but even when on good form with Julian, he'd simply prove how out of touch he was. Cynthia writes in her book, *John*: "Sometimes he'd come home with the car full of toys, usually meant for eight or nine-year-olds, John having forgotten, in his enthusiasm, that his son was only two."

Once John found his soulmate in conceptual Japanese artist Yoko Ono (after no small amount of persistence on her part), he was able to retreat and avoid responsibility concerning not just Julian, but anything else that wasn't in their immediate bubble. Ono herself had a young daughter, Kyoko Chan, with her first husband, Tony Cox, but Ono and Lennon agreed to keep themselves separate from anyone who might pull their focus from each other.

"We try to keep a slight distance from everybody, even our own children," she said. "We know if we love our children too much, it will draw us slightly apart."

Fans and friends might not have liked it but being with Yoko gave John licence to be himself, which wasn't always a particularly nice person. "I realised somebody else was as barmy as me," he said of his new companion. There were no limits. They caterwauled together for hours, became extremely thin on a macrobiotic diet, wandered about naked and took copious amounts of drugs – something John couldn't share with Cynthia. Crucially, John and Yoko would become addicted to heroin together. Mutual drug-taking creates a cast-iron bond; if one partner wants to experiment and the other doesn't, the resulting gulf is destructive. Heroin served as the glue that would attach Yoko and John even more powerfully to each other. But eventually they would also soften together. At least they were in sync in this respect, although the dynamics were totally different from his relationship with Cynthia; he proved himself to be a child in need of parenting himself, expressing this in his reference to Yoko as 'Mother', and in the iconic image taken of himself and Yoko by Annie Leibowitz a few days before he was murdered, in which he poses, naked and foetal, next to a clothed, serene Yoko.

John and Yoko would wed on March 20, 1969 in Gibraltar, flying to Paris and then Amsterdam, and inviting the press to their honeymoon at the Hilton for their 'bed-in for peace'. A befuddled Julian watched 'Hokey Cokey' (his childhood malapropism for Yoko) and his dad on TV. Cynthia: "'What's dad doing in bed on the telly?' he asked. 'Telling everyone it's very important to have peace,' I answered through gritted teeth."

Lennon famously became a house-husband when baby Sean arrived on Lennon's 35th birthday, October 9, 1975. He changed nappies (despite being unable to bear even being near the nappy-changing process when Julian was tiny), cooked, sang his child to sleep and wrote about him in songs like 'Beautiful Boy'. (John wrote the lullaby 'Goodnight' for Julian, but in the end gave it to Ringo to sing instead on *The Beatles* – the record known as 'The White Album').

Lennon confessed after Sean's birth that when it came to being a dad, it pained him that he'd got it wrong with Julian, and wanted to get it right with Sean. But he still didn't manage to make amends with his eldest son until it was too late. Julian and his mother, John's first love, had watched as the man they doted on changed from, in Julian's words, "John Lennon (dad) to John Ono Lennon (manipulated lost soul)". One thing that didn't change was his temper.

In later years Julian spent some time in the States with his dad, Yoko and his little brother. On one occasion, when they were making pancakes together in the kitchen and Julian was finally learning to relax, something made him laugh, and all hell broke loose. John started yelling: "I can't stand the way you fucking laugh! Never let me hear your fucking horrible laugh again." He continued his tirade until Julian fled, as he often had to, in shock. Cynthia remembers having to deal with the fall out: "It was monstrously cruel and has affected him ever since. To this day he seldom laughs."

John might have mollycoddled Sean but this didn't mean he wouldn't also get bawled out occasionally – there is a well-known story of how Sean was playing with his food (aged four) and John yelled so ferociously it damaged Sean's hearing. This mirrors how John blew up at three-year-old Julian at the dinner table for eating messily. Cynthia retaliated, telling her husband that if he was around a bit more he might understand that that's how toddlers eat.

Something worth bearing in mind when it comes to the treatment of first offspring in contrast to their younger siblings or contemporaries is that, unlike Zak and Julian, Sean and Dhani Harrison were both born well after the peak of their respective parents' careers; in both cases their dads had withdrawn from the public gaze altogether and become quite content to be stay-at-home dads. Their kids were, as they should be, a priority. The Beatles were in a different mindset by the mid-Seventies, and would be very different fathers from the kind they were or would have been had they had kids at the height of Beatlemania. When Sean was born, Lennon and Ono were at a new stage in their lives and in their union, and this was reflected in their parenting of him. Harry Waters put it succinctly when he said, "My sister (India) often wishes she was brought up in the family I was brought up in." Dylan Howe's experience of growing up also cannot be compared to that of his younger siblings.

Dhani Harrison, an only child, was born in 1978 when his father, George, was anxious to concentrate on his family and continue his spiritual journey. Dhani grew up going on CND marches, chanting with his dad, going to Ravi Shankar gigs, practising with his band upstairs in his father's Hare Krishna retreat and probably watching a prodigious amount of Monty Python, which his father adored and credited with continuing the irreverent spirit of The Beatles. George even mortgaged their home to finance *Life Of Brian*, so Dhani will have grown up with a fine sense of the important things in life.

Life was, as one would expect, generally peaceful within the Harrison household at Henley-on-Thames. George was understandably shaken when Lennon was murdered in 1980 however, and paranoia sank its claws into him, not relenting for some years. George put up barbed wire around the family home, the magnificent Friary Park, retreating into relative obscurity. Hard as it may be to believe, in 1982 Harrison was listed in the 'Whatever Happened To...' section of a pop nostalgia book, while Macca was a star feature of the annual *Who's Who*. But this didn't bother George. It must have been quite a relief after years of intense scrutiny and hysteria.

Dhani would have been ten when his dad formed the supergroup The Travelling Wilburys with Bob Dylan, Tom Petty, Jeff Lynne and Roy Orbison, who died in 1988, the same year the Wilburys' first album was released. By now George had become more inclined to view death with total dispassion, convinced of the eternity of the spirit, and this was an attitude he would pass on to his son, no doubt making George's own passing in December 2001 a little easier to bear. Watching his dad act with grace and courage in his final months was certainly inspiring to Dhani. He said: "He never sat around moping. He was never afraid. He wasn't attached to this world in the way most people would be. He was on to bigger and better things."

X Ray Spex singer Poly Styrene left the hardbitten Seventies life behind after her initial foray into music, bringing up her child Celeste in Harrison's Hare Krishna retreat in Surrey. Preconceptions of a life of rock 'n' roll clichés are dissolved when it comes to Celeste's childhood. She was born of punk stock for a start, and punks rejected rock 'n' roll excess, but it was life in the commune that ensured her innocence was preserved. She didn't even hear a swear word until the age of ten, when she was taken out of the retreat to go to state school in Brixton, which must have been something of a contrast.

"We lived in the commune growing our own potatoes and that kind of thing," she says. "It was in the stately home George Harrison donated to the Hare Krishnas. It was completely cut off from society. I have this gap in my memory of popular culture, the late Eighties/early Nineties." She missed out on Bros, the tail end of Thatcherism, heroin chic, Jive Bunny... Maybe not a bad time to have a gap.

"I was very innocent. I think the hardest word I'd known up to the age of ten was 'brat'. It was strange, I was very nerdy as you can imagine, sandals and socks, vegetarian..."

Celeste's ultimate and inevitable rebellion, as a result, was a kind of anti-rebellion. She turned her nose up at arty hippiedom, went to university and became an English teacher before making her own way back to music.

"We were living in another world, really. A lot of my mum's artistic friends I just thought were airy-fairy, spacey people," says Celeste. "I rebelled against that, people taking themselves a bit too seriously, art becoming an ego thing. I wanted to keep it real and work. Now I've worked at a proper job for four years, well, it kind of sucks but I needed to go there! My mum is very proud, I'm the first person in the family to go to university. And I never wanted to drop out or take loads of drugs or anything like that."

Mamas and Papas star John Phillips' palatial Hollywood home was something of a haven for Los Angeles' counterculture community, but it was far from innocent or wholesome. His daughter Mackenzie, who has struggled with drug addiction throughout her life, recalls in her autobiography seeing her father's once grand mansion in Malibu deteriorate into ruins as a claustrophobic mess of rock stars and hippies turned on, tuned in and dropped out within its peeling walls.

While still living with her mother, Mackenzie remembers being driven either to John's house in Bel Air or his house in Malibu in a limousine (he was never in the car himself). Eventually, however, Papa John's (not the pizza chain) was where Mackenzie would end up living full time but it was no place for a child. It was a pharmaceutically charged other world where the Sixties ideals of 'free love' had become an excuse for increasing depravity. "Hollywood trash (was) streaming in and out of his home," she says. "I watched my father's lovers and wives crisscross paths. Love and lust ebbed and flowed and my parents and their lovers were just splinters of driftwood bobbing along with the tide.

"The house was full of priceless antiques but if something got broken it was never fixed. The housekeeper hadn't been paid, or was fucking my father. It was a bizarre mix of excess and oblivion, luxury and incompetence. I had no idea what I might hear or see on any given night."

Mackenzie's story is sobering because of its sheer lack of sobriety. But when flower-child ethics in their purest forms work, they really work. Back to the brighter end of the psychedelic scale, Soft Machine maverick Kevin Ayers brought up his daughter Galen, now a singer-songwriter in the critically acclaimed duo Siskin, in a commune in Majorca. "It was idyllic. It was where the poet Robert Graves lived and died," reminisces Galen over a soya latte in London's Hammersmith (which also has its charms). "All my friends were musicians, everyone's a poet or an artist, everyone was your mum, everyone was your dad, you slept anywhere, your parents would play music…"

But tear yourself away from the jewel-like colours and drifting calm of the groovy Spanish communes (we'll return for a veggie burger later) and come with me, if you will, to the opposite pole… Namely, in this case, Buckinghamshire, where a Brummie rocker from a heavy metal band is hanging out at his mansion, tripping over toys and shouting, "SHAAAAROOOOON!"

Like Ronnie Wood's children, Ozzy and Sharon Osbourne's kids were born during the height of their father's fame and, thus, inebriation. It is touching that the Black Sabbath singer was insistent on being physically present at the births of his children, even if he did bellow, "Fuck her, give the painkillers to me," as Sharon was in labour with Aimee on September 2, 1983. Sharon admits she "smiled through the whole thing", however, and it wasn't entirely due to the morphine: Ozzy disappeared to buy her a diamond ring, which he returned to put on her finger just before she gave birth. This was all the more thrilling for Sharon because she initially thought he'd just gone to the pub.

The following October, Kelly was born, and her entry into the world was a little less romantic – Sharon underwent 18 "horrendous hours" of labour, during which Ozzy asked her, "If you could make it a boy, please do." He then went off to tour with the mad, bad Mötley Crüe, in Sharon's words, "a toxic combination." Not a comforting thought to a young mother nursing a newborn baby and a one-year-old back home. Sharon would force Ozzy into rehab as soon as she possibly could after Kelly's birth as she feared for his life.

The robust Ozzy obviously did stay alive, as he fathered a third child, born in November 1985. Osbourne senior's euphoria at seeing his son, Jack, pop out of his wife's business end was too much for him and he blacked out on the hospital floor, a dozen cognac miniatures tumbling out of his pockets as he went – a prophetic greeting for a child who would later be known, temporarily, for indulging in similar excesses.

Ozzy's daughter Aimee became doggedly sensible, but Kelly and Jack initially veered decidedly dad-wards in their habits and inclinations. Ozzy lived in a grandiose world far away from his harsh working-class background in the Midlands, and he made the most of it in terms of excess and indulgence. At worst, he would behave violently towards Sharon (who gave as good as she got), but while the kids were generally shielded from seeing their father's darker side, they were always aware of what was happening, and absorbed it like a sponge.

They knew his behaviour was unacceptable, but on the other hand seeing their parent act this way normalised the sort of antics that would be seriously unusual in any other setting. If you see your parent being indulged when they are behaving unreasonably, then why shouldn't you be if you decide to act the same way?

The Osbournes' screaming matches provided much of the entertainment on their TV series; Sharon appeared almost proud of the way they could freely tear into each other with supposedly no permanent damage once peace was restored.

American therapist Sheenah Hankin voiced the concern during the *ABC News Show* that living this way meant the kids could grow up to be "yellers and screamers", potentially harming their future personal and professional lives. Sharon told her anyone who thought that could "kiss (her) freshly lipo'd ass, if they want to grow up to be yellers and screamers, so what?" Sharon was used to shouting and aggression from her own family life at home with her infamous music mogul father, Don Arden. Maybe she felt it was healthy and unrestricted to grow up in such a way, or maybe she was acting like the school bully who was once bullied themselves. Either way, it's hard to say 'so what?' to the following story.

Jack: "There were always fights going on, it was a war zone. I'd trash my room and get into really nasty, vicious fist fights with my sisters. The tipping point came when I held a knife to Kelly's throat."

Living under the constant gaze of cameras only added to the teenage angst of Kelly and Jack. While Sharon insisted she wanted to raise her kids in the "real world", understandably her kids longed for simpler, pre-MTV times.

Ex-Boomtown Rat and all round modern-day saint Bob Geldof could be a volatile character to be around (although perhaps not to Osbourne proportions). Geldof's tougher side was at least balanced by his wife Paula Yates' fluffier influence in the homestead. He thus had to restrain his desire to gaffer-tape his three noisy little girls' mouths while on endless car journeys, as Paula insisted that none of their personalities should be stifled. (Interestingly, Paula's description of Peaches as an eight-year-old shows that little has changed – she was all blonde flick-ups and heart-shaped pink plastic sunglasses, glittery make-up and party dresses.)

It is amusing to imagine Bob Geldof gritting his teeth silently at the wheel as his little princesses chattered and argued away in the back seat. They'd also threaten to fine him every time he swore, which wasn't an infrequent occurrence. "Bob would get incredibly stressed," Paula wrote in her eponymous autobiography. "At one point he said, 'If you ever have another baby I'll shoot my dick off.'"

The Geldof kids certainly learned plenty of new words and phrases from Daddy G, and between this and hanging out at TV studios as Paula shot *The Tube* with Jools Holland, or playing with your toys as Bob organised Live Aid, it's unlikely you'd get an education of this ilk at school. But school, I'm sorry to say, is where we are going next. So tuck your shirt in and get in the car, we'll be there before you can say 'Ozzy Osbourne ate my homework'.

CHAPTER 4

School

'Well, we got no class / And we got no principles / And we got no innocence / We can't even think of a word that rhymes…'
'School's Out', Alice Cooper

It is a fact that many celebrities' children go to expensive schools. It is also a fact that many don't. It is equally true that some of those who did go prefer giving the impression they didn't, and plenty of those who didn't go wish they did. Still with me? Good. Yes, it's deemed uncool by inverted snobs to go to a 'posh' school, but a rock star sending their child to the local comprehensive in a bid to retain his or her working-class hero credentials, or to ensure the little ones have a taste of the 'real world', isn't always the best way to go.

Movie critic Cosmo Landesman wrote a book, *Star Struck,* about the effects of coping with his famous/fame-hungry parents, the songwriter and poet Fran Landesman and publisher Jay. Cosmo himself still shudders to think of his boyhood in Holloway, a rough area of north London, where he was terminally isolated because of his 'weird' folks.

"My father likes to boast, 'I sent my children to the worst school that money could buy!'" he groans. "It wasn't his fault. I wanted to go there, kids from my primary school were going there. I didn't really know what it was like. But being a Cosmo in Holloway, believe you me… there weren't any! If you weren't a Dave or Bill or Martin you were doomed to be beaten." Callum Adamson also complained bitterly of his father, Stuart's, "champagne socialism" by continuing to buy expensive cars but insisting on his son going to the rough local school.

What's a parent to do? 'Betray' his roots (and supporters) and brave the criticism? Admit he has transcended his initial status and act accordingly because his children will suffer if they go to a school in which the other kids and parents are likely to find the concept of artistic success unusual? Or does he cling to every last vestige of youthful punk ideals and advertise this through his kids? Everything he does sends out a message, so he'd better choose carefully. But he also has to choose what he feels is more important.

Christian Davies, Kinks guitarist Dave's son, was fortunate enough to go to King Alfred School in Hampstead, where it was accepted that rock stars – and actors, sportspeople and TV personalities – are a) actual people and b) have children that go to school, but even then, Christian was keen to stay under the radar. It didn't really matter if your parents were immediately recognisable to your classmates, it's more that the rock star *je ne sais quoi* pulses off them with every step they take, it's dusted on their hair and coming off their clothes in waves of grooviness. "Sometimes if he came to pick us up from school he'd be wearing his leather trousers…" says Christian, with an air of confidentiality. "I was 11 or 12 and didn't want to stand out. When I was 15 or 16 I was like, 'Actually he's pretty cool,' but there were just a couple of years where I may have lied about what dad did, 'Oh he's a greengrocer…'"

The 'grocer' tag wouldn't have cut it when, in 1984, The Kinks surged back into the charts with 'Come Dancing', but this was also the point at which The Kinks' respective broods truly became aware of their fathers' pop currency in their own lifetimes. What's more, the appearance of Muswell Hill's favourite rock heroes on *Top Of The Pops* came at the right time for Christian, old enough to throw off any embarrassment and just enjoy being proud of his father, Dave, and Uncle Ray. Christian: "I remember me and my brothers went down to the BBC to watch it, that was one of the biggest memories I have of realising at about 13, 'Wow! Dad's a pop star!'

While one might imagine that the families of rock superstars are probably set up for life, with private schooling par for the course, it can be a very different story should the breadwinner die tragically before managing to put their house in order.

After T Rex frontman Marc Bolan was killed in a car accident in 1977 at the age of just 29, with his partner, Gloria Jones, at the wheel, the singer's young family was catapulted from a privileged lifestyle to one of relative poverty when it transpired that Bolan had left his financial affairs in disarray. To complicate matters further, he was also still technically married to his first wife, June Child.

"He wanted to provide for our future, but he found he was paying tax at 83 per cent so he set up an offshore trust in the Bahamas," Bolan's son, Rolan, explained in an interview. "Unfortunately, he hadn't had time to sort out all the details before he died, so there was no provision for us, and the trustees told us their hands were tied."

David Bowie, Bolan's friend, glam-rock contemporary and occasional rival, generously stepped in after learning about their plight and covered various expenses, including Rolan's education in Los Angeles. "The money allowed me to go to a good private school and meet (other) children of celebrities," said Rolan. "They knew I didn't have any money. They always took me to one side and said: 'Keep your character. Stay who you are.'"

Stella McCartney, who is usually adamant about the virtues of going to a more humble school, has admitted that "when you go to a comprehensive and you come from my background, they don't love you for it. You get a hard time. And that is valuable... otherwise you would go through life thinking you are fabulous. People would say, 'Oh your dad's great, you're great.' They would have been impressed by all the money and stuff."

The Beatles' kids are as different from each other as their parents were from each other but, generally speaking, the onus is largely on 'being normal', particularly in the case of the McCartneys: they are keen to remind us they went to regular schools. They did go to a state school in Sussex, but what is rarely mentioned is that they also received some of their education at the expensive, bohemian King Alfred School, rubbing shoulders with the Davies*es*, Starkeys, Howes and, intriguingly, the Prince of Tonga.

"King Alfred…" begins former alumnus Dylan Howe. "I don't know if there's any other school like it. It was a new progressive idea of schooling – if you had money and were quite open-minded you would go for that school. Zak and Lee Starkey were there, the McCartneys for a while… that school could be seen as a Hampstead cliché, but it was good. If my parents had taken more of a socialist approach and sent me to a regular school, just me turning up in my nice jeans and jumpers would have singled me out immediately, and I don't have the same reference points, so I either say nothing but am thought a spoilt brat… or open my mouth and remove all doubt!"

Teachers at King Alfred would be referred to by first names, you didn't have to wear a uniform and (I hate to tell you this, Mr Landesman) there were and continue to be plenty of Cosmos. One of whom is Baxter, Ian Dury's son, and this is something that amazes Baxter himself: he was sent to KAS in his early teens but managed to get kicked out after only two days, an episode that is included in the 2010 Ian Dury biopic, *Sex and Drugs and Rock 'n' Roll*, which was in production during our interviews.

"I was watching the film thinking, 'Uh-oh!' I wonder what the school is going to think about the Dury bunch now," he laughs. "We're a force now, there are three Durys in the school at the moment (including younger brothers Billy and Albert). And I was there for two days…

"It's fucked when you don't go to the right school, that's what happened to me. All the way through, I became the naughtiest kid to get away from it. I wish I'd gone somewhere like (KAS), totally, utterly wish I'd gone… I got battered at school. 'Hit me with your rhythm stick', the whole predictable thing, 'cripple'. It was like an episode of *Grange Hill*.

"To be fair, they did try to send me to King Alfred and I just started throwing all the chairs (around) in a maths lesson. I was there for a two-day trial, and I was thinking, 'This is a bit different!' They put that bit in the film. Then I took my kid there for the first time yesterday."

The school's radical, secular ethos continues to attract the great and the good, and for Baxter, the novelty of who you might bump into at the school gates is not likely to wear off. "The fucking celebs! Thandie Newton walks up, Liam Gallagher. I was quite excited. I was sort of ticking them off, Thandie Newton, seen her, Bobby Gillespie, Jonathan

Ross... it just went on and on..." Even the teachers aren't necessarily immune to getting a bit star-struck, or at the very least, opportunistic. Georgia Howe remembers, "The music teachers would be like, 'Can you give your dad a tape of my music?'"

Alongside the young rock aristocrats at the school are also various genuine royals, heirs and heiresses. This can seem paradoxical, particularly as many of the musicians themselves came from basic, working-class backgrounds. But children shouldn't be embarrassed if their rock 'n' roll parents sent them to a rock 'n' roll school – it's probably what kept their self-esteem intact. It's no small matter if your dad or mum is one of the biggest stars in popular culture – and you look like him.

It didn't stop them having problems, but at least they'd be among some like-minded souls. If someone asked about your weekend, you really could say that you went clay-pigeon shooting with Grace Jones without getting headbutted.

Christian Davies remembers: "I remember Jason Starkey came up to me in the playground and said, 'Oh, are you Dave Davies' son?' I'd just started at the school, and that was the first other famous person's kid I met. I felt, 'At least I'm not the only one...' I know if I was a famous parent I'd be concerned about the environment my child was in."

Will Hunt, son of Wizzard's Bill Hunt, wasn't under scrutiny at school because his father wasn't 'pop star' famous, although every Christmas he did have to endure having 'I Wish It Could Be Christmas' being conveyed vigorously by everyone who knew him. And if you think it's irritating that Christmas seems to be celebrated earlier every year, spare a thought for Will, for whom it practically *is* Christmas every day... "Every Christmas I'd get it," he says. "It was fun up to a point. I get it even now, but nowadays it gets played earlier and earlier. You walk into a supermarket in mid-October and it will be playing already, on Argos adverts. Never-ending. But it's fun." It keeps the Hunt, Wood and associated Wizzard families in top quality stuffing balls too, one would imagine.

As if being known as 'Christmas boy' wasn't enough, when Will went to sixth form college, he became the focus of attention for the non-Yuletide part of the year because of a certain film that appeared to be written about him. It wasn't, in reality, but the circumstances of the plot were uncannily familiar...

"Oh... the *About A Boy* thing," groans Will, so accustomed to this ever-present spectre that he's almost surprised he has to explain it to me. "Hugh Grant plays a guy called Will who lives off his dad's royalties because his dad wrote a one-hit wonder Christmas song..." Ah.

"It was weird to watch," he continues. "I went to see that in the cinema and the girlfriend I was with at the time was like, 'Is this about you? Is this a joke?' Once that came out, it *exploded* at school."

Another issue Will certainly had was that he was literally too cool for school. As a trendy kid at a regular school in the Black Country, his haircut became a matter of concern for his teachers. "I had longish blonde hair with a massive undercut. It was looked down upon. I remember in the school hall hearing the deputy head, who didn't realise I was there, saying to the head teacher, 'What are we going to do about Will Hunt's haircut? I think we should speak to his parents.' And the head teacher said, 'We can't speak to his parents, his dad's a hippie as well.'"

Spandau Ballet star Martin Kemp and his wife, Wham! singer Shirlie Holliman, sent their daughter Harleymoon, now a music and fashion photographer, to a private school in Hertfordshire. This at least meant there was a likelihood of everyone being slightly more on a level and the fascination with fame and status would be less intrusive. But the usual presumptions about celebrity kids sprang up predictably as soon as the other girls had a whiff of her background.

"They'd be like, 'Did you know about her? I bet she's really arrogant...' Or you would get a lot of people going, 'Can I come round your house?' But I never got affected by anything, I just ignored it completely. And dad's used to it, he's had people staring at him his whole life.

"My brother Roman was always fine with the fame thing. When he was five or six, a fireman came in to do a talk at school, 'This is what I do,' sort of thing. Everyone was saying, 'Oh isn't this cool?' But my little brother said: 'This is crap. You should have got my dad to come in! He's much better than that fire chap.'"

When the identity of Harleymoon's famous parents was still relatively under wraps there were times when being the child of someone with a less conventional occupation could be awkward. Most people seem to find it hard to compute the reality of being a musician or an actor at the best of times, but when the school announced it was Take Your

Daughter To Work Day during a protracted 'resting' period for Martin Kemp, Harleymoon's own acting skills had to come into play. "Everyone was saying, 'Yeah, I'm going to the office,' 'I'm going to the car dealers...' and I was like, 'My dad's not working, he's been at home for about a year.' So we just made up a job! I pretended my mum worked in a recording studio, we didn't know what else to do. We had to take pictures of ourselves in a studio, pretending, basically."

Not all children wanted to stay under the radar. Surprise, surprise, Peaches Geldof "always made a glamorous entrance at school", according to Gerry Agar's book *Paula, Michael and Bob*. Gerry was also a mother at the school, Newton Prep in Battersea, south-west London. Peaches was a super-confident child according to Agar, and just as well: she and her family were under the microscope of bored, bitchy yummy mummies because of their success, natural charisma and popularity.

Agar recalls there would be as many fawners and flatterers as there were those who felt threatened by the Geldof phenomenon swept into school every day – sometimes with bubbly Paula, sometimes with scowling Bob. One exchange between two Sloane Rangers, according to Agar's book, went like this: 'God, she looks like a precocious little tyke, doesn't she?' 'What the daughter or the mother?' came the catty reply. 'I know, she looks different in the flesh without an army of make-up artists to paint her up.' 'Obviously doesn't look after herself. But then I suppose you would get like that, living with Bob Geldof...'

Teachers aren't always much better. The temptation to cut the 'overprivileged brat' down to size is clearly irresistible for some, but life gets tough when that's how everyone treats you, all the time. "People in positions of power like teachers or instructors think they're going to be the first person to show you you can't do whatever you want," says Calico Cooper. "But the problem is that a lot of people think like that, so we catch the butt end of a raw deal a lot of times. When I was a kid, if everybody in the class was talking, I would be the one who's name would end up on the board.

"It's the same for my dad, people can be really nice, but then there's the people who are like, 'Frickin' rock star, gets everything for free, let's double charge them or make them wait longer than everyone else,' just to show him he's not as big and wonderful as he thinks he is...' I've watched my brother and sister go through it too: my sister comes home and says, 'Is there any reason my teacher always makes me go last, or makes me leave my hand up the longest?' and I'm like, 'Yep, let me tell you why...'"

It can't be denied, though, that the child-of-celebrity phenomenon can have its advantages too, even in the harsh, judgemental world of school, where kids are at their cruellest, parents at their most resentful and power-freak teachers at their most sadistic. Spending hours watching your parent sign autograph after autograph (usually when you're waiting to have a chat with him yourself) can arm you with something that can excuse you from school altogether.

"You know when you have to sign pieces of paper when you're sick or you need to take a day off?" begins Callum, with a conspiratorial air. "I'd seen my dad sign autographs 1,000 times, so I could quite easily forge his signature. No matter what I did, if I'd got a note from my dad with my 'dad's signature' on it, the teacher was like, 'Wicked, I've got Stuart Adamson's autograph!' and they wouldn't question it. I got away with fucking murder."

Two children who weren't likely to get away with anything approaching murder or even a light Chinese burn were Kelly and Nicholas Brilleaux, daughter and son of the late firebrand Dr Feelgood singer Lee Brilleaux. Brilleaux senior came across as a wild-eyed, hard-drinking maniac onstage – in fact the entire group looked as if they weren't averse to a bit of criminal activity – and during one of his famous benders he once plunged his arms inside the aquarium in an expensive restaurant in order to try and eat the tropical fish. He also, according to his own mother, while touring America was "racking his brains" to work out which states had capital punishment, just in case he decided he had to kill Feelgood guitarist Wilko Johnson once and for all (they didn't get on).

But he also, by all accounts, had possibly the most solid moral code in rock and was something of a Superdad, taking care of his children when his wife Shirley retrained as a nurse. Woe betide his kids if they didn't toe the line though: one day Kelly came home from primary school claiming to have 'found' a ten pound note. Not only did Brilleaux not believe her, he frog-marched the little girl back to school and turned her in to her headmistress (who probably, to be fair, pocketed the dosh for herself, but never mind). She didn't do that again.

Depending on the level of your parent's renown, you also come ready-packaged with your own celebrity by association, which is fun before kids' envy muscle becomes more honed. "My very first day at school, someone asked for my autograph," says Callum. "I was four. I was like, 'What's an autograph?' I wrote my address." (This sort of misunderstanding is not an unusual occurrence: a five-year-old Dylan Howe was approached by a fan of his father, Steve's, after a Yes concert in Edinburgh in the early Seventies, and handed a programme to sign. Dylan wrote his name on it and then presumed that it thus belonged to him, and wouldn't hand it back.)

While it is definitely kinder (on the parent as well as the child) to send your kids to a school in which they are likely to assimilate in their formative years, at least if finances allow, one wonders whether Madonna's motives were at least partly image-based when she decided to send her daughter Lourdes Ciccone Leon to the elite, French-speaking Lycee Francais in London's Kensington. They live in England and the US, Lourdes' mother is Italian-American, her father is Cuban, she is being educated in... French. *Pour quoi?* It's hard not to see it as a bit of a pose, but it's one that's already biting the pop businesswoman in that diamond-hard derriere: Lourdes takes advantage of the fact her mother *can't* speak French by switching languages to talk to her friends, so poor Madonna is denied her god-given maternal right to eavesdrop.

Otis Ferry, Bryan's fox-bothering son, was also urged to embrace his inner Gaul, but no such luck. He informed *Country Life*: "My mother told me when I was 10 that I had to learn languages. I hated that and said:'I don't want to speak bloody French. I like speaking English, thank you.'" He didn't go back to the "boredom" of school anyway once he'd discovered his passion for blood sports. (Bryan Ferry appears to approve of his son's questionable hobbies, for which Otis has become a kind of poster boy. At the 2004 Q Awards ceremony, Ferry braved a chorus of boos when he dedicated his Lifetime Achievement Award to his "brave son", who had recently stormed the House Of Commons with fellow pro-fox-hunting protesters.)

Lourdes has also enrolled for a course in the Manhattan Professional Children's School (previous alumni include Macaulay Culkin and Scarlett Johansson) as, hi-diddly-dee, 'tis an actor's life for she. Interestingly,

Madonna, who also has a son, Rocco, and two adoptive Malawian children, David and Mercy, initially disapproved of the idea of her firstborn becoming a performer, although since this stand-off Lourdes has appeared as a slightly uncomfortable-looking bride in her pelvic-thrusting, knicker-flashing mother's pop video for 'Celebration'. The deal was this: if she earned good grades at the Lycee, she could study acting. And she appears to have got her way, although Madonna could also reveal some of her acting secrets to Lourdes in the meantime, should she be willing to pass on some of the magic movie-going audiences witnessed (possibly through their fingers) in the likes of *Swept Away* and *Body Of Evidence*.

To be fair to Madonna, her reluctance to allow Lourdes to enrol in an acting school without proving herself first is a common mindset for many parents. They might not have been to a good school themselves or had the opportunity to go to college. They might have left school early to fulfil their dreams, but later regret not finishing their education and bullishly insist their kids don't limit their options in the same way.

But sometimes you get the kind of parents who take a different, arguably radical, route. Toto guitarist Steve Lukather was instinctive when it came to his son Trev after realising that, through no coercing on his part, his boy was born to play guitar. Steve's theory was that he would make no bones about how difficult life in the music industry could be, but if Trev was going to do it anyway, he wanted to give him the best chance possible. He wanted him to be alert to the pitfalls and the logistics of what he was getting himself into, and this has saved Trev from many issues that other musicians, including those who come from a 'good pedigree', are tripped up by if they are simply not aware.

"He believed in me so much he took me out of everyday school and put me into independent studies," explained Trev. "He said, 'Let's get you into the school of making sure you own what you're doing, and focus on playing, writing, singing, getting this together.' That's how much of a support system my dad was. If he hadn't have done that I wouldn't have got the Lindsay (Lohan) gig. I owe him for that. He's an amazing dude."

Frank Zappa was dubious about the Californian education system and wanted his children out of it as soon as possible. He'd raised his children to question, learn, observe and think freely, and this was reflected in their precocious intelligence and independence. When Moon reached school age, she thought she was going to help the teacher out.

"She didn't know anything about education," wrote Zappa proudly in his autobiography. "She was surprised to find that none of the other children had names like Moon or Dweezil – though this being Hollywood, there were other unusual names. Nor did they dress like her: Moon sometimes wore her underwear on her head. Nor did they know anything about R&B or make Barbie and Ken fuck and orgasm loudly. They didn't find inflatable sex devices or pornographic cartoons lying around the living room." How boring of them. From the way in which Zappa boasts about his 'kerrazy' inclinations, it is hard not to perceive his determination to be subversive at all costs, and like other examples discussed here, his children are placed in various situations just to serve the purpose of supporting the pose.

Zappa discouraged his children from going to college, but whatever his feelings on American schooling, this opposition would be detrimental to Moon in particular. "As a child I was given free rein, now I am only employable as an empress of the universe or something in the 'arts'," she said, in Barry Miles' book on Zappa.

Miles himself remarked that she had "wasted years appearing in bit parts in third-rate sitcoms and movies before finding her metier as a writer. She would have benefited from studying at a good university, both her journalism and her first novel, *America The Beautiful* (which is apparently *not* based on her own strange home life despite widespread belief to the contrary) reveal her to be a talented writer. Blame must be laid at Zappa's door for imposing his own bizarre ideas about the American education system on his children. Maybe he didn't want her to be one of those 'college-educated women' he wrote about in the song 'The Illinois Enema Bandit'..." *

The whims and changing decisions of a parent under the influence (not including Zappa in this, he was just strange) means that the stability of

---

* For those of you unfamiliar with this particular opus, they are forced to have their colons sluiced by the rogue irrigator, and are none too happy about it. I'm sure Zappa realised this is not necessarily what happens as a rule when women embark on further education... although that all depends on which society you sign up to in Freshers' Week.

their children can be compromised if one minute dad wants to be in the English countryside to dry out, and the next needs to leave the country – family in tow – because of the bad vibes he's left behind after kicking his various habits. This is what happened to the Osbournes on numerous occasions, leaving Buckinghamshire behind for LA, uprooting their little seedlings and replanting them in a school in the Pacific Palisades. The children despised it, the focus on fame ruled their daily lives in the classroom and they were terrorised by teachers and children alike. Idiotic but unsurprising remarks would be levelled at them: 'There's the girl whose dad bit the head off a bat…' 'Can your dad get me cocaine?'

They also informed the Osbourne children that they and their family were 'Satanic'. It was a Christian school, incidentally. (The Osbournes are at least in good company with Alice Cooper's family – when Calico was a little girl, one of her schoolmates told her, "I can't come to your birthday party, Mum said your dad is the Devil.")

Fortunately for them, and unfortunately for the kids and teachers who had nothing better to think about, the Osbournes moved back to Buckinghamshire when Aimee was accepted by the Arts Educational school in Tring. The children were happy … for a while. Aimee had finally found something she wanted to do for herself but again, they were whisked back to Los Angeles before she'd finished her dance training.

Sharon, who had the often tough task of managing Ozzy in more ways than one at the time, is defensive about the moves: "I think it gave them a great education in life. My kids from age eight could find their way around New York, LA and London…" Fair enough, the University of Life is not to be sniffed at. But when would an eight-year-old really be expected to make their own way alone around the perhaps ironically named City of Angels, or New York or indeed London?

The second time the Osbournes hit Los Angeles, the kids were in their early teens, which ensured they had a different experience from their first time in the US. Jack admits that he was a "mummy's boy" and often wouldn't go to school at all, tagging along with Sharon to the hairdressers. But when he did go, he would often be picked up by fearsome, flowing-haired rock stars such as System Of A Down, which caused a few jaws to drop at the school gates. In your face, bullies!

"They would pull up in an old white Bronco with clouds of smoke billowing out of the window. They took me under their wing, and the drummer, John, used to give me the occasional lesson in chatting up women." Now *that's* an education.

Natascha Eleanore, daughter of Jack Bruce, came up against similar preconceptions and for comparable reasons. This is inevitable as it is for most of the kids of addicts, or former addicts. However, Natascha just found assumptions that she went home to a fug of crack smoke and a house full of wasted rockers rather amusing.

"I went to the normal primary school and some of the older kids said, 'Does Eric Clapton come round your house?' And I'd be like, 'No! Never met him.' But it came more from people's parents, they'd always be asking, 'How's your dad?'

"I remember one girl wasn't allowed to come round my house because they thought there would be drugs there. We just joke about stuff like that. I didn't grow up in a crack den, it's not quite how people think!"

Fame + well-publicised problems with drugs or alcohol = curiosity and stupid questions, and because of the notoriety, parental issues with substance abuse, which children would ordinarily be oblivious to, are public property, and have to thus be processed at an early age.

It's something that isn't always considered, although Nirvana icon Kurt Cobain was pained by the idea that his daughter, Frances, would grow up hearing about her parents' heroin addiction from school gossips or outside sources. "I don't want my daughter to grow up and be hassled by kids at school," he told the *LA Times*. "I don't want people telling her that her parents were junkies. I can't tell you how much my attitude has changed since we've got Frances. Holding my baby is the best drug in the world."

For Papa John Phillips, drugs were the best drugs in the world, and, if his daughter Mackenzie's book *High On Arrival* is to be believed, he gave no thought to how his habits would affect his children. In fact they were heartily encouraged to join in.

The Svengali-like singer did have ideas about how he wanted his daughter to be educated; he was already seeing her as a miniature version of himself, and she certainly modelled herself on him. So he chose a school called Summerhill, in California, where smoking was permitted, classes were optional, the teachers were hippies and the pupils were "rich and undisciplined", as Mackenzie put it. A dangerous combination.

"I was a person with no boundaries going to school with no boundaries," wrote Mackenzie. "My father wanted me to live and learn as he did, through experience and experimentation. Our class was called 'Electric Bananas', from the Donovan song 'Mellow Yellow'. People thought the line meant smoking banana peels to get high, but Donovan ultimately revealed it referred to a yellow vibrator. Either way, as a name for a class, it set a clear tone.

"Sometimes I had to hitch-hike because nobody was awake or willing to drive me. I was allowed to go to school on acid if I wanted, and dad signed a ream of blank paper on which I could write notes (excusing myself from class)."

Baxter Dury was also eventually sent to a school for the "rich and undisciplined" after being continually thrown out of school throughout his childhood and early teens. But while, as we know, it is the right thing for a celebrity to send their child to a more liberal school for the sake of their happiness, don't expect them to do any work.

"Mum persuaded Dad to cough up money to send me to what they call a crammer college called Collingham Tutors, basically a posh school mostly for kids who'd been thrown out of public school. It was full of kids who'd kind of been abandoned at the age of three by wealthy parents and had incubated themselves in institutions like these, and were parentless, emotionless and absolutely mad.

"I thought, 'Fuck, this is brilliant.' It was like a volcano... I had a ball for about six months and then I got thrown out of there. I had such an amazing time. It was loose, it wasn't about discipline, it was about befriending you and *then* teaching you. It kind of worked in a way. There were so many wild people there and it was the end of the Eighties ecstasy thing, it just went off. Best six months I've ever had."

There are plenty of high-profile parents who pack their kids off to boarding school, sometimes because it's easier if they are in a single-parent situation, but often, according to some rock 'n' roll offspring, because they had some hard partying to get on with themselves, and they didn't want any little people getting in the way.

"My godmother was married to Phil Carson*," says Charlie 'Harris, daughter of Whispering Bob'. "They had a massive banquet table in their house in Chiswick. They had this big white room and the kids weren't allowed in there. It was so rock star-crazy.

"We were like kids that should be seen and not heard, the adults were getting pissed and having fun, 'Shut up, kids, get out of the room, go and play.' Phil Carson's daughter Jody, when we were in Ibiza, she wasn't allowed to get out of bed before 11am. Now if you're a kid and you're in Ibiza and it's sunny and there's a pool outside… you know? Jody was not allowed out of the bedroom. The parents were having so much fun they just wanted the kids out the way."

Back across the Atlantic, life changed for Mackenzie Phillips after she shot *American Graffiti*. She was sent off to a prohibitively expensive boarding school in Switzerland, apparently to avoid the madness that would ensue once the film was on general release. But one wonders whether that would have been a drop in the ocean knowing what her family life was like. It was frightening and pointless being sent to a school where she couldn't understand anyone nor they her, and she ended up stranded when it transpired that John hadn't paid the bill, nor paid for a ticket home, and had become uncontactable. She'd been tidied out of his way and, it appears, he'd actually managed to forget about her in his strung-out state.

Back in the US, she bagged a role as a rebellious big sister in the US TV show *One Day At A Time*. She would now study at Hollywood Professional School, where all the children were in showbiz and classes stopped at 12.45 so they could go to auditions. But it was hard for Mackenzie, already older than her years and fiercely independent, to even come close to finding an adult role model in this setting. One of the teachers, "who wore more make-up than a showgirl" and played belly-dancing music in class, was arrested for prostitution in front of the school.

Teenagers often say pretentious things for effect, or obnoxious things that get them in trouble. They might say they hate school, but if you're

---

* At the time Carson was an executive with Atlantic Records in London. He has since gone on to manage several successful heavy metal bands.

in the public eye, as Mackenzie was, these adolescent moans would be splashed all over the tabloid press. Mackenzie was also worse than the average teenager: she lived in a freewheeling microcosm where anything was acceptable, and this made interacting with the outside world doubly hazardous. She was kicked out of Hollywood Professional School after *People* magazine published a conversation they'd had with her in which she stated that Hollywood Professional School was 'ugly, boring and a fire trap'. Oops.

I think it's time to dig out one of those ready-made absence notes, scribble a forged signature and sign yourself off for a few weeks. After the madness of school we're going to hurl ourselves into another kind of insanity – that of the tour bus, the hotel, the backstage area and the arena. Music and everything that goes with it – the studios, the musicians, the business side and touring life – is indelibly stamped onto these children from birth, and informs how they spend the rest of their lives. Also, heading out on the road means you can spend hours with the parent that, more often than not, you might not see much of at other times, and those are magical times. Lisa Marie Presley knows what we're talking about.

"I wasn't crazy about school, and I'd look out of the window waiting for a car of his to come and pick me up. When the car pulled up that meant my father was yanking me out of school and I was going to see him somewhere on the road…"

Well, the car's here, so grab a toothbrush and let's get a move on.

CHAPTER 5

On The Road, In The Studio,
In The Blood

"If The Rolling Stones is a travelling circus, at least it's a family circus"
Ronnie Wood

For Jeff Buckley, music was his first 'toy'. Kelly Osbourne's toddlerhood was spent terrorising a tour bus in a frilly dress. Moon Zappa's first word was 'werp', reflecting the sound of tape reels being run back and forth in the living room. For Emma Townshend, The Who's anthem 'Baba O'Riley' simply means being a little girl, listening to the curious synthesised sounds coming from the 24-track "squeezed next to the washing machine" outside her bedroom. It took an afternoon watching *The Brady Bunch* for Ahmet Zappa to wonder who were the weird ones: the Bradys or the Zappas? The Bradys went camping, but the Zappas went on tour…

"I remember going to see Yes at the Rainbow when I was three or four," remembers Dylan Howe. "It was a packed house. I was up in a box with mum and I was like, 'Everyone's excited, what's going to happen?' Then somebody started to play guitar and I realised, 'That's my dad!' The realisation was profound."

One way or another, whether these children chose to become musicians themselves or not, they were surrounded by music, absorbing and responding and sometimes not even realising what was actually there because it was so close.

They might become savvy to the nuts and bolts of the business from an early age, or they might be blissfully unaware even of how known their parent is. As a child Stella McCartney would ask her dad when he was going to "put a song in the charts again" without realising you had to achieve a certain number of record sales. She had no real concept of how famous he was until she went to a Wings show with 200,000 people in the audience.

Similarly, the photographer Natalie Curtis, only child of Joy Division singer Ian Curtis, was aware of her late father having been a singer but "it just seemed normal, like having an uncle who was a tradesman or whatever". She was perfectly aware of how powerful her father's music was when she was growing up, the shock was discovering that "not everything was that amazing. I assumed all music was done with that level of style and intelligence." Ian died in 1980, when Natalie was just one, and there are many other examples who barely knew their parents. But however close they were or are does not diminish the fact that, directly or indirectly, these children's lives would be ruled by music. And they'd certainly come to know when it was a higher priority than themselves.

On December 18, 1971, Baxter was born to Betty and Ian Dury, a brother for Jemima. He arrived bang in the middle of a chaotic rehearsal for Ian's pre-Blockheads group, the pub rock/proto-punk band Kilburn & The High Roads. Betty gave birth in the upstairs bedroom while the Kilburns roared through their set. "At one stage Ian left the session to see his wife before returning with the words, 'It's a boy,'" writes Jim Drury in *Ian Dury and the Blockheads: Song By Song*. "He then picked up his microphone to carry on where he had left off."

Ian Dury was in his thirties when his career in music started to blossom, and there was a sense that time was running out. He wasn't going to risk missing out on his chance of success by spending his nights at home taking care of the kids. Baxter admits he eventually became feral, while Jemima was neatly absorbed into boarding school life at the Tring Arts Educational School near their Aylesbury home. After Betty and Ian split up, Baxter was sent to stay at his errant father's in Hammersmith. He found himself, as we now know, at the coalface of Dury's lawless life – although he was lucky if he saw him much at all.

One of the greatest chances of spending time with your nomadic parent and experiencing life as a musician yourself, is being allowed on the tour bus. This is a place where there are few illusions of rock stardom – it can be incredibly boring and is often full of people who have started to smell funny. You also have to accept that while your parent may be happy to have you there, there might be others who aren't so thrilled about the presence of excited young children in their personal space, what there is of it (not all tour buses are the kind with two levels, a bar and a roller-skating waitress, you see.)

"The first time I met Ginger Baker I was five, my little sister was about three," remembers Natascha Eleanore. Her dad, Jack Bruce, had brought his daughters on the road with him, but the reception was far from warm from the gangling, red-haired figure barring their path.

"We were getting on the tour bus and Ginger had his legs across the seats. I was holding my sister's hand and trying to get past, and I was like, 'Excuse me…' and he looked at me and went, 'I fucking hate children! I fucking hate kids!' So funny! He doesn't care what people think about him."

Baker wasn't much warmer with his own son Kofi, now in his forties and living and teaching in Orange County, Florida. At the age of five, Kofi would have to go over one drum rudiment at a time until his little hands were covered in blisters. "I learned from fear. He would say, 'Do that until I get back.' Then he would leave for two or three hours. I'd be crying my eyes out!" said Kofi in an interview. But the seed had been planted and despite the obvious distress (and eventual abandonment as Ginger left his family for Italy to kick his heroin addiction when Kofi was a teenager) his son became a passionate and respected drummer himself, working with the likes of Soft Machine's John Etheridge and Randy California from Spirit. By the age of 15 he'd be obliged to help support his mother and two sisters when they were evicted from their home while the former man of the house contemplated his navel in the sunshine.

After a year, Kofi went to Italy to show Ginger how his playing had developed, only to be told he "had a great feel but no technique". After another few years of absence, Kofi played for him again to be told: "Too much technique. Stop playing for six months."

Baker now lives in Tulbagh, South Africa, after, according to his Wikipedia entry, "having been forced out of homes in England, Nigeria, Italy and the US for various offences, including tax evasion".

If luminaries like Baker used going on the road – touring or not – to get away from toys, tantrums and involuntary bodily expulsions (although this does sound rather like life within the confines of Mötley Crüe's tour bus), there were others within the rock pantheon who couldn't bear to be away from their brood. Ronnie and Jo Wood brought their children Tyrone and Leah with them on The Rolling Stones' *Steel Wheels* tour in 1989. Jamie and Jesse were at school and stayed behind, but Leah had a tutor who travelled with them. "We hated being separated from them," said Ronnie. "This was Tyrone's first tour – there was no way we were going to leave him home alone with a nanny."

Life with the Stones was always, in Ronnie's words, a "travelling circus, but a family circus", and all part of that University of Life education. Keith Richards would bring his children Marlon, Angela and Theodora on tour or to interviews (journalist Chris Welch recalls meeting a 14-year-old Marlon while conducting an interview with Keith, "who fell asleep! Marlon was most concerned."). Mick would bring Jade, Jimmy and Lizzie, and later Georgia, Gabriel and Lucas. Charlie's daughter Seraphina and granddaughter Charlotte could often be seen backstage too. Hopefully there was plenty of sugar-free Ribena and organic Smarties on the rider alongside Richards' consignment of 'Nuclear Waste' (ingredients: vodka, cranberry, orange juice and Fanta. At least two of your Five a Day in there).

They were having a great time being spoilt by the dressers and backing singers, helping out backstage where they could and generally enjoying being included in the thrilling chaos of a large-scale touring show. Tyrone was less impressed when he was small ("Too much noise, too much music, too much shouting and sleeping in strange places") but it didn't take long for Wood's children to adapt. "We didn't realise just how great a time they were having until Jo got a room-service bill for caviar, foie gras, champagne and chips," remembers Ronnie. "We were rocking up a storm across the world and so were our kids."

Dylan Howe, like the Woods, broke through the 'Little Lord Fauntleroy' preconceptions some might have of rock stars' kids and helped out the roadies whenever he could, making some lifelong friends as a result. 'I felt more akin to the crew and the people helping to make the show happen. I helped carry the rider in and out, I kind of mucked in, which didn't go unnoticed because some of my contemporaries in the 'son of' gang that were there at the same time didn't seem to want to get involved in the same way.

"I had a great time and it helped to dispel the wall of politeness or fear of losing jobs if they thought they were going to upset me somehow! I also met some great people I still know to this day, one of whom is Ferdy Unger-Hamilton, then runner for (Yes singer) Jon Anderson. He'd set up his in-dressing room tepee and basically run around for everybody. He might have been low on the food chain then but a couple of years later he's a record company boss (Go Beat/Polydor – he is now an executive at Virgin) after signing Portishead, Gabrielle and Keane to name a few. He remembered me and has put quite a lot of work my way. This might not have happened if I was just seen stepping in and out of a limo!"

Suzi Quatro's daughter Laura Tuckey would often tag along on the road, although the flamboyance of her mother often left Laura fighting not to be left in the shade. Put bluntly, she became a bit of a show-off to compensate. "I felt I had to compete with mum on these tours," she said in an interview with *The Times* in 2007. "I used to try and hog the limelight. If there was a microphone I would get up and sing, because I wanted the attention on me. If we were on a tour bus I'd get on the microphone and tell jokes."

The Osbourne children loved going on tour with their parents and the neo-family that was the road crew – it was better than being left at home with the "psycho nannies" (we'll be meeting them later). Kelly and Jack spent the first few years of their lives on tour with Ozzy, skipping school for months at a time and, like the Woods, helping the production team and road crew once they were old enough.

They were also spoiled rotten on the road. "We could just ask for something and there would be someone there to get it for us," says Jack. "One day I said to one of the production staff, 'I want a Playstation.' One hour later, a Playstation appears. It was like that with anything we asked for." When they were allowed onstage, Osbourne's drummer, Randy Castillo, would give them both a drumstick and let them play along. At night they'd bundle into the back of the bus with their parents and watch videos together.

They lived up to their hell-raising genes too, to the point they nearly got kicked out of shows by security who didn't realise who their dad was. It wasn't as if they had the best examples for good behaviour though – the adults on those tours were like big kids themselves, chucking eggs at the support band and getting into fights. On one occasion they had to fight for their lives, after Ozzy appeared to invite the entire audience to storm the stage and a riot kicked off, with fans trying to steal guitars, equipment, even tearing the mic out of Ozzy's hands. Jack remembers seeing his father fighting on the stage with a fan before the crowd started rushing the backstage area and dressing rooms. The kids were bustled into a van and driven away for their own safety.

But there were serious reasons why Sharon wanted the children on tour with them: she felt it was vital for them to see their father shine, appreciated by thousands. Wisely, she wanted them to understand that this was their father at work. Also, a positive consequence of witnessing people generating the sort of bedlam that occurs on tour is that it ceases to be a novelty. You see your elders lose control unattractively and vow never to do that yourself, simply from the point of view of your own teenage vanity.

"When you're on the road, especially with other bands, they feel as though they have to act up and live out that whole sex, drugs and rock 'n' roll lifestyle," tuts Kelly in the Osbournes book *Ordinary People*. "It bugs me to see these bands that go out there and are rude and trash dressing rooms. That's such an Eighties cocaine and booze lifestyle, it isn't about that any more."

Depeche Mode singer Dave Gahan would often bring his son Jack, named after Dave's stepfather (quite a lot of Jacks in this chapter), on tour with him. Jack was even featured (as a baby) in the Depeche Mode tour documentary *101*, much to fans' delight.

When I first see Jack strolling up to meet me on Westbourne Grove in his leather jacket, I find it hard not to be struck by how much he resembles both his mother, Joanne Fox, a former punk scenester, and his father. Jack and Dave are also alike in character, he tells me, sharing the same dark sense of humour. We have tea in his flat nearby, with *King Tubby Meets Rockers Uptown* echoing away in the background and a whiff of incense in the air. Our original interview was postponed by way of an apologetic email telling me that his dad was in town from LA and wanted to watch the football with him. I found this all the more touching when I later discovered that Dave Gahan wasn't originally into football at all, but is now developing a liking for it because he knows Jack is a fan. (This was also shortly after Gahan senior's operation on a malignant tumour in his bladder, discovered after he fell ill in his dressing room just before going onstage in Athens on Depeche Mode's *Tour of the Universe* in May 2009.)

Jack Gahan, 22 at the time of our interview, would have been too young to spend time with his dad on the road when Dave was in the throes of his heroin addiction, which finally came to a head in 1996 when the singer had a near-death experience after speedballing. (He recalls a 'blackness' and hearing his third and current wife, Jennifer, calling him back. It seems no coincidence she plays an angel in the video for Depeche Mode's 2006 single 'Suffer Well'.) But by the time Jack was 13, he'd be allowed to spend his school holidays hanging out with Depeche Mode when most 13-year-olds would be heading to summer camps or stacking shelves in Asda.

Being on tour with his father allowed Jack, like the Osbournes' children, to see his parent getting on with his job. As a result, he garnered insights about the music industry from the inside and learned to naturally behave respectfully on tour and in the studio.

"I was around when they'd be mixing or recording in London, but as I got older I realised it's like going to work. You don't want to be in the way, the last thing I want to do is intrude on anything. That was always quite a clear line, the same goes for being on tour. It's very much work for my dad and he sees it like anyone would a normal job."

The work ethic is strong, the long-standing crew is like a family and Dave Gahan for one is now more likely to head back to his hotel room than sniff out the nearest party. That's not to say they don't have fun when Jack and his family join the group on the road. "Playing 'foozeball', we do that quite a lot!" says Jack. "And I love the atmosphere building up before the show, chatting with the guys, travelling out with my family and being at all these venues in America where there'd be little games machines with mini basketballs and stuff. Being in amazing countries, seeing amazing landscapes.

"I love seeing the shows. I've grown up around it, it's embedded in me, I can listen and watch and appreciate it for different reasons than a fan would. When I was 13 I went out for the *Exciter* tour, it was all the craze at the time to have those little scooters, we (himself, his cousins and stepbrother) all had them and were going round and round the hotel on these things, and at the gig!

"Up until the last few years I'd just be with my dad, we'd go and see a movie or something. It's well past the phase, certainly for my dad, of the whole partying side, it's just nice to hang out."

In Dylan Howe's case, years spent standing in the wings watching Yes play live during the Seventies left their inevitable mark. Did he become a prog rocker himself then? No. Did he develop a horror of Chris Squire's rather form-fitting trousers? Well, probably. But this particular development is a little more cerebral. Every Yes concert was, and is, preceded by the dramatic sound of the finale to Igor Stravinsky's *Firebird Suite*. Every night this poetic, rousing music would etch itself onto Dylan's psyche. And in 2009, Dylan and jazz pianist Will Butterworth recorded their own adaptation of Stravinsky's *Rite Of Spring* and *Firebird Suite* for drums and piano.

"So many seeds were sewn at that impressionable stage," says Dylan. "It was such an exciting, exotic sound. I associate that music with feeling such wonder as a kid. Then to get to a point where I started to understand it musically, and feel I'd like to play drums inside it with another arrangement, it felt like a natural thing to do because it was kind of part of me.

"When you're exposed to such advanced music at a young age, and that begins to sound right to you, that's more the norm than simpler harmonies and structures, then that sets the bar. When people tell me they are a musician or an artist, I expect a lot because I'd been surrounded by virtuosic individuals. When you're young, anyone idolises their dad but if he's on a platform and you see physically some kind of mastery, that only adds to it."

'Prog' musicians such as Steve Howe and Rick Wakeman were often dismissively referred to as "trying to be classical musicians" but Pete Townshend was another artist, equally progressive in the true sense of the word, who was open to crossing over, and British music is richer for it.

"I started to think on a larger scale after meeting (Who manager) Kit Lambert who encouraged me to leap over snobbery in the classical establishment, and reverse-snobbery in the rock business, and just do what I felt was right, "says Pete. "I liked storytelling, and installation in rock. It's common now, and Steve (Howe) was definitely part of an experimental socio-musical art installation as well as a band, with a manifesto straight out of art school or the college canteen. We were all determined to cross boundaries.

"Record companies were idiots in the Sixties. Journalists were mostly twats who had failed to kick-start their own bands. We had to be a little blinkered, very brave, and thick-skinned. Look at how the most experimental and delightful period of British rock was pejoratively reduced to 'prog' rock by a few shithead punks who were still learning to play. Nothing wrong with punk. But there was nothing wrong with prog rock either, except, as always, the haircuts!"

Back to the subject of touring, as Joe Jackson rightly sang, it's different for girls: musicians' daughters often have to wave off their father and brothers as they board the bus. And in one little girl's case, with over 20 siblings, she had potentially quite a lot of waving to do.

Lovella Ellis is the daughter of Studio One rock-steady legend Alton Ellis (famous for his renditions of 'You've Made Me So Very Happy', 'Sitting In The Park' and 'Girl I've Got A Date') and Lovella herself is a singer at the forefront of a new generation of the Seventies reggae offshoot Lover's Rock.

Lovella and I meet in her cousin's immaculate flat, a picture of Alton propped up on top of the TV. We have retreated from the heat of a summer afternoon on her home turf of Vauxhall, an area of south London where her father, who died in October 2008 (less than a year before our interview), had his own record shop called The All-Tones, a play on his first name.

Going away with her father and his Jamaican band was largely a male preserve, she recalls. "Obviously you've got a girl child with all these men around on the road and in the studios for hours on end. Dad didn't think it was the right environment.

"He took me sometimes. I'd sit in the studio watching him, and people would say, 'That's your daddy there!' I enjoyed that. It was interesting, we'd stay for hours rehearsing, and then the next take and the next take, not knowing what they're saying, and then as you get older you start to understand. It does help you get used to studios. I know a lot of people who have talent but haven't been moulded into that studio mindset and so they get thrown in, they can sing, but it's like nothing comes out when they get in the studio, they get dumbstruck, on stage as well."

I'd first seen Lovella sing with Lover's Rock queen Janet Kay at the British Film Institute after a screening of a documentary about much-missed Dalston club The Four Aces. I had no idea at the time she was performing in place of her father, who had died just weeks before. Since Alton's death Lovella has billed herself as 'Lovella Ellis, Daughter of a Legend'.

Sharing the surname of a beloved tastemaker within the galaxy of rock, such as John Peel or Whispering Bob Harris, is indeed taken as a guarantee of quality, certainly in the case of Charlie Harris. Working in music and publishing, this never fails to impress men of a certain age, and she backs up her pedigree with a similar passion and knowledge for music, having been whisked from stadium rock concert to studio recording in her youth. This was also thanks to her mother, Jackie, who worked for the merchandising company Winterland during the glitzy Eighties.

"She did Prince's *Purple Rain*, Madonna's *Like A Virgin*, Michael Jackson's *Bad*..." lists Charlie, as we sit on the grass in Holland Park, accompanied by the tinkling chimes of a kids' outdoor percussion workshop nearby. "I went to all of those big Wembley Stadium concerts. I don't even know how many times I've seen Yes! Mum would take me and put me on a chair, blag security to let her little girl in and I was backstage from an early age."

Charlie was born during the Whispering one's early heyday, which in the Seventies saw him behaving as much like a rock star as the legends he partied with - Elton John, Marc Bolan, "You name it," says Charlie. "*The Old Grey Whistle Test* was massive and the people he was hanging out with were huge. He did the last interview with John Lennon, that was very much what he was up to.

"One of the best stories I know was while mum was heavily pregnant with me, dad got beaten up by the Sex Pistols because he wouldn't play their song on the show. He wasn't a massive supporter of punk really, but the main thing is *Whistle Test* only put people on who had albums. He actually got beaten up, they sent some guys round to our house. Mum remembers seeing this leather-studded fist come through the living room window.

"Also, Marc Bolan died in a car crash the September I was born," Charlie continues. "While my mum was pregnant with me, she was backstage at a concert that year (while my dad was on stage) – and Marc said to her: 'I have this terrible fear that something's going happen to me so that Roly (his son Rolan) won't remember me.'"

Callum Adamson's favourite memories include travelling with Big Country during the height of his father, Stuart's, fame during the Eighties, although the flip side to fun on the road can often be long periods of doing very little (some might see that as an advantage) and also being stared at in airports: "It was like meerkats everywhere peering over. I kept thinking, 'Have I stolen something?'"

But the tedium would be obliterated whenever there were other children to tear around with. "We were really nosy, opening flight cases backstage, stealing cans of hooch, running around hotels. The manager had kids who were a similar age, and I remember completely terrorising hotels with them, doing really stupid stuff. Do you know Barrowlands (Ballroom)? They have these stars on the walls, I stole two stars.

"I always got a lot of freedom. I'd be allowed to just wander off and come back. And there's something about being in a venue before the crowd's there. I'd get to play guitar at stage volume, that was very cool. Wandering around, things being screwed in, smoke machines being tested…"

Bands on tour find it notoriously hard to cope should they be vegetarian (unless, like Morrissey, you have the constitution that would cope with egg and chips every day for weeks), or keen to follow a healthy, regular diet. This is a particular concern if you have children aboard. "If catering's not there, you are eating tacos forever," explains Callum. The other problem with kids on the bus is that they are likely to get stuck in to anything that looks like sweeties (dangerous) and down anything that looks drinkable, as Callum himself experienced as a youngster: he picked up a glass of what he thought was water and drank it. It tasted funny. It made him feel funny too. It was, of course, vodka. "I was drunk for the rest of the day…"

He also had to learn the mixing desk was not a toy when Big Country recorded at Abbey Road. "He (his dad, Stuart) must have got so pissed off with me, I remember playing with the faders and annoying the engineers." Being a parent doesn't stop just because you're in the studio concentrating on mixing your latest masterpiece.

One pleasantly surprising studio story appears in J. Randy Taraborelli's Michael Jackson biography, *The Magic And The Madness.* During the recording of Jackson's 2001 album, *Invincible,* at the Hit Factory Criteria studio in North Miami, little Prince Michael I dropped popcorn on the floor. A producer was about to clear up the mess when Jackson said, "No, let me. He's my kid, I'll clean up after him." The producer told Tarborelli: "I look down and there's Michael Jackson on his hands and knees picking up his son's popcorn. I'm not sure you'd see Madonna doing that."

Spending time in touring or studio environments can obviously inform your own direction, and while it is lazy to suppose that all musicians' children would continue in the family trade, the sheer accessibility of all facets of the lifestyle can be a decisive factor.

"I've always played instruments and always wanted to be a musician," says Will Hunt, Dansette Junior frontman and son of ELO/Wizzard musician Bill. "I remember my mum said once that our breakfast table was the only breakfast table where if one of the kids said, 'I want to be a rock star' it was acceptable… rather than a doctor or an accountant. It's not unfeasible.

"I've never been forced into the music industry which is often a preconception. 'Oh, your dad must have made you play guitar?' Not really! I did karate, I played football, rugby, I was never forced into anything. It was cheaper for me to pick up a guitar because there was one in the house already. You haven't got to go and buy me a karate suit or a new pair of football boots for that. The instruments were already lying around, it wasn't like I even had to make a choice. It was there to pick up and do."

Marc Bolan with his baby son Rolan, September 1975.
(TERRY O'NEILL/HULTON ARCHIVE/GETTY IMAGES)

Ringo Starr with his children (l-r) Zak, Lee and Jason Starkey on their way to Los Angeles. 1977.
(EVENING NEWS/REX FEATURES)

Paul McCartney poses with his first wife Linda, and their daughters, left to right, Heather, Stella and Mary, 1975.
(DAILY EXPRESS/ARCHIVE PHOTOS/GETTY IMAGES)

John Lennon with Yoko Ono and his son Julian at Internel Studios in Stonebridge Park, Wembley, during a rehearsal for the Rolling Stones' *Rock And Roll Circus* TV special, London, December 10, 1968.
(MICHAEL WEBB/KEYSTONE/HULTON ARCHIVE/GETTY IMAGES)

George Harrison with his son Dhani, London 1987.
(TERRY O'NEILL/GETTY IMAGES)

Ronnie and Jo Wood with Jamie, Jesse, Leah and Tyrone. (DAVE HOGAN/GETTY IMAGES)

Keith Richards with wife, model Patti Hansen,
and their daughters Theodora and Alexandra.
(TIME LIFE PICTURES/DMI/TIME LIFE PICTURES/GETTY IMAGES)

Mick Jagger with his wife Bianca and their daughter
Jade, circa 1974. (ARCHIVE PHOTOS/GETTY IMAGES)

Beach Boy Brian Wilson with daughters Carnie (L), Wendy (C) & wife Marilyn (R).
(JULIAN WASSER//TIME LIFE PICTURES/GETTY IMAGES)

Recording at Panda Sound studios, Norma and Mike Waterson with Martin and Eliza Carthy. (DAVE PEABODY/REDFERNS)

Rod Stewart with Kimberly and Sean, 1983. (DAVE HOGAN/HULTON ARCHIVE/GETTY IMAGES)

Ginger Baker at home with his children Ginette and Kofi. (D. MORRISON/EXPRESS/GETTY IMAGES)

Big Country frontman Stuart Adamson
stacking videotapes with son Callum.
(TERRY SMITH/TIME & LIFE PICTURES/GETTY IMAGES)

Kurt Cobain and daughter Frances Bean
(KEVIN MAZUR/WIREIMAGE)

Paula Yates, Michael Hutchence and Paula's children at Planet Hollywood in London, February 5, 1996.
(DAVE BENETT/GETTY IMAGES)

Ozzy Osbourne and his children Kelly, Jack and Aimee. (GAB/ARCHIVE/REDFERNS)

Yoko Ono and son Sean Lennon visit Strawberry Field in Liverpool. (HOWARD BARLOW)

The instruments were there, as were the records, but equally important was the fact that Will would often come home to find influential musicians and producers just sitting around on the sofa. "Steve Winwood would be there... I'd come home and Slade would be in the lounge..." (I didn't ask whether they have Christmas anthem sing-offs.)

"Dave Hill, the guitarist, and my dad would write together, they do still. And there were people through my cousin (Wonderstuff's Miles Hunt) as well. When he was number one with 'Dizzy' with Vic Reeves and Bob Mortimer, you'd end up going out with Shane MacGowan, Eddie Izzard. That's more of a cool thing than anything that really influenced me, you know, I had a beer with Shane MacGowan!

"I remember being eight years old and going to a Wonderstuff gig at the Walsall football club. We were in the family box, and just seeing all these fans singing your song back at you... I thought, 'I want this!' Going to so many gigs at a young age inspires you to keep going because eventually it might happen."

Trev Lukather's experience was similar – he wasn't coerced into embracing the guitar like his power-chord Pop, indeed he was bought a mini drum kit when he was four, but watching his father's virtuosity, and the reaction it would spark, persuaded Trev to put down his drumsticks and change direction. But that's not to say that Steve modelled him in his own image.

Trev: "I'd done this Fender photo-shoot when I was 10 (as you do) and I had this guitar collecting dust under my bed, and I said, 'Dad, I want to play guitar just like you! Teach me, teach me!' And my dad being the awesome cat he is, he takes my low E string, put his index finger on the first four strings to make like a power chord, and said, 'Have fun!' and walked out the room. He had no patience to teach me anything!

"I'd watch videos of my dad playing and learn licks. He's not a very patient guy, he's not going to sit and teach me something. If I don't get it in the first few tries he'd be like, 'Argh! Do it on your own, I've got to do like a million things right now!'

"But it felt natural to me, I never got lessons, that's why I believe it's in the genes. It's like the colour of your hair. And you can take it and run with it."

From girlhood, Calico Cooper was running with it big-style as she toured with her father Alice and the travelling Cooper show. She credits the testosterone-packed experience for her predominantly male approach, *and*, she quips, for moulding her into the 'perfect woman' (does that mean the perfect woman is thus male? Let's not go there). In all seriousness, being brought up around strong alpha males taught her to stand up for herself and fight her own corner, qualities that are twice as important to one likely to be dismissed as a "celebrity brat."

"I grew up with men on a tour bus. No women," she tells me. "It was interesting, it was cool. They showed me the perfect girl without knowing it. They'd hang up the phone from their girlfriends and go, 'Dammit! I hate it when she says I don't this and I don't that…' and I'd be listening at formative ages like 10, and I'd be like 'OK, note to self, don't say you're going to call and then don't.' Got it. Then when I came of age I was like, 'Look who's perfect!' (laughs).

"I tend to have a male approach, not aggressive, but I don't like to be talked down to, I don't like to be told 'No'! I wish I could send a message to all the young girls out there: don't roll over so easy. You don't have to be a jerk about it, but if you go, 'Hey I have this great idea for a screenplay,' and you hand it over and they push it aside, I will walk to the other side of the desk and point and say, 'Especially on page 12' and make sure that they know I'm not just some celebrity kid who wrote a story. I put my heart into this."

This isn't to say she didn't have her moments, but the sobering (no pun intended) experience of being inadvertently abandoned in a foreign country soon changed that. She'd reached a stage in her teens when she'd started behaving more 'rock 'n' roll' than her own dad, who was abstaining from booze while his little girl quaffed away with his entourage. "I got a little too comfortable with the touring lifestyle, I went a bit Britney Spears," Calico chuckles. "We were drinking and listening to jazz in the bus; my dad wasn't there, he'd decided to fly. He'd come to a point where he was comfortable to leave me with the band because I could handle myself. And I proved him wrong…

"We pull up to this truck stop to use the bathroom. I had had way too much to drink, and I got off the bus in my pyjamas with no shoes on. When I came out the sun was coming up and I had no idea where we were – turns out Belgium but I didn't know that. It's starting to rain, I look up, and the bus is driving onto the freeway.

"I laughed because we are the worst with pranks, ask any band that opens for us, we're brutal. We've thrown guys out of the building in the middle of their own show. So I just think this is some elaborate prank. I'm standing in the rain going, 'Ha ha! OK I get it, hilarious.' Then it disappears off into the distance. I am drunk and shoeless with no wallet and no phone and I don't speak any other language but English. So I wait and wait – this is the glamorous side of being a celebrity kid – and it doesn't come back. I start panicking, 'Oh my God, everybody on that bus is passed out and nobody knows I'm not on it.' We have a show that night, and we are in the middle of nowhere. I go inside, and I'm trying to explain to the clerk that my bus left me and I need to use the phone but I don't have any money. I've never felt like such a princess in all my life. I just realise nobody here knows who I am and they're not going to do me any favours. And I look like a homeless person.

"Finally this nice man who spoke a bit of English showed me to the pay phone and I had to collect call my mother in the States who had to call the tour manager and my father on a plane, who had to call the bus driver to turn around and come and get me. I'm crying because I'm a complete idiot, and then the lady comes up to me and said, 'You cannot stay here…' I was like, 'WHAT?' What she was trying to say was I couldn't loiter, she thought I was some crazy drunk hippy. I said, 'Oh no, my bus is coming for me. My bus?' And she keeps pointing outside to the bus stop, 'Here is the bus…' and I'm trying to explain it's the Alice Cooper bus, trying to demonstrate the make-up on my face, 'Alice Cooper?' 'Oh! Alice Cooper!' And I'm like, 'Yeah, that's me! I mean, not me, but I'm in the band,' I'm doing air guitar, and she's not getting it, and going, 'Stand outside for the bus?'

"So I have to go outside in the rain. The hangover is kicking in and she comes out again and says I can't stand there either, it's on the property. So she makes me walk across to the bus stop and sit in the rain. I was so angry. That was a low point, you want to picture champagne and flashbulbs and all the nice things associated with my life? I was shoeless and wet and she did not want me there. Like a total rock star I kick over the trash can, and the trash goes everywhere in the rain and I look at her as if to say, 'You'll have to pick that up…'

"Finally the bus comes and, totally out of character for me, I slipped the girl the finger. I went on about that for weeks, I'd say to my dad, 'Ooh I really like these shoes… maybe you should buy them for me seeing as I GOT LEFT AT A TRUCK STOP!'"

The offspring of New Romantic groups like Spandau Ballet, which originally split when the children were still very young (or not yet born), are less likely to have had the opportunity of even seeing their parent on stage up to now. Martin Kemp's photographer daughter Harleymoon, an impressively motivated and witty 19-year-old, saw her father and uncle (Gary Kemp) and their Spandau Ballet cohorts on stage for the first time just months after our interview in the summer of 2009.

"I'm putting together a photographic book for Spandau Ballet," she said. "I've been photographing their rehearsals and it's cool because half of the songs I'd never heard. It's so exciting, but I just couldn't imagine him in a band! He's so soft… but he plays real baddies." (Reggie Kray in Peter Medak's *The Krays* in 1990 and the soap *EastEnders'* calculating Steve Owen.)

Harleymoon and her little brother Roman were always made to feel they could go into music if they wanted to. When she expressed an interest in putting a band together, her parents immediately went out and bought a PA system for the music room. "I was just thinking about maybe practising downstairs, the next thing my dad's gone out and bought a PA system! Just going too far!" she laughs.

But this is not always the general *modus operandi* for musical parents – in some cases the children are actively discouraged from exploring a life in music, which is confusing and frustrating because they were born into it, and in many cases they come back to it eventually anyway. By the time they do, they're pretty annoyed they weren't nurtured in the first place.

Galen Ayers: "I bumped into Leonard Cohen's son Aaron, and we had this same conversation about encouragement.

"He was like, 'I was completely encouraged, and now I'm really annoyed that I was. Why wasn't I told what a nightmare it is?' and I burst out laughing and said, 'I wasn't encouraged at all! Why didn't they encourage me?' and we were laughing – you can't win, is my point."

Aaron Horn, son of super-producer Trevor Horn, co-founder of legendary independent label ZTT (Zang Tuum Tumb) with wife Jill

Sinclair, Paul Morley and Anne Dudley, was hanging around their studios (Sarm) in West London from a very early age, but he isn't afraid to admit he too is irritated his father didn't cultivate his musicality more.

Aaron (an educated Jewish north Londoner in his mid-twenties with a tinge of what I think the youth of today call 'street') met me at Chalk Farm tube where he had come to walk me down to his Camden flat. Or rather, I was walking, he was gliding on a skateboard and eating an ice cream in celebration of it being a prematurely summery day in March. We have a cup of tea in his flat, a pleasing tangle of wires, mixing desks, as one might expect, and sky-blue walls decorated with wispily painted white clouds, a homage to his mother, Sinclair: "She always insisted studios should be painted blue."

Aaron was born in 1983, at the peak of ZTT's success with their controversial pop protégés Frankie Goes To Hollywood. As a result, Aaron tells me, his father was barely there, let alone around to encourage him. To Aaron, the glamour and mystique of the studio was in part because it contained his hard-working and inevitably enigmatic dad.

"When I was little, I was like: 'Wow, the studios are cool, dad's always going in there, something's going on,'" remembers Aaron. "I got banned as a little kid; when he'd leave me in there I'd just press everything and re-programme stuff, so it was like, 'Don't leave Aaron in the control room!' He didn't really want me to be a musician so he never used to teach me anything musical, which was something I got angry with.

"When I was 11 or 12, they started to use Pro-tools and digital stuff, and it would just ruin things. He'd come home stressed, and it would be like, 'What's wrong?' 'Pro-tools went down!' It was like this evil thing. I remember having a conversation with him when we were walking around Primrose Hill. I must have been 13, 14, and I was like, 'I could never learn Pro-tools!' It sounded so insanely technical.

"But I've always been interested in the technology side of it because I wasn't ever shown the acoustic guitar, although it would be sitting around at home. It was never like, 'Look, this is really good fun, you can do stuff on this.'

"And he was always busy when I was a kid as well, some days he'd come back from a session when I'd be having breakfast. I remember for about two years of my life I'd see him more in the mornings. He'd be in a good mood though because he'd be stoned after a long session! He'd be chilling and we'd have a chat for a minute while I was having my breakfast, but it wasn't like he was around when I'd come back from school.

"Whatever you see you probably don't want your kid to get into, but I'm still kind of pissed off with him for that in some ways, as I don't have certain musical rudiments. Because I don't have that, I can't always 100 per cent understand what I'm technically doing, I'll just try and do what works and it's usually quite basic. It will feed into what he's doing sometimes. I can't say, 'You should try going into this key,' I can't competently explain it, so I just say obvious things like, 'Those bits are a bit gay… you might need to give it a bit more space,' or 'Why did you need to do that? That bit's really good.'" Obvious stuff.

"Because he's such a musical purist, he didn't really get what I was doing in the beginning. When I was doing lots of DJ-ing and scratching, because there are two levels to him, as a father he's like, 'Cool that you're into it,' and then on a music level, you could feel he'd be like, 'Essentially, you're just playing with toys…'

"But I think he sees me as sort of 'the youth'. I play him bits of music and he starts to cotton on, and understand what I'm into and how that feeds into things. And he bites some ideas sometimes!"

Aaron is now a DJ and a producer himself, and he knows much of what he picked up organically throughout his childhood from engineers has stood him in good stead, if only because he was forced to learn for himself. Trevor certainly didn't have time to stand over him and teach him the ropes, 'One day, all this will be yours' style. But this served to demystify the process of production.

"He would say, 'There isn't a rulebook, just don't blow the speakers!' But it's not like there's a magical mathematical equation to recording a band anyway. Microphone, sound goes in through this channel and into a recording device. That's it. Once I'd worked that out, I just learnt through mistakes, which is how most people learn. I was lucky to have the stuff there, so people are right when they go, 'Oh lucky him…' That's right. I didn't make the choice, it's not something I can change, but wouldn't it have been worse to waste it?"

CHAPTER 6

Absence

"The dirtiest word was 'goodbye', and we seemed to say it all the time."
Kelly Osbourne

Absence has always stalked the family of the rock star; days that turn into weeks and often months spent in the womb of a studio, seemingly endless tours, often a whirlwind social life. Then there's the marathon sleeping sessions during which children bound into the bedroom to show off their new trainers as their squinting, jet-lagged parent with a pillow-creased face mumbles incoherently.

Robert Plant's eldest child, Carmen, was so unfamiliar with her own father that she once mistook him for a burglar when he came home from tour. Jack and Kelly Osbourne tried to surreptitiously pack themselves into a suitcase when they weren't allowed to join their parents on tour. Ringo Starr biographer Alan Clayson describes the drummer's 'Count Dracula hours' during his son Zak's teens as damaging in many ways, not least because of the example it set: Zak saw his father disappear off to party his way around the world. So what was the point in turning up to school when you could be doing something more fun? He'd skip class and then skip off to see another potentially questionable role model.

"During my puberty, Moonie (Keith Moon) was always there while my old man was far away in Monte Carlo or somewhere," Zak said in later years. It wasn't enough that Ringo was there for him when he was a child, his sons needed a strong, loving patriarch when they were teenagers.

Keith Moon might have provided Zak with a quasi-father figure, but his own daughter Mandy was less fortunate – Moon was apparently indifferent to his little girl most of the time, and Mandy, in turn, was terrified of her father, and would be 'semi-rigid' when she was around him, according to Tony Fletcher's Keith Moon biography, *Dear Boy*. Mandy was whisked away from him when she was just six when her mother, Kim, left Keith in 1973, eventually marrying the Small Faces' Ian McLagan in 1978 and leaving the UK to settle in Austin, Texas. "I don't really remember him as a person," says Mandy of Keith. "I know he was my father, but I don't really think of him as my dad. When he was at home, it was like, 'Who is this strange person?'"

In many cases, if the oft-absent parent is the father, the mother and child would become a tight-knit team. Rufus Wainwright became so close to his mother, Kate McGarrigle, and so distant from his father that he longed for a man in his life to fill the void, sometimes dreaming of finding an egg in the forest that contained a brother for him.

Similarly Frank Zappa's children had trouble piquing their dad's attention; even when he was at home, he was 'absent'. He slept when the children were awake, or worked obsessively in his studio. Moon's collaboration with Frank on the track 'Valley Girl' came about only because she was trying to find a way to spend time with him. The note she slipped under his door was addressed to 'Daddy', not 'Frank' as he'd instructed his children to call him. She introduced herself and told him she wanted to sing on his album, suggesting she could do some freestyling in her party-piece mock-Encino accent. She included the home telephone number and told him to call her agent: her mum.

Moon: "It was me saying, 'Pay attention to me!'" It took him several months to respond, however. (Moon and Frank would be at their closest when he became ill with cancer in 1990. She spent three years looking after him up until his death on December 6, 1993. He still refused to discuss anything personal whenever she tried to talk about her childhood.)

The emotional absence caused by addiction, egomania or psychological complexes can be an even more distressing unavailability than that of physical absence. In many cases the parent remains the child, wrapped up in their own needs, development arrested by dependencies or delusions of grandeur and having their superiority complex, often fuelled by inferiority, stoked by exposure and the indulgence of cronies and yes-men. Like children, everything is done for them.

When they come home and are expected to put their usual priorities on hold, difficulties arise that are confusing for everyone involved. If this balance is thrown, the child can respond by becoming over-responsible and extra-protective of the parent who is 'left behind' with them. They might behave like the 'man of the house' like Julian Lennon at just 10 years old, or, like the 11-year-old Frances Bean Cobain who nursed her mother Courtney Love through an OxyContin overdose by making her green tea while they waited for an ambulance. (Child Services took Frances Bean away from Love the following week.)

There is the inevitable absence caused by marital breakdown, the lack of father figure when the union that created you was a one-night stand, and, there is the final, irrevocable absence if the parent dies, leaving a family to evolve and continue without them (their presence still remaining, not just personally but culturally, depending on the level of their profile. Their name, their music, their face could pop up to haunt you at any time). Jazz saxophonist and Duke Special collaborator Ben Castle also tells me the frequently asked question "How's your dad?" turned into a sympathetic "How's your mum?" after his much-loved father, Roy, passed away in 1994.

In some cases, the child might never have known the deceased/ estranged, but still relate to what they related to, share their expressions, inherit their gifts.

Whispering Bob Harris walked back into his daughter Charlie's life when she was 15, after the break-up of the relationship between her mother, Jackie, and stepfather, radio DJ Richard Skinner. Charlie might have been estranged from her father during her formative years, but she was amazed by how similar they were. "The most interesting thing is when you meet them you're exactly the same, same smile, same voice, same interests. It takes a little time to break through the wall, but we've done it.

"We had to get to know each other again. You hit 13, first boyfriend, all that stuff, Dad wasn't there. My first gig, Dad wasn't there. We had to rediscover each other, how we'd changed and learn about our music again together. We're like peas in a pod now.

"When dad left mum he was off with the fairies, and it's only been over the last 25 years he came down to earth. The reason he's doing so well now and holding it down where others don't is because he completely sorted his life out. Obviously the cancer (Harris was diagnosed with prostate cancer in 2007) had a massive impact – he's got into exercising, cut down smoking, he barely drinks, the rock 'n' roll lifestyle has gone out of the window but he's still a big groupie at the end of the day!"

Big Country's Stuart Adamson fortunately put home life before rock'n'roll during his children's early years, and a certain pop mega-star had to go to great lengths to persuade him out of the bosom of his family at all. "It was Christmas time," remembers Callum Adamson. "We were all at home in Scotland. Elton John was playing at Wembley, and he *had* to have Big Country play with him, but they wanted to stay at home.

"They ended up sending a private jet to pick everyone up, fly them down. They played Wembley and then flew straight back home the same night so they didn't have to be away from home. That was very cool."

Family life for the Adamsons was largely this warm and cohesive throughout Callum's child and teenhood. However, sadly, after the divorce of his parents and Stuart's eventual descent into alcoholism, Callum didn't speak to his father for years. "I don't know why, I just decided, 'Fuck this, I'm just going to smoke hash,' and that's really all I did," he says. "But then after a while he started talking to me about Alcoholics Anonymous, and how you can't control anything else except your surroundings and your decisions, you can remove yourself from certain situations. That's a good thing."

Jack Bruce is keenly aware that his family from his first marriage to sometime writing partner Janet Godfrey suffered because of the long periods he had to spend on the road. Touring was even more important to Bruce and Cream as a result of unsatisfactory business deals, so heading out on the road was often the best way to stay afloat. He also drank a lot, and had developed a considerable heroin habit to support.

The group split in 1968 when it became apparent that Bruce and drummer Ginger Baker could stand each other no more. (It wasn't a cold war, they would sabotage each other's equipment. Even during their tenure in the pre-Cream Graham Bond Organisation, Baker would throw sticks at Bruce's head, Bruce threw a double bass at Baker, decimating his drums. Baker also went at Bruce with a large knife, which led to Bruce walking away from the GBO – it's amazing they decided to work together again at all, and the antipathy hasn't mellowed. "Nowadays, we're happily co-existing in different continents," said Bruce after the Cream reunion in 2005. "Although I was thinking of asking him to move. He's still a bit too close…")

The years beyond psychedelia and into the Seventies saw the star bassist's finances slump disastrously, and his marriage to Janet fell apart. It wasn't the best time to be a dad to his sons Malcolm and Jonas, or 'Joey'. Jonas would tragically pass away in 1997 after an asthma attack when he was 28. Just a few years before, in 1991, Bruce's old bandmate Eric Clapton lost his four-year-old son Conor, after the child fell from a 53rd floor apartment window in New York. But while Clapton chose to grieve publicly with the ballad 'Tears In Heaven', Bruce later admitted he "couldn't have done that"; he didn't want to upset Jonas' mother, and his was a very private mourning that led to him going "insane" for the following two years, unable to go near a piano, which was his late son's main instrument. The untimely passing of a parent may be hard to bear, but the loss of a child must be indescribably heart-breaking.

In 1979, Bruce married Margrit Seyffer, mother of his children Natascha, Kyla and Corin. Margrit became his manager and continues to take care of the business side of his career to this day. Jack's life began to pull together, and he would put his children first and get his priorities in place. While he isn't going to pretend rock stars and family life always correlate perfectly, he insists there are plenty of devoted dads out there.

"There are some of my peers, and I'm not going to name names, who have been awful fathers," he explained to *The Times*. "You could argue that it's the nature of the business, but I wouldn't agree with that. Some musicians I know are incredible fathers. Like Keith Richards. A fantastic dad. If times were tough, Keith would be there. If you needed somebody to do the school run, Keith was your man."

Jack Bruce acknowledges that even during his most troubled years he always "did his best", but without wishing to take sides in the tumultuous Cream camp, we already know Ginger Baker's son Kofi has a different view of his own dad. In the early Noughties, Kofi received an email from a woman claiming she was Ginger Baker's love child. Possibly Kofi suspected there was a whiff of opportunism about this, perhaps it was someone who wanted to squeeze money out of Ginger, or maybe it really was Kofi's half-sister, desperate for a loving relationship with her long-lost father. Either way, Kofi wanted to warn her against any disappointment.

He wrote back: 'Let me tell you about my dad. He never gave me a Christmas present. He never remembered my birthday. In my whole life he gave me maybe $5,000...'' He continued in this unflattering description of how Baker fared as a parent. When the woman wrote to say she would still like to speak to Ginger, Kofi forwarded the email to his dad, forgetting his own, lengthy, brutally honest response was underneath. Ginger read it in horror and practically combusted with rage, announcing to Kofi that he was disowning him. While this renunciation was apparently short-lived, how this would have even changed their relationship is hard to imagine.

Kilauren Gibb, only daughter of Grammy-winning singer-songwriter Joni Mitchell, didn't even know Mitchell was her mother for 32 years. Mitchell was just 20, studying art on a shoestring in Calgary in her native Canada when she became pregnant with Kilauren (or Kelly Dale as she was known originally) in 1964 by photographer Brad MacMath.

Joni moved to Toronto, and after the birth of Kelly in February 1965, she married folk singer Chuck Mitchell. When their marriage faltered and Joni poured her energies into making a name for herself as a musician, she put her daughter up for adoption, later insisting that an "unhappy mother" should not bring up a child. She would write 'Little Green', a track that would appear on her seminal album *Blue*, about her. It contains poignant lyrics about her situation when she gave the child up: 'Child with a child pretending/Weary of lies you are sending home/ So you sign all the papers in the family name/You're sad and sorry but not ashamed/Little green, have a happy ending.'

The child was adopted by David and Ida Gibb, a well-heeled couple from Toronto, and they would give her the more exotic name Kilauren, a tranquil suburban upbringing and a private education. Kilauren, having inherited her mother's high cheekbones and limpid eyes, would become a successful model in the Eighties. She had no idea she was even adopted until she herself fell pregnant with her son Marlin in 1992, and the Gibbs decided it was time for her to know the truth.

Kilauren sought out Joni in the late Nineties, and the pair would enjoy an emotional reunion. "It was a great relief to me in every way," Kilauren told the press at the time. "It made me feel whole. It made me feel complete. I don't have any expectations. I just wanted to find my mom." Joni also was blessed with the news that she was a grandma without having even seen her own daughter grow up, which must have stirred up mixed emotions for all concerned.

Having lived a life without Joni in relative normality in the straight-laced Toronto suburbs, Kilauren still feels glad she grew up the way she did rather than living out her teens as a pop star's daughter in Los Angeles. "I had a great childhood," she told the *Toronto Sun*. "I could have been raised in California and been a Bel Air brat. I'm really happy that I got my family to raise me, in a down-to-earth style."

At least, as neither she nor anyone around her (apart from her adoptive family) knew the truth about her parentage as she was growing up, she was free from the preconceptions and expectations that come with being the child of a celebrated musician, she was never surrounded by star-struck users or false friends only interested in what she could potentially do for them in her privileged position.

Brit-pack model Daisy Lowe grew up thinking she knew exactly who her parents were – singer Pearl Lowe (often seen drifting around Primrose Hill in witchy black lace) and holistic fertility specialist Bronner Handwerger. Bronner was based in San Diego and Daisy also had a loving godfather in Bush frontman Gavin Rossdale. But when she was 15, life changed dramatically. Bronner had given Daisy the book *Eat Right 4 Your Type*, which advises on diet according to your personal blood type. Daisy passed it on to Pearl (who, Daisy has claimed, spent much of the time getting stoned and succumbing to the resulting munchies), and Pearl went ahead and chose the diet for what she believed was her blood type, O. After an unsuccessful attempt at losing weight, she was tested and it transpired that she was a type A. Daisy knew she was type O, she also was aware that Bronner was not type O. If neither of her 'parents' shared her blood type, there was only one conclusion she could draw.

A DNA test would prove that Daisy was the product of a flash in the pan sexual relationship between old friends Pearl Lowe and Gavin Rossdale back in the Eighties, a tryst deemed so insignificant that neither assumed there was any link with Pearl's subsequent pregnancy. Naturally, the discovery shook Daisy's foundations, but the situation worsened when Rossdale, married to No Doubt singer Gwen Stefani, apparently decided to cut ties with the Lowes all together.

Rossdale is, obviously, *persona non grata* in the Lowe household now, but Pearl's current partner, Supergrass drummer Danny Goffey, is, according to Daisy, "a brilliant father" to her, and her admiration of Goffey also underlines her feelings toward her biological father. "(Goffey) will be there for me when no one else will," Daisy tells *The Times*. "I'm proud to call him my father."

When a child knows his or her estranged parent is famous and respected, but literally never sees them because of a messy family break-up, a kind of cognitive dissonance can result. You might not want to discuss them at all out of loyalty to the other parent, perhaps, or because of your anger at being 'abandoned', but his or her music or face is everywhere and everyone wants to talk to you about them. Singer Norah Jones felt this way when she was growing up – she didn't see her father, sitar virtuoso Ravi Shankar, until she actively sought him out herself at the age of 18.

Maybe you *do* want to talk about him, you're excited about what he is doing even though he has no contact with you, but no one believes you when you say you're related. If you were, surely you'd be living in luxury and he'd be spotted picking you up from school at least *sometimes*…

Hip-hop artist QD3 (the wisely ambiguous soubriquet of Quincy Jones III) barely saw his father between the ages of four and 18 after moving to his mother's native Sweden. The awareness of how Jones senior lived compared with how he and his mother and sister scraped by only served to exacerbate the gulf between them. The nature of QD3's upbringing was also in direct contrast to how he was welcomed into the world. Just after his birth two days before Christmas day, 1968, his parents received a letter and a $5,000 bond from Old Blue Eyes himself. 'Dear Quincy Delight Jones III,' the letter read. 'WELCOME! And let Uncle Frank start your college fund with the hope that you will find friendship, knowledge, and happiness in what will no doubt be a far better world. Love, Francis.' But for Quincy III, certainly up until he reached adulthood and could escape Stockholm, this 'better world' would still be the one his father lived in, not him.

Quincy Delight Jones II, a former jazz trumpeter and one of the most successful record producers in history, worked with the likes of Michael Jackson, Marvin Gaye, Frank Sinatra and Stevie Wonder. He had the Midas touch, but to give his child with Swedish model Ulla Anderson his name would be both a blessing and a curse. Quincy Jones III was proud of his father's work. But living with his name would serve as a stark reminder of how near and yet how far he was from Quincy Jones. It was only when he was in his teens that he decided he wanted to find out more about his father and spend time with him in LA, where he now lives himself.

"I was going through a photo album when I was 15, and I was like, 'Wait a minute, we don't really know each other that well. I'd visit him in LA on summer break, but for the rest of the year I was in another country. I would sometimes bring Michael Jackson records to school to show my friends what my father did, and they would think I was lying because we lived in public housing. It kind of struck a nerve.

"A lot of people may assume I had a silver spoon in my mouth, but the way my parents divorced, that wasn't really the case. We got evicted every 8-12 months, I went to 16 schools before 10th grade… but I was able to see both extremes and it's given me a unique vantage point for my line of work."

At least ZTT bosses Trevor Horn and Jill Sinclair stuck together as romantic and business partners amid the choppy waters of the music industry, but their son Aaron also came to understand that work came first for his father. "However much I want to deny it, there is an element of that in him," Aaron explains. "Not that he's not an amazing guy, but his primary thing is producing records, so that's what he is really good at, over other things… even being a father in some ways. He's good at it, but it's what you spend time on.

"When I was born he wasn't there, he was in New York. That was a good year for him, '83, Frankie Goes To Hollywood and the Art Of

Noise, there were other things going on that were important and he wasn't around because of those things. It's not something I grumble about too much, that's the way it rolls. They're busy."

Jill Sinclair ran the business and home with a rod of iron; Trevor was the good cop to her bad cop. "Dad would say, 'You shouldn't be naughty because it makes mum angry...' He wouldn't be around for ages and then he'd suddenly be around loads, or he wouldn't be up some days, on a weekend he'd show up halfway through the day. When you're a kid you get up at six or seven in the morning – adults take ages!"

As we know, John Lennon's absence from his son Julian was threefold. Often it was physical, when The Beatles were still touring, but it was also mental, particularly when John Lennon was using LSD and other drugs, and emotional, because even when you took the pressures of touring and the effects of various substances away, he appeared to be largely switched off towards his child save for the occasional ostracising explosion of fury or deep pang of guilt.

In a burst of emotion, John wrote to Cynthia during The Beatles' frenzied tour of the States in August 1965.

"I really miss him as a person now," wrote John. "He's not so much 'the baby' or 'my baby' any more, he's a real living part of me now – you know, he's Julian and everything and I can't wait to see him, I miss him more than I've ever done before – I think it's been a slow process my feeling like a real father! I spend hours in dressing rooms and things thinking about the times I've wasted not being with him – and playing with him – you know I keep thinking of those stupid bastard times when I keep reading bloody newspapers and other shit whilst he's in the room with me and I've decided it's ALL WRONG! He doesn't see enough of me as it is and I really want him to know and love me, and miss me like I seem to be missing both of you so much..."

Cynthia sold this letter among others after their divorce, desperate for any money she could raise, but Paul McCartney bought it back for her, framing it for Julian. The letter elicits sadness for Cynthia; despite John's intentions and the love displayed in this missive, he never changed.

Cynthia wrote in her book, *John*: "There were periods when he tried harder with Julian, but he was too preoccupied with other things. John would arrive home from tours exhausted and spend the next few days more or less asleep, which meant I had to keep Julian quiet and away from our bedroom. The rule was that at two in the afternoon John had a wake-up call and a cup of tea. Julian, who had waited impatiently all morning, would go in as soon as I gave the signal."

Hopes were high for the Beatle families when, after a year almost constantly away, the band decided that was it, no more touring. Their last official live show was at Candlestick Park, San Francisco, on August 29, 1966. Cynthia for one was optimistic that she would have "the old John" back.

However, that year, *Evening Standard* writer Maureen Cleave became concerned when John showed her around his Surrey pile for her piece 'How does a Beatle live? John Lennon lives like this...' The guided tour was conducted with Julian, just three at the time, forever at his father's heels as John told Maureen airily: "I'm just stopping (here) like a bus stop... I'll get my real house when I know what I want ... there's something else I'm going to do, only I don't know what it is. All I know is this isn't for me.'

In the final article, Cleave omitted his comment that he wished he'd made love with his mother, Julia, when he was a teenager. (He had lain next to her during one of her afternoon naps, accidentally brushed her breast, and then, in a rush of hormones, considered having sex with her. He apparently still regretted denying his Oedipal urges.)

It was in November 1966 that Lennon first met the Japanese artist Yoko Ono at her exhibition at the left-field Indica Gallery in Ham Yard, Soho. One exhibit was an apple bearing a £200 price tag. Lennon cheekily, and symbolically, took a bite out of it before leaving.

When John and Cynthia finally divorced in November 1968, almost two years to the day of Ono and Lennon's first meeting, Lennon falsely accused Cynthia of adultery in a bid to win custody of Julian, but the tables were turned when Yoko fell pregnant, thus proving Lennon's own infidelity. (The child was miscarried, and Lennon recorded its dying heartbeats. He called the baby John Lennon II, but surely Julian was officially John Lennon II, his full name being John Charles Julian Lennon?)

Cynthia and Julian were given a comparatively paltry settlement of £75,000 to support them until Julian was 21. A further £100,000 was put into a trust fund for Julian's school fees. Withdrawals had to be approved by John and Yoko, who were co-trustees. The fund would also be shared with any of John's future children. When Cynthia tried to persuade John to part with a little more money for their welfare, he snapped back, "You're not worth more. Christ, it's like winning the pools."

Cynthia had custody of Julian, agreeing to regular visits from John, although the reality was that she had no idea if or when her former husband would ever get in touch. "There was no word from him between 1971 and 1974," said Cynthia. "Apart from birthday and Christmas presents for Julian each year, sent by his London office with no personal note or card. All Julian had were newspaper cuttings to tell him where his dad was." John was also gradually cutting ties with old friends and relatives in Liverpool, as if he was shedding his skin and becoming a different person.

After the birth of Sean Ono Lennon in 1975, *Playboy* magazine would ask Lennon senior about his relationship with his sons. Certainly John was acting like a more devoted father to Sean than he ever had with Julian. He announced rather insensitively in the interview that "Sean was a planned child, and therein lies the difference. I don't love Julian any less. He's still my son, whether he came from a bottle of whiskey or because they didn't have pills in those days."

He told *Newsweek* he was looking forward to having more of a relationship with Julian in the future: "I hadn't seen my first son grow up and now there's a 17-year-old man on the phone talking about motorbikes. I was not there for his childhood, I was on tour. I don't know how the game works, but there's a price to pay for inattention to children. And if I don't give him attention from zero to five, then I'm damn well going to give it to him from 16 to twenty, because it's owed. It's like the law of the universe." Tragically, John Lennon was murdered by Mark Chapman shortly after making this statement.

"Julian (grieved) for the father he never really knew and so badly needed," writes Cynthia. "For some months he appeared to be spiralling out of control. He was angry with me, blaming me for the break-up with John, for not being stronger, for not making him behave like a proper father."

Julian travelled to New York after Lennon's murder on December 8, 1980, in a state of shock, surrounded by people reading newspapers on the flight, all bearing his father's face on the front page. Julian would also endure a public appearance with Yoko in Central Park in which she insisted he wore John's scarf and cap so he looked even more like him. He couldn't wait to take them off. Being obliged to associate with Yoko, who apart from the odd show of public unity made him feel as if he was invisible, continued to sting for years afterwards. Yoko also held the purse strings of Lennon's massive financial legacy.

Getting any money for Julian was, predictably, a struggle initially. Ono's sources claimed he had been granted $20 million, Julian insisted the amount was far smaller. But despite the antipathy between Lennon's firstborn and Ono, Julian has overcome any bitterness towards his father, and he expressed his forgiveness publicly at the launch in 2009 of *White Feather*, an exhibition at Liverpool's Beatles Story of his father's possessions that had been previously auctioned off by Yoko. Julian had used part of the multimillion pound settlement he finally received to buy back items over time.

"One of the obvious reasons (behind this) was that nothing was passed down to me after Dad had passed," he said. "The only way I could regain any of his belongings was to go out and buy them myself, for not only my sake but for my mum's. If in the future I have a family, I would want them to have part of their heritage."

The bridges between John and Julian Lennon were never truly burnt. However, John's American pop rival, Beach Boy Brian Wilson, went several steps further down the 'questionable dad' road and didn't even pretend to be interested in his daughters at any point during their early years.

Brian Wilson and his wife Marilyn were still together (thanks to Marilyn's stoicism) during Carnie and Wendy's childhood in the late Sixties and early Seventies, but Brian, despite being home almost all of the time, simply didn't want to be around them. He was confused by them at best, indifferent the rest of the time, and he admits in his autobiography, *Wouldn't It Be Nice,* that he told his long-suffering wife, "You raise them. There's too much weirdness in my head. I'll love them but I don't know if I'll ever be able to show it."

He couldn't understand the love Marilyn felt for them, and seemed able only to equate it with the strong emotions he felt for his songs, because he'd "given birth to them". Wilson had a difficult upbringing and a fractious relationship with his often brutal father, and he used this as his excuse for 'not knowing how to be a dad'.

This gifted songwriter, who dreamt up the halcyon soundtrack that millions still identify with a kind of utopian California, would redefine the concept of addiction. Wilson's daily existence consisted of hiding inside a cotton-wool cocoon of consumption – from cocaine to black heroin, his self-medication was boundless, but he also gorged on junk food and coffee, consumed literally by the catering urn-load. He was obese, he didn't wash or clean his teeth, he reeked not only because he was unwashed, but because of the toxins seeping out of his pores. He made himself bedridden and he would snub people's efforts to communicate by lolling his head back and rolling his eyes into his head to shut them out.

He made no effort to emerge from this state until he was forced to by Marilyn and the now-legendary therapist Dr Eugene Landy. Wilson would later complain that Carnie and Wendy became "like strangers" to him. It's not difficult to do the maths…

Brian writes that he'd "ignored (Marilyn's) pregnancy" with their first daughter, Carnie, assuming his wife was only having children in order to '"stake claim to a territory whose boundaries weren't always clearly defined – me. She might've given up hope of stimulating any normal, adult intimacy between us. She might also have made peace with my relationships with her sisters (with whom he had had sex). But by having my baby, Marilyn made it perfectly clear that she was Mrs Brian Wilson and entitled to the status and power that came with it."

Whether this was true or cynicism on the part of a jaded, narcotic-addled star is hard to know for sure. But he considered himself to have "nothing to do with Carnie" (despite presumably having been around at some point during her conception) and this excused himself from helping out in any way when she was a baby.

Dr Landy had a necessarily hard-line approach with Wilson, and his methods were unorthodox and viewed by many, including The Beach Boys, with suspicion. However, he attempted to save Wilson's family life, trying to reintegrate him with his wife and children, or at least not break their hearts by standing by and allowing birthdays or Christmasses to go by without a gift. But the break-up between Wilson and his family was inevitable.

Once Landy had managed to get Wilson to lose weight and start writing again, he continued trying to persuade the Beach Boy wunderkind to spend time with his family, but Wilson sneakily pretended Landy was stopping him from being with his kids – something he apparently found boring and awkward. "'Dr Landy won't let me' became my favourite catchphrase. I used him as an excuse for not doing things I found unpleasant. Everyone thought he kept me **from** seeing the kids. Wrong. The choice was mine and I chose not to. To me, family meant bummer time."

And so Carnie and Wendy would grow up without a father. He rarely returned their calls, he was like an errant teenager. But his lack of interest in his children came back to smack him in the face in years to come.

Fast forward to 1984, and Brian is backstage at the Universal Amphitheatre with the rest of The Beach Boys. Landy had been teaching him how to overcome his social paralysis and relearn how to simply say 'Hello, I'm Brian Wilson'. He needed complete retraining in even the basics of social interaction after years of being practically silent, even to his loved ones. This was a big moment for him, but the first person he tried it out on was the wrong person.

"A young overweight girl came toward me. As I'd practiced, I put out my hand and said, 'Hello, I'm Brian Wilson.' The girl stopped in her tracks and her smile turned into a look of shock. 'Daddy!' she exclaimed, aghast, 'Don't you know me? It's Carnie!'

"I was disturbed, she was crushed. Dr Landy took us into the dressing room. Then he located Wendy and brought her in too… She looked frightened and confused. What a scene. What a family!" he says in *Wouldn't It Be Nice?* What did he expect? What a family? What a father… his daughters were behaving the way any normal person would if their own parent had come towards them and introduced themselves as if they were a stranger.

What is frustrating about this situation is that Brian Wilson, like many who try to close the door on their own cold or even abusive parents and turn to the church of rock 'n' roll, refused to take responsibility himself as a parent. He claims that, as his two teenage daughters stared up at him waiting for him to react, he could only think of his violent, controlling dad "who was at the root of this mess. He'd fucked me up. I wondered if the girls knew..." But did he wonder if he was 'fucking them up' in his way? How his approach might affect them as adults?

Wilson reeled off a spiel about how he's "not a good daddy" but said he'd write a song for them one day (big deal. This is reminiscent of Loudon Wainwright writing the song 'Five Years Old' for Martha's birthday in 1981: 'Happy birthday, birthday girl, I'm sorry I can't be there for that party...' a gesture he presumably hoped would excuse him from being there physically). Wilson then went on the defensive, telling his daughters, "Your mommy's been a good mommy and a good daddy. I didn't have either. You've been lucky that way."

He then got up to leave, breathing a sigh of relief inwardly, until Carnie called, "Daddy! Don't you want to know anything about us?" It hadn't even occurred to him to ask how his own children were after years of absence.

"Carnie attempted to fill me in on a year's worth of stories... I was already concentrating on the show. The only bit of information I caught was something about making an album with Wendy and their friend Chynna Phillips."

Chynna, second daughter of Wilson's contemporary John and Michelle Phillips, of Mamas and Papas fame, must have had plenty in common with the Wilson girls. With their shared inherited vocal talent, like their respective parents they would form a successful vocal harmony group with a name that didn't even bother trying to shrug off their fathers' monikers: Wilson Phillips.

Indeed, when it must have been so hard to get close to their dads, the idea of using their surnames might have been a public declaration, celebration, even, of that bloodline, a way to publicly link themselves together. It was poignantly clear that many of Wilson Phillips' lyrics alluded to their fragmented relationships with their fathers, messages beamed out in song simply because they wouldn't be listened to any other way. When they topped the charts with 'Hold On' and 'Release Me' in 1990, Brian was "caught between joy and jealousy".

Growing up, Chynna fortunately had a relatively stabilising influence in her mother, but despite Michelle and John's split when Chynna was little, they still spent much of their time at John's twisted hippy haven with Mackenzie and her brother Jeffrey after they moved from their mother's in San Fernando Valley. It was a relief for Mackenzie to have a little girl to play with when most of the time she was running around with much older people, children of the flower variety. The desperation to grab John's attention, when he was generally out of it on drugs or absorbed in an intense relationship, led to Mackenzie choosing romantic partners whose behaviour in many cases would reflect the treatment she accepted from her father.

"Waiting for Dad. It happened a lot," she writes in her autobiography. "He became an unattainable figure, I'd watch him on TV and say, 'That's my dad,' but he wasn't a reality."

When Mackenzie was six and Jeffrey eight, John promised to take them to Pacific Ocean Park in Santa Monica, an attraction that even gets a mention in The Beach Boys song 'Amusement Parks USA', in which the Boys promise it is 'worth a trip to LA' for. Recommendation indeed. When the day finally came, the kids were driven to the park by John and Michelle, handed $100 and told to meet them in the car park later. John and Michelle then sped off in the car, leaving the kids to it.

When Jeffrey and Mackenzie eventually moved in with John, life was free and undisciplined but the dark side of this was neglect: neglect of the children, neglect of the house, their whole life started to decay around them as John disappeared whenever debt or responsibility loomed. Mackenzie remembers turning into a "maniac, a weird little savage" in this lawless world.

She remembers: "John and (second wife) Genevieve went for a long weekend to New York, which turned into several weeks, which turned into over a month before John bothered to call and explain they were trying to launch his play *Space Cowboy*."

He stopped paying rent on the house, leaving his children and sister Rosie, who was thankfully there to look after them, to pick up the pieces. "The tug of obligation must not have appealed to dad because he stopped calling or even returning calls. As dad would one day admit, he 'sort of forgot about California and the two kids.'"

414 St Pierre Road would be abandoned by the remaining Phillipses, who relinquished possessions in order to cover the back rent. Many of their belongings were kept in storage by the next owners, and according to Mackenzie, they are still kept there to this day, like a strange time capsule.

Coping with the death of a parent can sometimes be less painful than trying to come to terms with knowing your parent is alive and well but too busy to check in with you. Baxter Dury, as we know, has had to cope with both sides, but Natalie Curtis, daughter of Joy Division frontman Ian, never really knew her father, being just one when he died. Both Baxter and Natalie, however, have been involved in similar projects that saw their families being reinterpreted on screen.

Complicated feelings would arise for Natalie when photographer Anton Corbijn made *Control* (2007), an elegiac movie based on the book *Touching From A Distance* by Natalie's mother, Deborah, about life with Curtis and his bandmates from Manchester (Curtis himself was from the altogether leafier Macclesfield).

Baxter at least has plenty of memories of his father, even if he was left to his own devices most of the time, but Natalie grew up with pictures and music in place of her lost parent, hearing his voice only in recordings. However since the recent Joy Division renaissance, not only has his face and voice become ubiquitous, but so have pictures of her as a baby – being held by Ian in the garden, or lying on the changing table.

Natalie, herself a photographer, was born in April 1979, a year before her father committed suicide in the family home, and she is understandably protective of "that boy who is younger than me". But the film shone a light on Curtis' turmoil and sparked a new appreciation of his legacy, undoubtedly giving the formerly comparatively sidelined post-punk group's profile a substantial boost.

The pressure is always on when chronicling the life or at least part of the life of someone dear to people's hearts, and with Natalie on set, appearing as an extra (one of the lairy punks at the riotous 1980 gig in Bury, to be precise), the sense of responsibility must have been ever keener for those making the movie. Natalie's mixed feelings for the film weren't just because she felt the resemblance between her father and Sam Riley, the actor who played him, was iffy ("I look like my father, and Sam Riley doesn't look like me!" she said at the time). One of the issues that sat uncomfortably with her was the fact that, when they wrapped, everyone was happy. She wept. When the film was shown at Cannes, everyone shot to their feet and cheered. It was confusing to see people behaving as if they were enjoying themselves when the film is about someone very real who died a very lonely death. The film took a private heartbreak and exposed it to the world, over and over again.

Joy Division and Ian Curtis have been scrutinised and celebrated afresh, but Natalie and her mentor Kevin Cummins (the photographer responsible for many of the most iconic images of the band, including the ghostly, remote cover shots for *NME*) both feel it is frustrating that Joy Division, Curtis in particular, seem doomed to be remembered as perennially dour. To be fair, most of Cummins' better known pictures of them are cold, bleak and serious, underlining the jagged drama of their music, which of course reflected in turn the hard, monochromatic landscape of their backdrop, Manchester.

Natalie grew up poring over Cummins' pictures of her father, one day approaching him personally to ask, "Do you have any of my dad smiling?" The group did have fun and Cummins admits he had to wait for them to stop trying to make each other laugh in order to take those pictures of them looking so icy and stern. But the fact remains that Ian was also suffering from depression, believed to be exacerbated by prescription medication for his epilepsy.

"Bernard Sumner (Joy Division and New Order guitarist) told me my father used to drink before performing, which may explain his onstage fits," Natalie explained to *The Guardian*. "Alcohol is a seizure trigger. Seizures can also be triggered by flashing lights, lack of sleep and stress. He did the best he could; he was just very ill. I've never felt angry at my father for committing suicide."

Her reason for not listening to much Joy Division is that, she quipped in an interview (with writer Paul Connolly), "No one wants to listen to their dad singing. It's like watching your dad dance. It's dead embarrassing. Your dad's never cool, is he?" But one might also venture that the dark, troubled lyrics her father would write flag up his mental state too blatantly, like cries for help heard but unheard. Indeed the rest of the group, Sumner, bassist Peter Hook and drummer Stephen Morris, have since admitted these were signs they were missing – they were too young or too absorbed in their ambitions to see what was right in front of them.

Frances Bean Cobain has had to live without her father, Kurt, since the age of one and a half, but, like Natalie, Baxter, Julian and Sean, she lives with constant reminders of him. Frances saw her father for the last time on April 1, 1994 when she was taken to see him at Los Angeles' Exodus Recovery Centre. The following day he went missing. On April 8, his body was found outside his Lake Washington home, a gun pointing at his chin.

In his suicide note he describes how pained he feels when he sees in his baby daughter "too much of what I used to be. Full of love and joy, kissing every person she meets because everyone is good and will do her no harm. And that terrifies me to the point I can barely function. I can't stand the thought of Frances becoming the miserable, self-destructive death rocker I've become."

Killing himself was hardly going to make Frances any happier, but on the other hand, he wouldn't have to face her turmoil as she grew up discovering her parents had been addicts. He'd rather die than witness that. He also chose to kill himself in the shed so as not to "haunt the house, and not give his daughter the kind of nightmares he had lived with". Obviously one can't rationalise on behalf of someone who is not thinking rationally, under the influence of drugs or in the grip of depression, but surely if he didn't want to give his daughter nightmares…

Courtney Love would later freak out after realising Frances Bean had gone to see *Control*, which of course deals with the subject of suicide. However, Frances bizarrely threw a suicide-themed 16th birthday party in 2008, with a prize for 'who can look the most dead'. The birthday girl herself reportedly sported a dress her father had previously worn. This seems to suggest she is not overly sensitive about the theme.

Jeff Buckley was always irritated when interviewers insisted on shoehorning him and his father Tim together. It fits with the romantic image we have of the Buckleys – both were tousled, poetic and seemingly delicate 'dreamboats' whether they liked it or not. And, of course, both would die prematurely, leaving beautiful musical legacies. Jeff insisted he was not influenced by Tim musically and was often reluctant to speak to journalists unless he was assured they would not focus on his father. He hardly knew him anyway, or at least, he knew him as someone who chose to leave him behind.

Tim Buckley saw his son once backstage when Jeff was eight in 1975, and died soon after this meeting of an accidental heroin overdose. The grief and confusion would be intensified when it transpired that Jeff and his mother, Mary Guibert, were excluded from the funeral.

"I was not invited, and that kind of gnawed at me," Jeff said later in an interview with Ray Rogers. However when, in 1990, a memorial for Tim Buckley was held in New York, Jeff performed 'I Never Asked To Be Your Mountain', a song of Tim's that mentioned both Jeff and Mary, the tone of which seemed to typify Tim's decision to live the life of a travelling musician instead of a family man.

"It's a beautiful song," continued Jeff. "I both admired it and hated it, so that's what I sang. There are all these expectations that come with this 'Sixties offspring' bullshit, but I can't tell you how little he had to do with my music. The people who raised me musically are my mother, who is a classically trained pianist, and my stepfather."

His stepfather, Ron Moorhead, was a loving dad to Jeff, who would be brought up as Scott Moorhead (Scott being his middle name), and Jeff would often speak fondly of Ron. He gave him his first Led Zeppelin cassette after all, and Ron talked movingly of his final conversation with Jeff days before the singer drowned during a misguided swim in the treacherous Wolf River in 1997. Jeff had apparently assured Ron that he saw him, not Tim, as his father.

The role of others in the lives of children, whether it is a stepparent, a sibling or a close family friend, can never be underestimated. They might play the part your real parent never could for whatever reason. So fear not if you are starting to feel a little bruised and emotional. It is the nanny, the mentor, the honorary uncle and the rough but kindly roadie that we run to next.

CHAPTER 7

The Influence Of Others

"Winter, Spring, Summer or Fall, all you have to do is call..."
('You've Got A Friend', James Taylor)

Thank goodness for the entourage. Whether a nail needs fixing or the chihuahua needs its curlers taking out, they're always there to deal with the essentials. But more importantly, that gang of odd-looking, disparate characters often provide succour to the child of a rock or pop star when the going gets tough, which it invariably does. From the officially appointed, security-checked nanny to the big-hearted backing singer, all play their part in looking out for the children of rock and shaping who they would become. You might be taken to Thorpe Park by Damon Albarn (Daisy Lowe), baby-sat by one of Elvis Costello's Attractions (Dylan Howe), sung lullabies by Screaming Trees vocalist Mark Lanegan (Frances Bean Cobain) or shown how to restring a guitar by Maglite thanks to a friendly technician (Callum Adamson).

Some created a shield from the insanity, others contributed to it. Some were salt of the earth, some were sadistic, some were groupies, some meant well but were basically mad. But most of them did what they could with love and commitment – as much as they could before passing out at least...

111

On that note, it is about time you met the Sulphate Strangler, a former Led Zeppelin roadie and the man Baxter Dury describes as his "psychedelic nanny".

"My upbringing was pretty goddamn rock 'n' roll. It's amazing how normal I am now," mulls Dury over a coffee in Notting Hill's chic Electric Brasserie, breaking off to wave at Rough Trade boss Jeannette Lee on a neighbouring table. This, clearly, is the hub.

Baxter is a gentle soul with an unusual hybrid Estuary/posh accent, which bears testament to his rougher roots, "arts & crafts" upbringing, and sporadic public school education. He describes himself as "traditional", "nerdy", a "good dad". He has a son called Cosmo who goes to an expensive school, he runs marathons, he jokes that he makes "asthmatic, feminine music" in contrast with that of his father's visceral style. It was thanks to his quiet, strong mother, Betty Dury, that he and his sister Jemima even survived, he insists.

Baxter has left the insanity of his early life behind, but he's also having to relive it now more than ever, a) because of this book (sorry Baxter) and b) because of the 2010 biopic about his father, *Sex & Drugs & Rock & Roll,* starring Andy Serkis in the lead role, and for which he and Jemima were consultants. ("It's amazing. They've mixed up all the times, but it successfully shows the chaos," is Baxter's verdict.)

The film concentrates heavily on Baxter's childhood, and also focuses on the Sulphate Strangler, who would care for his charge in his own unique way. The Strangler's trademark, according to Blockheads organist Mickey Gallagher, was "grabbing people by the throat, lifting them up and biting their nose". He could drink a bottle of vodka in one go. He was not the first person one might think of as the ideal babysitter, particularly for a child who was, as Baxter himself admits, "ambitiously naughty".

"There were a lot of lunatics and drugs around," he continues. "The whole process of Dad suddenly becoming famous affected me in a funny way, I became very rebellious and I didn't go to school. I was eventually in dad's control (after Betty and Ian split up), and he couldn't handle that responsibility, so there were these odd people looking after me. Me and the Strangler, we brought each other up."

Ian Dury had a reputation for winding people up, dropping bombshells just to see what would happen, insulting the hardest men in the room to see if they'd lash out at a disabled person/celebrity. (They often would, and the Blockheads would have to finish the fights on Ian's behalf. This was known as 'Dury Duty'.) Baxter's theory on why Ian mystifyingly placed him in the care of a wild-card drug fiend is that it was just another of his mischievous social experiments.

"Mum couldn't handle me, Dad was going off to do a Bob Hoskins film, then this 6ft 7in speed freak turned up and Dad thought, 'Ah, that'll be good!' Like giving the baby a cigar: 'Let's see what happens here!'" Blockhead Mickey Gallagher suggests it was Dury's attempt to make sure Baxter was protected after he had heard his son was being bullied. Dury's "glamorised view of violence", according to Gallagher, will have had something to do with his choice of the Strangler as 'nanny'.

"I lived at Dad's house, this wild place overlooking Hammersmith Bridge. The Strangler took my bedroom. He'd come to stay for a week on the sofa, and five years later he'd got my room and I was sleeping on the chaise longue at the age of 15.

"The Strangler just got progressively madder. He tried hard though, he was responsible in the only way he knew how. He gave me all the love he knew, he made me pie and chips every night, but sometimes he'd go to sleep for four days. Or I'd find scales and drug paraphernalia. I once found a girl asleep in the middle of our front room with a nosebleed. I got a bit feral, but there were enough people keeping an eye on it."

For Maria, Ben and Luke, the children of Mickey Gallagher, the Dury camp was balanced by that of The Clash, as a result of Mickey's frequent collaborations with both groups. The Gallagher brood had their wild moments but they were bolstered by a strong network of friends and loved ones within the uniquely close-knit artistic community that continues to define the area in which they lived for some years: Ladbroke Grove.

Parties, happenings and the Notting Hill Carnival celebrations, usually culminating in a get-together at Joe Strummer's, were always family affairs. The wives and girlfriends of The Clash would look out for Maria in particular, being the youngest, and the three Gallagher kids would later babysit Strummer and Gaby Salter's first child, Jazz. "I remember lots of funky girlfriends taking care of us," says Maria Gallagher, who moved back to the area in recent years with her own teenage daughter, Amy Grace. "Gaby was always there. I remember (Clash and Blockheads crony) Kosmo Vinyl's girlfriend, I remember Pearl Harbour (American DJ and Paul Simonon's sometime girlfriend). She was in the Clash film *Hell W10,* which is like a home movie to us. My dad was in it, The Clash were in it. I remember going down to Westbourne Park bus station at night to make it, just like a home video. Twenty-five years ago."

Often, it is up to many more people than just the parents to ensure the child is kept in check, particularly if their parents' marriage breaks down (the Gallaghers' did not, incidentally). In the case of stars such as Elvis Presley there would be a multitude of staff around, and he kept his extended family close too. Little Lisa Marie was never alone, which was just as well because she was a law unto herself and no one knew what she was going to do next; her father couldn't bear to discipline her and so she ran riot. She described herself as "a holy terror", and even Elvis' gentle, ever-present cousin Patsy confessed that while she loved Lisa Marie like her own child, she "wanted to kill her a couple of times, but God helped me not to."

When the cooks, of whom there were quite a few (being Graceland), weren't rustling up Southern-style comfort food for the Presleys, they would watch out for Lisa Marie during the day, or sit with her at night if she was scared. (They had more reason to be scared themselves; while Elvis always showed them great respect, this hadn't yet rubbed off on Lisa Marie. The child once barked, "You're fired!" at one of the cooks who, on Elvis' orders, had told her she wasn't allowed any chocolate cake until after dinner. "For a while we didn't know who was running Graceland, Elvis or Lisa Marie," jokes Patsy through gritted teeth.)

Fissures appeared in Elvis and Priscilla's marriage when Lisa Marie was still a child, and when they split in 1973 she was just five. However, she found three fairy godmothers who would be there for her whenever she went on the road with her father. These women were appropriately known as The Sweet Inspirations – Sylvia Shemwell, Myrna Smith and Estelle Brown. They were Elvis' backing singers (although he called them his "analysts") and they indeed provided inspiration, support and a kindly ear to both Elvis and Lisa Marie when the madness became too much.

"When I think of my father touring, playing Vegas and stadiums all over the country, I think of The Sweet Inspirations," remembers Lisa Marie in *Elvis By The Presleys.* "They brought out his soul."

The vocal group, which had originally also included Dionne Warwick and Cissy Houston (Whitney's mother), worked extensively as an Atlantic recording group. Their voices can be heard on Jimi Hendrix's *Electric Ladyland* and Dusty Springfield's *Dusty In Memphis,* and they sang frequently with Aretha Franklin. They'd been around and viewed the world with no small measure of sagacity. Lisa Marie worshipped them.

"The Sweet Inspirations did an album on their own, which, next to my father's records, was my all-time favourite – I memorised every song," continues Lisa Marie. "When my father would take me on the road I'd practically live with The Sweet Inspirations. Soon as I got to the show, I ran to their dressing room. They were wonderful women, easy to talk to. I felt like they helped raise me."

In one's formative years, it's certainly important to have someone suitably maternal and grounded in your life, particularly if you're spending time in that anarchic netherland known as "on tour". But in the absence of such figures, Frank Zappa & The Mothers of Invention were nothing if not resourceful. Seemingly glued to the band was a kind of official association of 'super-groupies' known at this point as the GTOs (which stood for Girls Together Outrageously, or as some have sniggeringly and probably more accurately claimed, Girls Together Orally.) They're women, mused Zappa. They're around all the time. The kids need a babysitter…

Moon was eight months old when she became the unsuspecting project of star-groupie Pamela Miller (who as Pamela Des Barres, her subsequent married name, wrote the sexually voracious hanger-on's bible *I'm With The Band*) and Christine Frka, who was featured on the cover of Zappa's 1969 album *Hot Rats,* crawling out of a crypt. She died of an overdose in 1972.

They might have frolicked with Keith Moon in the kitchen as the kids had their breakfast, but they imparted enough knowledge to help the children get by in the wilds of Los Angeles: when Moon was just two she had the awareness (not to mention vocabulary) to shriek, "Fuck off, pervert!" after being approached by a man in the supermarket. Moon recalls, in later years, a nanny surrounding her nipples with masking tape and Magic Marker in order to cover up her areolae. Maybe the groupies weren't so bad after all.

Life was a little gentler on the bucolic Spanish hippy trail, and Galen Ayers remembers a colourful, eccentric woman who not only looked after her but took care of her father, Kevin, and the rest of Soft Machine and psychedelic groups such as Tangerine Dream when she had a flat in London. (It was at one of her London parties that Robert Wyatt fell from a window and tragically broke his back.).She was known as Lady June, and she moved out to Majorca to join her comrades who severally decided to leave the hard, grey, demanding metropolis behind in favour of sunshine, a slower pace and a bit of peace.

Every genre needs a quasi-matriarch like this. Jazz had the Baroness Nica Rothschild, who subsidised musicians in New York and cared for the dying Charlie Parker, who passed away in her home. Punk had Nora Forster, the heiress of German newspaper *Der Spiegel*, Slits singer Ari Up's mother and John Lydon's wife, who also put her money to good use and made sure The Slits, The Clash and the Pistols had something to eat and somewhere to sleep. The Rat Pack and their cronies even had a 'Den Mother' in Lauren Bacall… although they probably didn't have to bother her for a floor to sleep on.

"She was doing for adults what she ended up doing for kids… Lady June was an incredible woman, an artist," explains Galen. "She died recently but she was like a surrogate mother to me. I got so into art because of her. She would colour sand so you'd get bright pink sand, blue… she'd give you chemicals so you could make explosions, we'd spend hours drawing.

"Her crowning glory was that she created a treasure hunt for us; all the parents would play along. It led us to the beach where there was this old washed-up fridge, and she'd put masses of ice lollies inside. It was so creative and fun. I see that missing with kids now."

Some people are just good with children. It does seem to be a natural gift that some have and some don't. Not everyone knows instinctively what to do, or perhaps some people's instincts are rather different from others'.

Giving champagne to a baby might not be what childcare experts recommend, even one in the shape of the hedonistic Paula Yates, who wrote numerous books on the subject (childcare, not champagne). However, one dapper but inexperienced childminder felt driven to it. Paula and Bob Geldof had not had a 'date' for months after the birth of their first child, Fifi Trixibelle, in 1984. They had a wealth of friends, perhaps not all of whom would be suitable babysitting material, but they plumped for the designer Jasper Conran, who was the child's godfather after all. He was "delighted but not overqualified when it came to changing nappies", Paula recalled wryly.

"Fifi was blissfully asleep when we went out. When we got home, Jasper answered the door wild-eyed, hair flattened with sweat. We went into the sitting room where Fifi was propped up in a corner of the sofa, bright red and hiccupping sweetly. 'She woke up as soon as you left,' explained Jasper. 'She was fine all through *Top Of The Pops*, but she got really grumpy when I tried to watch Poirot and filled her nappy twice without pausing at all. It was ghastly. I'd rather do six collections in a year than change that child's drawers again… She got totally fed up, so I opened a bottle of champagne, wet her lips with the tiniest drop, sang a couple of my favourite numbers and she's been fine ever since.' With that, he gathered up his jacket and the remains of the bottle and went home to bed."

After the birth of Bob and Paula's daughters Peaches and Pixie, instead of risking the consequences of the alco-babysitting service again, they sensibly employed Anita Debney, an uber-capable nanny-turned-housekeeper who ran the childrens' schedules and, according to Paula's one-time publicist Gerry Agar, "even encouraged the two youngest kids to say their first word at the age of just eight months". I just hope it wasn't a squeaked demand of 'champagne'…

The Geldof girls had their own 'Lady June'-style mentors in the shape of Paula's glamorous friends, in particular Pretenders singer Chrissie Hynde, whom Paula first met when she was compiling her photographic book, *Rock Stars In Their Underpants*. There was also Anjelica Huston, who took the young Fifi under her wing when the Geldofs came to visit her in Hollywood, taking her horse-riding and holding egg-painting competitions "with ravishing actresses like Faye Dunaway", remembered Paula. "Michelle Phillips and Carrie Fisher sat with Fifi and glued sequins and feathers onto blown eggs very seriously for a grand prize of either sexy lingerie or a Barbie, depending on who won."

Chrissie Hynde's influence on the children was notable, if rather more serious. It was after a week at the Sunset Marquis hotel (a place that describes itself as a 'rock& roll epicentre') in West Hollywood with the militantly meat-free Hynde and her children that Peaches became a vegetarian.

Paula: "When I ill-advisedly succumbed to temptation and ate a hamburger, (Chrissie's) children stood there looking sorry for me, whispering 'murderer' every time I took a mouthful... It wasn't long after this that Peaches became a vegetarian. At Christmas, guests had to help themselves furtively to the turkey while Peaches, Pixie and Fifi all sobbed in unison, 'It's not a very happy Christmas for that turkey, is it?'" Good work, Ms Hynde.

A truly vital and beloved figure in the lives of the Geldof children, and obviously Paula (though not so much Bob), was the Australian singer and undisputed sex symbol Michael Hutchence. Paula was besotted with Michael from the minute she saw him when he appeared with his group, INXS, on *The Tube*. The clip of her flirting with him on the show has its place in TV history.

Paula left Geldof for Hutchence in 1995, ten years after their first fateful meeting in the TV studio in Newcastle, and all three daughters enthusiastically embraced the new man in their lives, as he did them. The singer taught Fifi how to kick-box and did pretend kung fu with the younger sisters. The children would paint him pictures and sing songs with him. He'd cancel studio sessions and meetings to attend their birthday parties, and he'd refer to them as "my girls". While some might assume this to be an extra dig at Geldof, Hutchence genuinely appeared to adore them despite a widespread belief he had taken on a rather unwelcome burden by hooking up with Yates, and thus, her extensive brood. He responded to this angrily; the real problem was the intrusive and often aggressive media interest. "The (kids) are not the problem, they're a privilege to be with," he said. "They should spend one afternoon with those kids. That's all it would take."

There's no doubt there was a lot of love in their lives, and they were jubilant when their baby sister, Heavenly Hiraani Tiger Lily, was born in 1996 to Paula and Michael. But while the grief experienced by their own father throughout the breakdown of their parents' marriage and subsequent separation was disquieting, the tragic and bizarre death by sexual misadventure of Michael Hutchence in 1997 was traumatising. "I'll never forget how Pixie cried," wrote Paula. "It was like someone had ripped her heart out."

Ordinarily, when it comes to family life with a rock star patriarch, it is the mother who provides the stability. But in the case of the Geldofs it was progressively the other way around. Yates had already started to unravel since before Michael's death, not least because she was trying to keep up with his sexual and chemical experimentation, which involved her taking Rohypnol. But what was worse, according to Gerry Agar, was that the Rohypnol as well as other substances, not to mention pornography, would be lying around in a house full of inquisitive little girls.

Fifi had wanted to stay with Bob after the split. When Paula realised this, she took it out on her eldest daughter, ensuring her sisters had beautiful presents at Christmas and Fifi did not. "It really hurt Fifi," said Bob. "I made it up to her as far as I could."

Paula would also turn against their the faithful nanny Anita, sacking her just after the divorce. This decision was heartbreaking to her daughters and Anita herself. Peaches wrote to her every single day. When welfare officers realised this they insisted they were allowed more time with her.

Bob and Paula had joint custody of the kids, but when Paula made her first suicide attempt after the death of Hutchence, the children stayed largely with Bob. Paula would come and visit, sometimes sleeping with the children, more for her own sense of security than theirs.

The deep depression and confused state into which she retreated after Michael's demise would eventually lead to another wretched and untimely death – her own. In 2000, Paula Yates was found (by four-year-old Tiger) dead on her bed from a heroin overdose, on the morning of Pixie's 10th birthday. When it was later explained that Paula had gone up to heaven to be with Tiger's father, the little girl asked, "Why didn't she take me?"

It was up to Bob Geldof to step in and deal with the fallout, organise the funeral and, most importantly, take over the brood, including Tiger. This was a decision that initially angered the Hutchence family who questioned why Geldof would want to take on the child of a man he hated. But he was taking on the child of a woman he loved. Paula's will stated that Tiger should grow up in Britain, not Australia, and because of enmity between Paula and the Hutchence family, she stated that Tiger's grandparents were to be denied access to her.

Patricia Hutchence, Michael's mother, was deeply concerned and the entire family were prepared to fight for Tiger. "People must not forget she is Michael's daughter. She is the image of Michael and when I see her little face, it brings back such memories of him. We just want to love her."

Anita ensured, in the meantime, that Tiger's bedroom in Bob's house was covered with pictures of her family in Australia so when they came over she recognised them all straight away. And when they did, for Paula's funeral, Hutchence's father, Kell, was struck by the warm, privileged life Tiger lived, deciding "she is best off with her sisters in England". And not only her sisters, but Bob, his partner, Jeanne Marine, and of course, Anita, whose presence ensured stability and love within the confusion. It becomes a little harder to judge or begrudge when one remembers the catalogue of traumatic incidents the Geldof girls had to endure.

The Osbournes always stuck together as a family but they were less fortunate than the Geldofs when it came to nannies, apparently getting through about 30 of them. To make matters worse, the good ones never wanted to stay and the worst ones were hard to get rid of. Maybe 'nanny to the Osbournes' was a job title that some of the freakier female fans would try to earn at any cost. However, the most successful babysitter ended up being a huge male Mohawk-sporting cartoon punk – Jack at least thought he was "cool" and was more likely to respect his attempts at discipline. But it took a while to find the right person. Some were verbally abusive (although I can't imagine why this would be deemed shocking in the Osbourne household), one drove Jack – who had a 'car-wash phobia' – through the car wash daily, another freaked the children out by munching raw, mud-covered vegetables in front of them (we all get our kicks somehow), others would help themselves to booze, get drunk and flirt with Ozzy… Perhaps expecting a normal nanny to come and work for one of the least normal families around was unrealistic.

"I got set on fire by a nanny once. She lied to mum and said she didn't smoke, but she did," says Jack (the telltale). "A few days later, she was driving me somewhere, cigarette in hand. I was in the back seat with my window open, so when she threw the butt out of the window, it flew straight back in and landed on me. It's amazing how combustible kids can be."

Another nanny chose to read aloud to the children a newspaper article that detailed a sermon by New York's archbishop Cardinal O'Connor, proclaiming how evil their father was, how he was assisting the devil in his works. O'Connor preached that Osbourne's music could lead to demonic possession and self-destruction. It was something the kids perhaps didn't need to hear, and should have been protected from, but the very person in charge of protecting them was exposing them to the worst and most disturbing perceptions of their father.

Growing up, Julian Lennon relied not so much on nannies but friends of his parents and kindly members of his elusive dad's staff in order to cope with the lack of father figure in his life. (One rather odd babysitting arrangement arose when John's estranged father, Alf, appeared at their house out of the blue, eventually grudgingly accepted by a suspicious John. Alf, then 54, was having a wild romance with a 19-year-old girl called Pauline Jones, who Cynthia soon recruited as a childminder for Julian, meaning that Julian was babysat by his teenage future grandma...)

Even if John was at home, Julian's fear of him meant he would often rather Lennon's driver Terry Doran put him to bed than John himself. Indeed the warmth of those on the edges of his immediate situation made a huge difference to his development. Another of those people was Paul McCartney.

"Paul and I used to hang about quite a bit... more than dad and I did," Julian said in later years. "There seem to be far more pictures of me and Paul playing together at that age than there are pictures of me and my dad."

It was only when he was in his teens that Julian learnt Paul had written 'Hey Jude' for him during the devastating period when John left Cynthia for Yoko. Everybody was intimidated by John and his ability to freeze people out and make their lives a misery if he wanted to, and this ensured that, at the time Cynthia needed her friends, the rest of the Beatles camp stayed away, even close friends Maureen Starkey and Patti Harrison, George's wife. Paul was the only member of The Beatles' inner circle who defied John, travelling to Lennon's former home in Weybridge on the train to present Cynthia with a rose and spend some time with her. He wrote the lyrics to 'Hey Jude' on the way, originally titling the song 'Hey Jules', before changing it.

Julian: "What it meant to me was that there were other people on the fringe of our life that had a great deal of love for myself and mum too, and to this day I still have to appreciate and be thankful for that love and care, it's a very kind gesture and one that will never be forgotten."

John believed 'Hey Jude' was for him when he first heard it, although I can't imagine why; it wasn't as if the rest of The Beatles were especially supportive of his union with Yoko anyway. But as both John and Yoko gazed ever more intently into their own navels, it's safe to assume that Julian was, for the most part, some distance from John's mind. Why would he have assumed it to be about anyone other than himself?

Fortunately in 1973 a new influence entered John's life that had a positive effect on Julian after a protracted absence from his father. May Pang, a then 22-year-old Chinese New Yorker working as an assistant for John and Yoko, was suddenly thrown into a situation she initially refused to partake in. Yoko was sensing a change in her husband, and believed he was going to start getting bored. If this was the case, Yoko wanted him to get this out of his system with someone of her own choosing (whether they liked it or not), so she still had ultimate control. (Later it was claimed that she herself wanted space from the marriage.) John enjoyed a very loving 18 months (the 'lost weekend') with May until it was terminated by 'Mother'. During that 18 months, however, Julian describes his time spent with his dad as the happiest he can remember. "Dad and I got on a great deal better then," he said in an interview.

John was at his most relaxed with Pang, who encouraged him to reconnect with his loved ones (he even hooked up with Paul McCartney) and becoming like a sister to Julian, and a friend to Cynthia. May dispelled the tensions in what would ordinarily be an unbearable situation when she urged John to invite his son over to the States to spend some quality time with him.

The trip was particularly memorable for the young Julian because, during time spent in the studio with his dad, he played drums that John recorded, later using the results on a track on his next album, *Walls And Bridges*, crediting his son. (The album is appropriately named, I think; Lennon *was* breaking down walls between himself and his family, and building bridges, temporarily at least.) May is still a special figure in Julian and Cynthia's lives, and Julian included some of her personal photographs of her time with John, and Julian himself, in his *White Feather* exhibition at Liverpool's Beatles Story in 2009.

A similar situation occurred between Rufus Wainwright and the flamboyant New York performance artist Penny Arcade, with whom Loudon had had a fling in the early Eighties. Arcade had appeared in Andy Warhol's 1973 satire *Women In Revolt,* and would become Rufus' 'New York mother', a vital influence artistically and personally, also to Martha. Rufus was staying with his father in New York when he was sent to see Arcade. Loudon might not have known what to say to his son about his burgeoning sexuality, but he knew Penny would be the perfect mentor.

"Loudon called me and said, 'If Rufus is gay then you're the best person for him to know,'" Penny Arcade told biographer Kirk Lake. "I understood some of the issues that would be created by Rufus being gay in that family at that time, clearly, as there would be in most families of young teens in the middle of the Aids epidemic. So I took Loudon's call very seriously."

Arcade's dazzling social and professional circle was also of greater interest to Loudon's children than their immediate one. She introduced them to empowering, inspirational friends of hers such as Quentin Crisp and Patti Smith, and gave them free tickets to her experimental and often eye-popping shows, in which naked genitalia would often be paraded about freely. Penny's most famous piece, *Bitch! Dyke! Faghag! Whore!*, shocked Loudon to the core, but Rufus felt he was home at last.

Arcade was also a close friend of Jeff Buckley, whom Rufus felt was a significant rival, particularly when he started to become a serious name. But in 1996 the pair would both perform at a show at the KGB Theatre on Arcade's invitation. When Rufus stepped up to perform, he had problems being heard. The audience became restless and started heckling but Arcade took the mic, shut them up and declared: "After you hear

Rufus sing you will be telling everyone for the rest of your life that you heard him first."

A similarly unconventional character who became an honorary parent to Ronnie Wood's children is Keith Richards. When Leah was born on September 22, 1978 there was a party in full swing, as there had been when her brother Jesse was born. And again, Ronnie was in a dilemma: "I was busy timing Jo's contractions, and also trying to be a good host to loads of people, many of whom I didn't know, except that a lot of them were dealers."

Keith would turn up to the hospital some hours later to visit Jo and little Leah (whom Ronnie affectionately dubs their 'love child'), and both men put on "operating room gear" in order to be allowed in. "The nurse in charge barked, 'Who's the father?' Keith and I answered at the same time, 'We both are.'"

A committed and supportive family friend he may have been, but all families have to have a mad uncle and Richards definitely took on that role, chopping up lines of cocaine on the dinner table in front of Ronnie's mother-in-law ("It's dessert!" he protested), screaming curses and chasing the kids around the garden after they put a banger in his cigarette and, during another visit, flinging a beloved family pet out of a window.

Ronnie explains in his book *Ronnie,* "Jamie (his third child) had a budgerigar that sang a very regular song. Keith wasn't turned on to the fact that the bird wasn't an alarm clock. He staggered down one morning/afternoon in his favourite leather trousers. He took one look at the chirping budgerigar and tossed the bird and the cage out of the open window.

"We screamed, 'What are you doing? That was Jamie's pet budgerigar!' Keith thought about it for a moment, then mumbled, 'Nobody told me it was a real fucking budgerigar.'"

Real or not, it makes one wonder whether this might actually be Keith Richards' general method of 'turning off' alarm clocks. This is also the man who purportedly snorted his dead father's ashes ("Went down a treat," he'd tell dumbstruck reporters as they tried to work out whether he was joking or not – he was). He also, when told by a concerned entourage-member that his son Marlon had taken to eating ants, responded: "He wants to eat fucking ants? No problem, man…" As I say, the perfect mad uncle.

When it comes to all influential figures in a child's life, it's hard not to want to copy every move they make. If one of their favourite moves appears to be lowering their head to a horizontal mirror and inhaling sharply, you could be in trouble…

CHAPTER 8

Drugs

'Drugs will turn you into your parents.'

Frank Zappa

"Children of addicts can go two ways. You become an addict yourself or you never touch anything. I went down the second path. Reality is scary enough for me," says Natascha Eleanore, whose father, Jack Bruce, lived within the grip of heroin addiction for many years.

There seems to be little grey area when it comes to children witnessing a parent's substance abuse, and I include alcohol under this (cocktail) umbrella. Witnessing a parent taking drugs can give the child an unspoken permission to do the same; maybe the emotional unavailability causes a void one tries to fill by using as well. Alternatively, the reality of living with the addiction of the person you love, and who is supposed to be taking care of you, may see you become more vehemently anti-drugs than the average person. Drug-taking can be a part of growing up, and it's certainly woven into the fabric of rock 'n' roll. However, if it dissolves one's capabilities in the parenting department and transforms an otherwise creative, exciting life into one of numb torpitude, we have to view it in connection with how the children of users evolve.

Daisy Lowe recalls that as a teenager she was like Saffy– the bookish, disapproving daughter to Jennifer Saunders' wild, posing mother in the sitcom *Absolutely Fabulous*. Her mother, Pearl, then addicted to heroin, would sleep long into the day, while Daisy became a mother figure for her young siblings, changing nappies and taking care of the home. She doesn't resent this period, insisting it was a learning curve and she loved looking after the kids. (Daisy was unaware her mother was an addict until her mid-teens, believing she was 'ill'.) But this first-hand experience no doubt played its part in ensuring the model is now resolute in never allowing drugs into her remit. Her 21st birthday invitations warned there would be no 'nose-powdering' at her party. Presumably she was referring to cocaine, although we should spare a thought for those who took it as a genteel reference to visiting the toilet.

Artist Trixie Garcia, daughter of Grateful Dead singer Jerry Garcia and Carolyn Adams (more famously known as Mountain Girl), was just 18 months old when she experienced her first magic mushroom, happening upon a bag that had been left lying around. Mountain Girl, a former Merry Prankster (the Pranksters were a group of hippies who travelled with countercultural author Ken Kesey, taking psychedelic drugs along the way), was rather pleased. "My mom was like, 'Oh, it made you more communicative!'" Trixie told *Rolling Stone*. "Most of the kids in the scene had some early dosing incident…"

There are plenty of drink and drug-related clichés that cling to our perceptions of what we deem 'rock 'n' roll' that in some people's cases are irritating and inaccurate, projected onto them by other people who think their own life is dull. For others, these clichés are lived out with full-bloodied enthusiasm. Some throw themselves into the music business just so they can become a living cliché, while others genuinely find the sometimes insane and exploitative process hard to cope with and need something to hide behind or to make them feel confident. In some cases, the drugs are just there, the musicians are young and curious. But there are those who stay clean and turn their backs on the advanced debauchery that might be going on around them. (Galen Ayers remembers her psych hero father, Kevin, blacking out frequently while on tour with Jimi Hendrix because of his spartan macrobiotic diet, not because of drugs.)

Those stories don't get heard because they aren't really stories – a life in balance isn't as interesting as a life in the balance. Although frequently fainting for any reason might suggest something is a little out of kilter, whether it's from living on nothing but vodka and pills or existing for weeks on alfalfa and soya milk. Good health doesn't fit in with the formula, and thus we continue happily to assume that every musician is 'on something', and is having a great time while they're at it. While the overexcited Waynes and Garths among us might prefer to imagine how brilliantly decadent life must have been for the pre-cold turkey John Lennon, Steve Tyler, David Bowie or Pete Townshend, the reality can be harsh, even more so for their children.

David and Angie Bowie's movie director son Duncan, aka Zowie (whose birth in 1971 inspired Bowie's song 'Kooks' – a sweetly hopeful, tenantative and rather apt song, inviting their baby to 'take a chance on a couple of hooks'), grew up with two drug-using parents. True or not, David famously announced he was gay to *Melody Maker* in 1972, a headline that became something of a *cause célèbre* at the time, while after their marriage broke up Angie would pen two volumes of autobiography that spared no blushes about their unconventional sex lives. Duncan's conversely grounded character, which must in part be thanks to his nanny Marion Skene (who "became his mother" according to Angie) meant he was able to help his father recover from some of his lowest periods. "He's seen me through some of the most awful, depressing times when I was really in absolute, abject agony over my emotional state," Bowie has said. "The heights of my drinking and drug-taking... he's seen the lot."

Jack Bruce could never hide his erstwhile heroin habit from his kids – the information was already out there in the press – but while he was "never high" in front of his daughter Natascha, she sensed something was wrong as a child growing up in their Suffolk home. The general vibrations of someone using class-A drugs, and the tension or sadness between them and a non-using partner, aren't hard to observe in the people you love.

Natascha: "My dad's always struggled with certain things and everyone has their own way of getting through them. It has been a part of growing up. As a child, even if whatever it is isn't actually done in front of you, you pick up on emotions and the ups and downs of your parents. You become perceptive to those things. That can be a positive, it helps you learn to be supportive even from a child's perspective.

"I think with anyone who's struggled with certain addictions it will always be part of their life, even if they've left certain aspects behind. I'm proud of him because he has got through it and a lot of people from his generation didn't."

At least Natascha and her siblings never needed the local policeman or well-meaning Theatre In Education troupe to pop by the school to give an anti-drugs talk. Her dad sat her down when she was 15 and relayed enough horror stories about friends who fell by the wayside, not to mention the sort of altered states that never quite alter back, to put her off hard drugs for life.

"Because he has been through it you listen, more than if someone's just giving you advice and you're like, 'Oh, you don't know what you're talking about, you've never lived! You're just old and boring...' I knew Dad knew what he was talking about.

"I feel my dad made a lot of mistakes for me, in a weird way that's a blessing; I didn't ever feel the need to do Class A drugs. There were a lot of people around me who didn't have that family background who were experimenting with a lot of stuff because it's different, it's exciting, it's new... with me, there was no novelty."

"(Being a dad) is not easy when you're a junkie," Jack Bruce said in an interview with *The Times*. "I had been getting through vast quantities of heroin for several years. When the doctors saw me, they said I was one of the worst cases they'd ever seen. It steals your soul and takes its place. It's not a particularly good substitute.

"I'm clean now, and it was (second wife) Margrit who helped me get my soul back. She gave me an ultimatum: her or the heroin. I'm not saying I immediately became Mr No Drugs, but I think I at least began to grasp the gravity of the situation. All my kids got on so well. They are all great people, kind and gentle and wise... All the stuff I don't do very well. If you knew me, you'd realise I'm a bit of a mental case..."

What is inspiring about Bruce, away from his obvious talent and creativity, is the fact he is such a strong character, a survivor with phoenix-like capabilities. He was seriously ill after a liver transplant in 2005, his liver damaged by years of methadone use during his battle with heroin. Loved ones feared the worst, but not only did he recover, he performed a run of Cream reunion concerts at the Royal Albert Hall in the same year. "If you look at the photos he looks very thin, he's just out of hospital," explains Natascha. "He didn't respond well to some of the medication, and there were concerns his body was going to reject the organ. He's lucky to have found a match.

"I'm grateful he's still here! But if you look at his palm, his lifeline goes all the way down his arm practically! He's a fighter, he's been through some mad things and he always pulls through."

Depeche Mode's Dave Gahan also cheated death several times. (They don't call him 'The Cat' for nothing.) He suffered a heart attack during the time of his marital split with first wife, Jo, but he defied advice and continued touring. Q magazine pronounced the band's 1993 *Devotional* tour 'The Most Debauched Rock 'n' Roll Tour Ever', in slaveringly congratulatory tone. His well-publicised problem with heroin and alcohol hurtled into further self-destruction when he survived a suicide attempt in 1995; he had slashed his wrists, later confessing it was a cry for help. The following year he overdosed on a speedball – a combination of cocaine and heroin – at the Sunset Marquis in Hollywood. He died for two minutes before being revived.

There is a clip of Gahan being interviewed by Johnny Vaughan on YouTube in his hotel room during the 1993 tour, Vaughan conducting the chat in typical cocky style, Gahan gracious but out of it. The comments beneath the clip range from amused to shocked to impressed, but the reality is heartbreaking considering it would not be long after this that Gahan would make an attempt on his own life.

There is a tinge of jovial mockery about the interview, but the interviewee is in trouble. When asked his 'top tips' for kids wanting to become a rock star, Gahan looks away and mumbles, "Stay away from the drink and drugs", and becomes briefly lost in a private moment. Vaughan then cheerily presents him with a gift: Gahan's camping knife from when he was a child, carved with his name. The singer laughs and immediately pretends to commit hara-kiri. Maybe it's hindsight that makes this clip particularly alarming.

Jack Gahan was very young when his father, at this point living in LA, was at his lowest ebb. (Fortunately Dave now insists his only addictions are dark chocolate and *Curb Your Enthusiasm*.) Jack, like Natascha, is philosophical on the subject of his father's past. It might have looked as if Dave Gahan was determined to embrace the life of a rock stereotype at seemingly any cost, but for Jack it is enough to know his dad did eventually gain control of his darker side for the sake of his family. Dave told the *Washington Post*: "I had a wake-up call and it's enabled me to not be afraid of growing. Facing up to real responsibilities in my life – I'm not talking about the band, I'm talking about my family, my beautiful wife, my children."

"I wasn't so much protected from knowing about it because I was just too young to know about it," explains Jack. "It was the same sort of time as the (marital) split, '92, '93, '94. I used to visit Dad like normal, it didn't change a lot for me, it was more my dad really. It was hard for my mum. I didn't really know what was going on.

"The worst thing would be to have to keep it a secret. It's just a part of what makes him who he is now. That was a stage in his life when he was doing something he may not be particularly proud of looking back on, but at the same time it happened, and he's very open about it. It's better for me that way too. Hiding things like that... it got to the point where it was so publicised he couldn't hide it anyway, but it's 13 or 14 years he's been sober, he's still very serious about that. It was something to learn from for everyone around him. That's the best way to look at it."

Unlike Gahan, Kurt Cobain never managed to turn his life around, though, perhaps at odds with his chaotic image, he had always longed for children. A typically morbid gesture indicating Cobain's nurturing instincts is detailed in Charles R Cross' book *Heavier Than Heaven*; during the early stages of Courtney and Kurt's courtship, the pair shot up together, then went for a walk, finding a dead bird on the roadside. "Kurt pulled three feathers off and passed one to Courtney, holding the others in his hand. 'This is for you, this is for me,' he said. And holding the third feather he added, 'And this is for the baby we're going to have.'"

When Courtney did become pregnant, she did apparently make an effort to get healthy for their child's sake, although 'friends' told *Vanity Fair* in 1992 that the mother-to-be was still using heroin and had abandoned a detox programme. "It's a sick scene in that apartment," said one source. Kurt was terrified their child would be deformed in some way as a result of their rampant drug use up to the time of conception and in those early months of expectancy (when they were still unaware they had conceived). The article added a new element of concern.

The shocking claims in *Vanity Fair* resulted in the world taking Cobain's fears and running with them, raging against the irresponsibility of the damaged king and queen of grunge. Even Guns n' Roses singer, Axl Rose, no friend of Cobain's, waded in, publicly declaring that 'Kurt Cobain is a fucking junkie with a junkie wife, and if the baby's born deformed, I think they both ought to go to prison'".

The Cobains were now terrified that the article and resulting furore would see their child taken away from them, and Kurt insisted he and Courtney should make a suicide pact should this disaster occur. Courtney, fortunately, was a little more rational. "What about Frances?" she said in an interview. "Sort of rude. 'Oh, your parents died the day after you were born.'"

Frances Bean Cobain (so named because Kurt thought she looked like a kidney bean on the sonogram) was born at 7.48am on August 18, 1992, at Cedars-Sinai Medical Center, Los Angeles. She was born healthy, to the Cobains' relief (although *The Globe* newspaper preferred to print a picture of a deformed baby, pretending it was Frances, with the headline: 'Rock Star Baby Is Born A Junkie'.)

Her arrival into the world was unconventional. Both parents were present, sort of. Kurt was in the same hospital suffering from withdrawal symptoms in the chemical dependency wing. Once her contractions started to become more frequent, Courtney hauled herself out of bed, marched to Kurt's room with her IV stand, shrieking, "Get out of this bed and come down now! You are not leaving me to do this by myself. Fuck you!"

Kurt was comparatively useless. He vomited profusely, was unable to breathe properly (so could offer no assistance to Courtney) and he blacked out just before Frances appeared. Courtney had to pay more attention to Kurt than to her own predicament, holding his hand and rubbing his stomach as he struggled to master his own pain while she was giving birth. (At least Kurt was there technically – after Keith Moon's daughter Mandy, who may or may not be named after Moon's drug of choice mandrax, was born on July 12 1966, Moon was called to bring clothes for his wife, Kim, and pick her up. Two days passed with no sign of him until he was finally brought to the hospital, tripping on acid and unable to recognise Kim, let alone work out who the baby was. He then wandered off, out of the hospital in Park Royal, West London, and into a neighbouring field, pursued by an incandescent Kim.)

Unfortunately but somewhat understandably, the *Vanity Fair* article did play its part in ensuring Frances would, as they feared, be taken from them. A social worker turned up at the hospital holding a copy of the magazine just two days after she was born.

It was argued by Kurt devotees around this time that despite the fact he had serious issues with drugs, there was never any question as to whether or not he'd be a good parent. However, individual good-heartedness aside, anyone who has witnessed a loved one's addiction might counter-argue that it's hard to be a good anything – parent, partner, lover, friend or indeed bandmate – when you're an addict. It's hard to be true even to yourself let alone anyone else when you are being ruled by a substance that takes precedence over your senses. There is no question that Frances, was deeply loved by Kurt but a child deserves their parents' full attention and protection. He doted on her, missed her when he had to go away, and loved playing with her, but a nanny would also have to be on hand to grab the baby if Kurt nodded out as he was holding her.

Caring, devoted parents the Cobains may have been, but this also didn't change the fact that the house contained guns and ammunition, which were seized by police who had been called to the house by Courtney after a fight broke out between the couple. Kurt had apparently been taunting his wife by declaring he was going to try crack. The pair then argued childishly over who should have the 'distinction' of getting arrested. According to Cross' book, "this was a mother lode of an opportunity to both emotionally retreat and play the martyr (for Kurt). He won." He was in jail for just a few hours before being bailed, and charges were dropped.

While John Lennon was a very different person than Kurt Cobain, it was, according to Cynthia, his addictive behaviour initially when using speed-like prescription drugs, LSD and marijuana that kept John's attentions away from his son, and indeed her. Julian relied on Cynthia being both parents, as Brian Wilson's daughters would with their mother, Marilyn. As a parent herself, former addict Mackenzie Phillips would take her baby son Shane (born in 1987 "jumpy from the cocaine" that had transferred from mother to baby in the womb) into crack dens – safer than leaving him in the car, she reasoned, in her book *High On Arrival*. She'd shoot up behind the shower curtain while she was bathing him, and let him fend for himself as she slept through the day, "committing the sins of the fathers", she laments.

Her father, John, during the height of his own addiction, would, she claims, allow his youngest child Tamerlane to play with needles as if they were water-pistols in his syringe-strewn flat. So, in many cases, it is hard to argue that an addict can truly make a good parent in that the addict is at best sadly never really there, and at worst is rarely capable of looking after themselves let alone a child. Boundaries get confused or ignored, instincts become mangled and misread.

There's a theory that drug users suffer a kind of arrested development the moment they become dependent — part of them stops maturing mentally from that point forth and they remain at the same age they were when they became addicted. This may explain such childlike, attention-seeking antics from otherwise sensitive, bright people.

This infantile behaviour, which sees young adults become bereft of the opportunity to evolve organically into the older, wiser people they could be and depositing them in an artificial stasis, was never more stomach-turningly demonstrated than by Brian Wilson. He married Marilyn Rovell, despite sleeping with both of her sisters, because he deemed her the most capable of mothering him. And mother him she did, to the point she couldn't bear it any more. Throughout the early to mid-Seventies Brian lived in bed, stuffing his face with junk food and snorting coke, too paranoid to brush his teeth or shower (in case blood gushed from the taps) and watching "soothing children's shows", as he puts it. The children who weren't feeling particularly soothed were his own — Carnie and Wendy.

Brian himself admits that by 1975 he "had no control. I cried in front of the children. I screamed and yelled, terrorised by voices that no one else heard. Marilyn found me in the hallway, incoherent, frightened, in need of more babying than the children."

Marilyn tried her best to keep life normal for her children but Brian's strange dominance over the household reached its nadir as Christmas 1975 approached. Wilson had procured some black heroin — a deadly variant that can lead to botulism and 'tissue death'. Before long he was in the hall trying to persuade his little girls to try it in a kind of junkie father-daughter bonding session. Marilyn stopped him just in time, before electing to hire a heavy, namely Stan Love, brother of Beach Boy Mike, to watch his every move out of sheer desperation.

The real (and eventually exploitative) genius who would blow this farce apart, Dr Eugene Landy, was introduced soon after the black heroin incident. One morning Stan Love rushed into the kitchen when he heard Marilyn screaming. Carnie and Wendy were at the breakfast table. Marilyn pointed at the floor where Brian was quivering in a foetal position, a bottle of heroin inches from his fingers. Marilyn ordered Stan to get him out. Wilson's expensive 'Landy Years' were about to begin, for better or worse. Eugene Landy had previously treated hell-raising actor Richard Harris and Alice Cooper before crossing paths with Wilson. He seemed to be the only one able to force him into any kind of sane routine, but it was intermittent.

After splitting from Marilyn in 1978, Brian Wilson fell into further decline and would be told by a conventional doctor that, in a manner of speaking, he had chemically destroyed himself. This was a fine opportunity once again to try to blame others for his fate. "My mother was the first one I called with the news… I wanted to lay a heavy guilt trip on her. I wanted her to know how she and Dad had fucked me up."

However, the fact Wilson had cut everybody who loved him out of his life meant he had ceased to become a priority himself. Wilson's mother, if his book is to be believed, appeared to be unmoved by the news (unless he was attempting to effect a double guilt trip by including this story). "The doctor says I'm probably going to die,' I groaned, 'Can you come and see me?' 'No, I'm making dinner for Carl and his kids and Marilyn and the girls.'"

While Wilson repeatedly and almost gleefully gushes forth information in *Wouldn't It Be Nice?* about his indulgences and addictions, Elvis Presley didn't even realise that, from 1973 onwards, he *was* a drug addict. The fact he was taking prescription drugs – barbiturates, painkillers, Quaaludes and uppers like the diet pill Dexedrine – was what made the difference in his opinion. He was a vociferous campaigner against 'street drugs', and therefore couldn't possibly have a problem himself. Presley clearly knew how to obtain whatever prescription drugs he wanted, but he apparently would carry a physician's reference book with him so he knew what to ask for and, if necessary, which symptoms to feign.

Lisa Marie observed her father's deteriorating state with distress each time she visited Graceland after her parents' break-up. "I could see he was struggling," she remembers in *Elvis By The Presleys.* "He was very sad. He'd come into my room walking so unsteadily that sometimes he'd start to fall and I've have to catch him."

Toward the end of Elvis' jumpsuited 'Vegas years', it transpired that the singer had been writing notes in his hotel suite, begging God for guidance. He was lost, confused and alone. Some months later, back at Graceland at 4am on August 16, 1977, Lisa Marie would see her father alive for the last time. "He found me and said go to bed," she says. "I said OK. And he came in and kissed me goodnight." Elvis was just 42 years old when he died of a heart attack. In autopsy, his body would reveal he had taken a staggering cocktail of drugs that included morphine, Demerol, Valium, the opiate codeine, Quaaludes, diazepam, Nembutal and Sinutab.

"It's hard to be in that place that my father was in," says Lisa Marie. She clearly wishes the people around her father could have prevented his self-destructive use of prescription drugs but they were unable to do so. Elvis was a victim of his extraordinary celebrity: the more stratospheric the rise to fame, the easier it can be to lose a sense of reality. Add substance abuse into the mix and unless you have a strong partner, you'll have to fight to regain control.

In 1979, the session saxophonist Bobby Keys, who had worked with Presley, the Stones and Eric Clapton among other luminaries, visited Ronnie Wood in his new home in Mandeville Canyon to introduce him to the 'nose-saving' concept of freebasing cocaine. A house-warming gift, if you will. Five years of paranoia, obsession and questionable house guests would follow for Ronnie and his family as a result.

"Once Jo [Wood] found a queue of people, mostly strangers queuing outside our bathroom for a hit on the pipe," recalls Wood in *Ronnie.* "We had people letting themselves in in the middle of the night with stash and pipes." The children would presumably have witnessed the entire bizarre and increasingly dark pantomime. The Wood clan grew up fast.

A shaft of light would cut through the clouds of powder and smoke when Tyrone Wood was born on August 21, 1983 at the Mount Sinai hospital in New York, but the drug use continued. "After his birth, while

Jo was still in hospital, I offered her a line of coke to celebrate," remembers Ronnie. She didn't take it. But soon after Tyrone's arrival, Ronnie started using 'dirty cigarettes' – tobacco laced with heroin. His consumption was considerable but he is still here to tell the tale, which is sadly more than can be said for Paula Yates and Michael Hutchence.

In the cases of some rock 'n' roll couples there is no 'straight' parent to create even an illusion of normality. They are just slightly bigger, wrinklier kids and drugs are their favourite toy, their security blanket.

When Heavenly Hiraani Tiger Lily Hutchence was born to Paula and Michael in July 1996, it was a joyous if rather public occasion (although it's not unusual for celebrities' children to be in the public eye the minute they've popped out of the womb. Sting and Trudie Styler's son Jake was rather graphically filmed being born. Talk about a crowning moment...). In order to get herself out of debt and raise her profile, Paula was writing a column for *The Sun* newspaper that pulled in £100,000 per year, and she had promised them exclusive first pictures of her child.

Tiger was born at home in the bath. Press banked up outside the house, and Michael, practically bursting with paternal took a moment to serenade them with Frank Sinatra tunes before disappearing to look after his partner and firstborn. "It was like a royal occasion," remembers Yates' former press agent Gerry Agar. "Tiger was the most famous baby to be born since Prince Harry. Flowers from every newspaper and television company kept arriving at the house and I had to fill the bath to keep the flowers from wilting in the heat."

Gerry Agar, according to her own book, *Paula, Michael and Bob – Everything You Know Is Wrong*, had become something of a Girl Friday and constant support to Yates, and it was thanks largely to her and nanny Anita Debney that the Geldof children were shielded from some of the wanton drug abuse that was occurring in the supposedly safe haven of their home.

After placing the flowers carefully in the bath, she opened a bathroom cupboard to find a towel. "There, among the bubble bath and Nina Ricci scent, was a folded slip of paper and a couple of white pills, imprinted with the symbol of a bird in flight," she writes. "I unfolded the wrap to reveal half a teaspoon of white powder. I was paralysed."

While Paula and Michael were on an extended stay in Australia, visiting his family with their newborn daughter, Hutchence's motorbike alarm went off outside Yates' home. Anita, in her attempts to find the manual, came across some brown envelopes addressed to 'Mr Kipper'. She tore one open but only found several Smarties tubes, and discarded them as she continued searching. The following morning she found Fifi, Peaches and Pixie in Paula's bedroom with Gerry's daughter Sophie watching TV. The envelope was open on the bed and the children had tipped out the sweets. Anita's suspicions were raised when she spotted Sophie playing with a strange brown stick – she knew it was drugs immediately, and quickly gathered up all the items, asking if they'd eaten anything. "Sophie said the brown sticks were too hard to bite," writes Agar. "Bob was due back later, but we were not about to ask him what they were." Bob Geldof was dubious about Hutchence and still scarred by the split, but Agar decided they had to tell Bob his "children were in mortal danger".

In order to save the children, and save Paula and Michael from themselves, the police were notified and the house was raided. Geldof took his children back to his home in Kent to keep them away from the chaos as much as possible. When they eventually returned to London they were met by the press at the beginning of every school day.

Meanwhile, Anita rang Paula and Michael to inform them of the raid, and of the storm they would return to. They responded with a dreamy, "Oh, that's nice," before telling Anita they loved her and hanging up. They were on ecstasy.

What is worth bearing in mind in relaying this unfolding nightmare is that some people may be unaware of or have forgotten quite what the Geldof daughters have grown up through. The loss of a mother seems to be a defining theme for both sides of the family – from the beginning of their courtship, Yates felt deeply for Geldof, who had lost his mother at the age of six; she could relate to the void as, while her mother hadn't died during her childhood, she had pined for the glamorous, footloose parent who had made herself unavailable. "I knew what it was like to long for someone," she wrote in her autobiography. "I spent most of my days longing for my mother to spend more time with me. My mother taught me how desperately attractive what you cannot have can be…"

According to Paula, her mother, Helene Thornton, a former Bluebell Girl, suffered an increasingly tense marriage to the manic depressive TV organist Jess Yates, who Paula would later discover was not her father at all. In fact, she would discover that she was the child of *Opportunity Knocks* presenter (and Jess Yates' nemesis) Hughie Green, a serial adulterer and alcoholic. Paula did not enjoy the warmest childhood with Yates but had just started to feel more at ease with her upbringing when she was to be destabilised with this unwelcome news.

The press invoke the shadow of Yates and Hutchence's drug abuse generally when they feel they can link the Geldof daughters' own antics with theirs. This is inappropriate, such as when Fifi was 'snapped' while drunk and enjoying herself one evening (comparisons drawn immediately with her mother), but sometimes it appears that whether consciously or not, history is repeating itself, such as when Peaches was secretly filmed allegedly buying drugs (or 'DRUGS', as the *News Of The World* referred to them), and in July 2008 when she was reported to have been treated after allegedly collapsing from a suspected overdose according to the same Sunday tabloid. Peaches has a strong role model in her father, but whether she was just indulging herself as a teenager who has more money than the average (and is invited to more parties than the average) or whether there were more sinister undertones to her actions, some children do inevitably go out of their way to become their parent – particularly the parent they can't reach. Both Jack Osbourne and Mackenzie Phillips admitted they were copying their unavailable fathers. To paraphrase Zappa, drugs really *did* turn them into their parents, that was the point.

"Ever since I was old enough to understand it, I've known Dad was an alcoholic and a drug addict," reflects Jack Osbourne in *Ordinary People*. "I thought it was what dads did. I'd see my dad taking pills, and I'd buy a box of Tic-Tacs and swallow them, to be like him."

Tic-Tacs would later be replaced by OxyContin, and Jack admitted he was high throughout the second series of *The Osbournes*. Kelly similarly experimented with alcohol and prescription drugs. Both spent their teens in and out of rehabilitation. "There wasn't a second in a 24-hour day I wasn't high," Kelly confessed on ITV's *Tonight* programme in 2004.

Jack and Kelly would drink, Ozzy would drink and Ozzy's father, Jack, was a drinker too – the young Ozzy used to follow him daily to the pub. Jack senior's alcoholism often led to violence, and for Ozzy, the by-product of copious drug-taking and booze was also violence. Jack Jr's own indulgence as a teenager, stoked by self-esteem issues, led him down a similar path of aggression while under the influence, on one occasion punching Kelly in the face.

Eldest Osborne sister Aimee, rather than following her father's descent into self-abuse, ended up reversing her role, acting almost as a parent would with a wayward teenager during the height of Ozzy's alcoholism, and feeling the guilt a parent often does when a child loses their way. "I remember I sat down next to him and said, 'Daddy, why are you doing this to us? Please don't do this.' He looked at me and said, 'Fuck you, I work hard, I get bread for this family, I have the right to do whatever the fuck I like, get away from me.' I remember knowing that this was not how daddies were meant to speak to their little girls. I just remember him being so hard, and I felt it was my fault for some weird reason."

It is said we never truly forget anything, everything is filed away in our minds, maybe appearing in dreams or not emerging as memories for years. When Ozzy Osbourne attacked Sharon in a drug-addled stupor in 1989, the incident and subsequent attention left its imprint on the children. Ozzy had staggered downstairs in his underpants and announced to Sharon that "we've decided you're going to have to die". Before she knew it Ozzy was trying to strangle her. Sharon hit the panic button just in time, the police rushed to the house and arrested Ozzy.

Despite Sharon's wishful thinking that the children were oblivious to the chaos, they were very much aware of what was happening; they had to face the publicity aftermath and classroom whispers every day. It wasn't enough that something traumatic had occurred at home, it was all over the press as well.

Seeing how Sharon tried to deal with her husband's addictions could also be unnerving. Jack: "One day, Dad was sitting on his balcony smoking pot. Mum was so pissed off that she found the bag of pot, removed the contents and shat inside it. When Dad tried to roll his next joint, he went nuts." (Fortunately he was too stoned to cause any real trouble – he managed to shout at Sharon for a bit before passing out on the bed.)

In Rufus Wainwright's case, it was his desire to become his father – a man who resolutely did what was right for himself – that would tear him away from drugs as opposed to push him towards them. Rufus became addicted to crystal meth during the early Noughties: his gums would bleed, he'd embarrass himself (once marching into Yoko Ono's apartment shouting, 'Hey Yoko! Where's the champagne?'), and he'd also go temporarily blind. Rufus was flirting with death, assuming it to be the "ultimate orgasm", and it was finally during a stint in rehab that he realised he had to address his issues with Loudon. "There was a common thread through a lot of men – once you get to issues with fathers, that's when we break down," he told *Paster* magazine. "For all the crap he's done to me and leaving me as a child, he's always been honest and taken care of himself. My father's always been able to survive, musically and career-wise … that's when I realised I wanted to be my dad, in a lot of ways."

It was a desire to become John Phillips, seemingly in the face of his absence and unpredictability, that led his eldest daughter, Mackenzie, to embrace drugs with tragic passion. (Perhaps choosing to become the parent that is never there is an attempt to make sure they are *always* there in you, because you have assumed his or her personality, habits and expressions.) Drugs and 'daddy issues' appear to be at the root of many of the twisted consequences for Mackenzie.

Mackenzie (who was congratulated by her father as a 'true Phillips' when she was arrested for the first time, wasted on Quaaludes, at 18) believes she was "genetically predisposed" to live a life of extreme indulgence akin to that of her father and his friends, but there is much to be said for exposure to a lifestyle. Couple this with the fact she was desperate for acceptance and totally open to her surroundings and the results are inevitable.

She detailed her first dalliance with cocaine, alongside her brother Jeff, at 11 years old in her disturbing autobiography, *High On Arrival* – a terrifying account of how life as a 'pioneer celebrity kid' can go very, very wrong. John and Genevieve snorted coke from a cereal bowl in front of the two fascinated kids during a stay at the Chateau Marmont. Why wouldn't Mackenzie and Jeff try it once the bigger kids had gone for a 'nap'? "It made me feel grown-up… If my father set out to raise a drug addict, he did everything right."

Around the same age, Mackenzie was home alone when John's hippy pal Donovan walked in, and they decided to bake brownies. He then told her, "You can't have any, these are special grown-up brownies." (He'd added some of her father's hash to the mix). Try telling a child not to eat brownies – especially when she's helped to make them. It's unjust and basically futile. Before long though, Mackenzie writes, "everything was funny"…

While many young girls would view being allowed to wear make-up, buy a first record or go shopping on their own as a rite of passage, Mackenzie's metaphorical druggy bat mitzvah was to become official joint-roller for her father and his friends. She also knew how to take care of anyone who was having a bad trip, having learned how to talk people down from the age of five. She was just trying to make sure everything she did met with her father's approval, presumably to stop him from going away, unexplained, unannounced and regardless of her needs. Of course, nothing he did had anything to do with anyone other than himself. He was the sun blazing, magnetic, terrible, and everyone else just happened to orbit him, hoping for a few warm rays but more often than not getting scorched.

It was no secret that Mackenzie had become a troubled, damaged casualty even in her early twenties. Elderly ladies approached her in the street. "I'm praying for you, dear," they'd tell her. "I've been praying for you since you were a little girl." Well-intentioned but slightly alarming. Such is life, or at least life in the spotlight.

On one of Mackenzie's attempts to get clean in the Nineties, this time at Eric Clapton's Crossroads clinic in Antigua, she was accompanied by her sister Bijou and her then boyfriend Sean Lennon. Much as she appreciated the support she became exasperated by the high-profile nature of every aspect of her life when, during group sessions of the family programme, Sean unintentionally stole the show by talking about the loss of his father. "Needless to say, his audience was rapt," wrote Mackenzie. "I wanted my loved ones there, but I was tired of having a family so colourful that their presence outshone everything else. Everyone at Crossroads was having family week, but mine had to be spectacular and sensationalised."

Mackenzie's own addiction problems are directly linked to her father – far from protect her from exposure to his own issues, he injected her with cocaine when she was in her late teens; he kept her as dependent on him as on the substances they would both abuse. If Frank Zappa truly believed his theory that children develop regardless of their parents' activities, this must prove otherwise.

The child of a user often tries to take care of their parent, and when they can't, become racked with guilt and a sense of misplaced responsibility. Hip-hop artist QD3, Quincy Jones' son, spent his childhood unsuccessfully trying to help his mother fight her demons. He has, however, managed to turn the heartbreak of the past into something he can use creatively. "I tried to help her my entire life and tried to 'fix' the situation. I would say (to someone in this position), try to be as objective as you can, try to have compassion for your parents. Also know that it's not your fault.

"It's up to you if you want to break the family cycles. My advice is to find a way to turn your past into a benefit," he told *411 Mania*. "Painful experiences give you drive, strength and compassion to do bigger things than you would otherwise have been capable of. Use it as fuel."

So, drug use is almost inescapable within the often hedonistic web of rock 'n' roll – almost but not completely. For Frank Zappa's kids, freedom was the bedrock of their home life, but narcotics were banned from the house. When little is off limits as far as your folks are concerned, you're likely to listen when they tell you what to avoid. He'd inform his children drugs gave people an "excuse to be an asshole". To be an idiot in the eyes of Frank was the last thing his kids wanted. Despite this, most people assume the likes of Zappa, with his floridly multi-dimensional ideas and intensely colourful approach, must have been on drugs.

"People think if you have an imagination you must be using some mind-altering substance," Ahmet Zappa told *The Guardian* in 2006. "Otherwise how could you think of that? That saddens me. I've never smoked or taken a drug, and ideas pop into my head all day long."

Galen Ayers is similarly nonplussed by the behaviour she witnessed when she entered further education. To be fair, most students were making the most of being away from home and enjoying the liberty that entailed. But Galen's life with her father, Kevin Ayers, in Majorca was free enough to encourage moderation, as opposed to extremes. Nothing was restricted, so why would anyone binge? "When I went to university everyone was getting trashed. I was like, 'Why are you doing that? Stop it! What's binge-drinking anyway?' Did not get it. Just have a little bit of wine!"

It's comforting to end on a less tormented example, but it's high time we waded out of the smoky fug, washed the stench of detox out of our hair and shook off the darkness. Extreme lows are always balanced by extreme highs, and not only of a chemical nature. Whether it's a pony, a your own fun-sized Corvette or a personal meeting with Bob Dylan, it's time to cheer ourselves up by experiencing some of the seriously cool benefits afforded to rock 'n' roll's children.

CHAPTER 9

The Bright Side

'The luxury of having the parents I had was that if all this goes horribly wrong I'll be all right…'
Stella McCartney to Jess Cartner-Morley, 2009

The progeny of rock stars might not always have it easy, but when it's good, it can be *really* good… from being four years old and having your drawing of a beetle used as artwork for a Beatles flexidisc (Zak Starkey), waking up in the Malibu Colony to see Larry Hagman patrolling the private beach in full Native American regalia (Dylan Howe), having a private jet named after you (Lisa Marie Presley), wearing genuine Sergeant Pepper outfits for a party (Jason and Lee Starkey) or simply revelling in the knowledge your mum once sewed up the crotch of Jimi Hendrix's trousers after he demonstrated a particularly elaborate dance move (the Zappa brood).

You might have a song dedicated just to you: 'Scarlet' was written and recorded by Jimmy Page for his daughter of the same name, 'Isn't She Lovely?' of course, was Stevie Wonder's joyous welcome to his daughter Aisha Morris. John Lennon's 'Serve Yourself', about Sean and featuring his baby chortles, is "essential – 'Beautiful Boy's bastard twin'", according to music writer Gavin Martin. Then there is John Martyn's tender blues

'May You Never', for his son Spencer, and Bob Dylan's gently instructive blessing 'Forever Young', for Jakob. Your face might even grace the album cover, like Mary McCartney did as a babe in arms on her dad's first solo record.

Some of the children in this chapter know how lucky they are. Others lost all sense of perspective long ago, sliding into a pampered apathy after suffering too much of a good thing. At the very least they lose their ability to monitor their own easy way of snubbing that which another might dream of: one child of a Rolling Stone once amusingly pronounced Bermuda "boring", for example. Jack Osbourne similarly complained of the tiresome fate of being taken to Hawaii "year in, year out… I dream of going anywhere but". (Tried Skegness? It's very bracing.) But, it may surprise you to learn, the latter appear to be very much in the minority.

The material benefits can be fabulous, let's not beat around the bush. Christmas would be an even bigger event than for most: Dylan Howe and his younger brother Virgil awoke one year to find two miniature Italian motorbikes under the tree, with which they terrorised Hampstead Garden Suburb. Aimee Osbourne zoomed about in a fun-sized Corvette, pets scattering as she approached.

It gets complicated when the family unit becomes divided of course. Competition can become fearsome, particularly if it transpires the attention (or money) is not being shared equally. Rod Stewart's daughter Ruby describes the house her sister Kimberly grew up in (ie, separate to Ruby) as "palatial, a beautiful house in Beverly Hills with pillars and stuff. She had way more stuff than I did. Not that it makes her a bad person, just that she was mistaken in thinking that was important." Ouch.

But it is often the experiences, the opportunities, the heroes you meet and the magnitude of some of the concerts in which you might even bag a starring role that can be the most memorable positives. "I got to sing on stage with The Beach Boys when I was about eight," says pianist Harry Waters, son of Roger, over a cup of tea in his instrument-packed front room. His eyes widen at the memory. "I was obsessed with The Beach Boys. Bruce Johnston sang on *The Wall*. That's the context.

"We went to this gig of theirs on Long Island, and they're really cool with kids, their kids run around and go onstage and all that kind of thing. He said, 'I understand you're a Beach Boys freak. Do you know any songs?' and I was like, 'I know *all* your songs!' He said, 'Do you want to come and sing?' I sang 'Barbara Ann', one of the harmonies. It was amazing."

Trev Lukather had his first taste of rock stardom when he was 13. His dad, Steve, might have left him to his own devices when it came to learning the guitar, but he must have noticed how advanced he was in developing his own style, because he trusted him with an audience of 20,000. "My dad took me on the road on the Toto reunion tour and on the first night it was sold out, it was crazy. I was sitting on the side of the stage just blown away by these shows.

"During the first show my dad says into the mic, 'Not only is this very special because we're all back together, but I also have my son here,' and he just took off his guitar – he never told me he was going to do this – and he said, 'Just play whatever you want.' I was so short he had to hold the guitar strap. I just started doing some riff I wrote and the whole band backed me up, 20,000 people started screaming my name, and that was it! I was changed for life, that experience will forever be imprinted on my soul and I thank my dad for that every day of my life."

Trev's appearance was such a success he appeared onstage with them every night on the tour, much to the fans' and his own delight. "I even made out with a 13-year-old French model," he froths, "I was like, 'Oh my God! You get gorgeous girls too?!'" As far as this young man was concerned, his fate was sealed. He was to the manor born.

This is all very well for kids of a certain age, but what about the little ones? Fifi Geldof was fortunate to be carted around by her mother, Paula Yates, wherever she went – to the TV studio in Newcastle where Paula recorded *The Tube* with Jools Holland, and notably to the recording of the historic 1984 Band Aid single 'Do They Know It's Christmas?/Feed The World' at Sarm Studios in west London. Fifi would also attend the legendary Live Aid show itself, in 1985, which her father, Bob, organised with Midge Ure.

Fifi was only 16 months old, so she could be forgiven for not being fully able to appreciate the motive behind the event; she was more moved by the prospect of rummaging through gender-bending Boy George cohort Marilyn's handbag and trying on his perfume.

"The Live Aid concert at Wembley was an unforgettable day," writes

Paula Yates in her autobiography. "Fifi wandered over to Prince Charles and wiped her mouth on his trouser leg. Prince Charles, however, grinned and admired her pinstriped shorts, obviously used to this sort of rowdy behaviour at home…"

Meeting people is one benefit, whether those experiences are remembered as fleeting encounters or meetings that led to lifelong friendship. Dhani Harrison found hanging around with the Traveling Wilburys inspiring, particularly when he struck up a friendship with Tom Petty; Scarlet Page remembers her father, Jimmy, making sure she always met her heroes as a little girl: The Osmonds, Abba, Adam & The Ants… "all the cool ones", she insists; Ronnie Wood and family spent a lot of time with the actor John Hurt, who would swim naked in their pool and occasionally recreate gory scenes from *Alien* while the rest of them were trying to eat. The Woods would also tour America in a Winnebago with John Lee Hooker on board.

Yes, the idea of meeting our heroes is an enviable one, but in many cases there's just one drawback – you're too young to appreciate who they are. Dylan Howe is a serious admirer of David Bowie's music, and has adapted some of *Low* and *"Heroes"* for his own jazz project *Subterraneans*, featuring Portishead guitarist Adrian Utley. Dylan hasn't yet managed to make contact with Bowie for his opinion on this work, and this is all the more frustrating considering Dylan, as a child, once fell asleep at one of Bowie's parties.

Dylan: "We'd moved to Montreux, Switzerland, for a bit when I was small and I remember we were invited to a party up in the hills. I was all sleepy and there was a lovely room near the front door where everyone had piled their coats up. I just went in there, lay on the coats and went to sleep. It happened to be David and Angie Bowie's party – and I must say now, I wished I'd stayed awake! I'd have liked to have had a bit of a chat with him. I don't even know if Zowie was there, I think I went straight to sleep almost immediately after arriving!

"Then when we spent some summers in lovely Malibu, we were staying next door to Miles Davis, and I had no idea who he was either! I saw him on the balcony a few times. Two of my heroes, and when I was young I was near them and had no idea who they were… On the other side was Larry Hagman who would arrange all these flags on the beach, doing his morning rituals. He had clothes on thankfully but he also was wearing a Native American headdress. I've seen him in interviews and he seems a very witty individual, so maybe he was having a joke on all of us."

Jack Bruce's daughter Natascha Eleanore had a similar experience with Bob Dylan. At least she spoke to him, but looking back it was not quite the conversation she'd want to have with him now. "One time at a show dad was doing, Bob Dylan was performing (on the same bill), and my headmaster, who had given me permission to be taken out of school, told me in a jokey way that it was on the condition I got him an autograph from Bob Dylan.

"When the time came, after the show my dad wanted to say hi to Bob – my dad generally keeps himself to himself and he was just kind of getting ready to talk to him, and apparently I just ran up to Bob Dylan and said, 'I need you to sign this for my headmaster!' That was all that was in my head! I embarrassed my dad no end. If that was now, I'd be like, 'Oh my God!' I wish I'd been a bit older…"

The children of Mickey Gallagher were allowed to sing on The Clash's epic 1980 double album, *Sandinista!*, to give early favourites such as 'Career Opportunities' and 'Guns of Brixton' a pre-school breath of fresh air. Gallagher senior played keyboards on the album, and accompanies his sons' (Luke and Ben) version of 'Career Opportunities' on what sounds like a spinet, subverting the original breakneck version into something rather more cute . His daughter Maria, then four, bravely sings on her own on the menacing 'Guns Of Brixton'.

"I remember it clearly," Maria says, with more than a hint of excitement at the memory. "I remember the stool I sat on, the size of the headphones, and the night it was. I remember singing it and my brothers pulling faces through the glass. I sound quite excitable towards the end of the song because they're messing around.

"The Clash were just playing 'Guns of Brixton' over and over again. I would get all the words wrong. My dad funnily enough felt it was because I had a crush on Paul Simonon! I was so in awe of Paul, and it was his song, I always thought he was lovely. So they decided to do that and my brothers did 'Career Opportunities'. Ben doesn't come in for a while, he's so shy; Luke starts it off and then they get into it.

"Dad's on the piano, it might have been Wessex Studios. Having grown up at gigs and in studios… it was interesting because there was a lot of crossing over. The Blockheads were at their height and also The Clash were doing all this work, but we were just kids hanging around in the studio."

Fellow Blockheads bass player Norman Watt Roy and saxophonist Davey Payne would also play on *Sandinista!* It was like an extended family album – sonic, as opposed to photographic. (Like all families, there was a healthy measure of tension: particularly regarding 'The Magnificent Seven', which Watt Roy and Gallagher contested was based on a tune they had composed.)

Had Strummer's children been around during this time, there is no doubt they would have made an appearance on the album as well. But they were born after the peak of their father's success, which would at least mean they had a bit more time to spend with him at home. Die-hard punks raged at the idea of The Clash living in luxury, supposedly at odds with their anarchic ideals of yore, but it might make them feel a bit better to know that Strummer had his children rummaging through skips and making do and mending, all skills that have stood them in good stead.

"I remember him saying he was having trouble singing 'Career Opportunities' after making a success of things," remembers Strummer's eldest daughter, Jazz. "It's all right for people like the Stones to do well because they were always about excess, but punk artists, when they started making money it just didn't work. Especially with Dad, he was considered a kind of punk prophet hero, but these guys were just real people at the end of the day.

"I grew up in the sort of world where it was about making things, and I've brought that through in what I do now," she continues. (Jazz now runs the Shoreditch Sisters, a youthful new branch of the Women's Institute, and is writing a book about the revival of the domestic arts. Before you argue that tea cosies and cupcakes are not very 'punk', the DIY ethic definitely is.)

"Dad always was like, 'You've got to do it yourself,' he was very resourceful. If something broke we'd fix it somehow. It wasn't about buying things. If you want to do something you do it, you don't sit around and wait for someone else to, or until someone's given it to you.

"He was a charismatic father, and it was always about the next adventure! We were always doing silly things like pulling stuff out of skips... no matter how much money he made or how famous he seemed to other people, we still lived in a funny house where boxes became tables and stuff."

At least in the case of most elite rock groups like Led Zeppelin, The Who and Yes, while they may have come from unglamorous backgrounds, they were never cast as 'working class heroes' like The Clash, Doctor Feelgood or Ian Dury, so they never had to worry about how fans would react to seeing them living like kings. In fact, they carried an air of majesty about them from the start, so their subsequent chart success only ensured they could live a life that seemed to befit them, and, as Steve Howe's son Dylan observes, their children would, for a golden period at least, live like princes and princesses. Until they mixed with anyone outside of this strange, fantastic sphere, no one ever had to feel embarrassed or uncomfortable.

"It was like an aristocratic bubble," remembers Dylan. "But when I would speak to my Grandpa, well, they all grew up in Holloway, north London, so that normalised things. My dad is the only one in the family who has made it big in that way.

"But there's always someone above you as well. If I felt like, 'Wow, we have a nice house...' then there's someone else who has a bigger house *and* a yacht... I started to understand this feeling as a bit of an illusion, a fantasy. It didn't feel very real a lot of the time."

At least during his childhood, Dylan could enjoy the high-end advantages of his father's success and hard work with a sense of wonder instead of awkwardness – his pre-teen utopia was during Yes' heyday. While Dylan may have been spoilt in one sense, he insists he never stopped appreciating the goodies and incredible experiences that appeared to be delivered on a semi-constant conveyer belt of luxury and fun.

"I was able to experience the travel, the hotels, the trips to the model dinosaur shop... (laughs). That era will never come again and I was fortunate to be able to experience a lot of that stuff. To go to this toy shop in LA, I think it was called Schwartz, and be told you can have anything you want is unbelievable! You might think, 'That sounds so spoilt', but I would actually really treasure every object I would get. I knew other people who didn't have anything like what I had, so sometimes when I would go to their houses and see the difference I did start to feel a kind of embarrassment, or at least the realisation that something is a bit different."

Charlie Harris, daughter of Whispering Bob, was on the inside but also felt she was on the outside. She was teetering on the outskirts of rock star nirvana because of those her family associated with. She remembers her mother, Jackie, in particular being close friends with the Yes camp, and Charlie's own, comparatively ordinary, upbringing was brought into sharp focus by contrast whenever she was in the company of bass-playing Yes titan Chris Squire and his family during the Eighties. "They used to do the maddest things," remembers Charlie. "Like take us in the limo to Harrods on Christmas Eve just before it was closing.

"Squire's wife, Nikki, only washed her hair in Evian, and she had hair down to her knees, and she'd be on the phone in the limo going, 'Nigel, get my knickers out the bath, they've been soaking in the Evian...' and you're just like, 'What the fuck?' They'd take the kids to Hamley's, 'Have whatever you want!' You're just in this bubble looking at all these crazy grown-ups going, 'What is going on?'"

Obviously there are two ways of being spoilt – the most abhorrent version is the one that manifests itself in the bratty, foot-stampy, demanding child (or adult) with no appreciation for anything that comes their way. It's important not to get them confused.

"You're only spoilt when you don't see what you have," says Calico Cooper, daughter of Alice. "If you do see what you have and you're generous, it's hard to stomach when people go, 'You wouldn't understand.' Or when I meet someone new and say, 'God, the recession is so bad, I can barely fill up my car with gas,' and they go, 'What are you complaining about? You must have millions of dollars!' *I* do not have millions of dollars. I'm 27, I'm not going to call my dad and say (affects Valley Girl voice), 'Daddy, I need money for gas...'

"We, meaning celebrity kids, tend to be apologetic for the hand we've been dealt, 'Oh God, I've been given so much'. Some become these great world-peace workers, and go and build churches for orphans in Mexico, *or* they're totally self-serving and feel they deserve never to wait in line or pay for a drink. Somewhere in the middle is the balance, where you go, 'Awesome, I'm so glad I have this life, I'm going to do everything I can with it for other people but also for me too.'"

It is all about perspective, and while the more socially conscious children of the rock royals might indeed feel a tinge of guilt, they can also rest assured there will always be someone richer and more extravagant than them. When the pre-teen Mackenzie Phillips moved into her father, John's, pink Hollywood palace after her parents split up, she was given an entire *wing* of the house, which was a classic Tinseltown abode originally designed for the Olympic swimmer and screen Tarzan Jonny Weissmuller. Mackenzie describes the decadent pile as a house "built for rich people to play".

Calico recalls not being able to visit Disneyland in case they were mobbed, particularly because her father would never turn a fan away – and when you have a lot of fans, it turns into a long day of not getting very far... but it was an important lesson. "Dad always says he'll never not sign an autograph because that's the reason we have such nice things," says Calico. "He's right, how hard is it to sign a piece of paper and smile for a photograph? Those people are basically the ones who paid for me to go to college. I really appreciate that."

The classic situation in which the difference between rock stars' kids and their less advantaged pals becomes glaringly apparent is at birthday parties. Keith Richards' youngest daughter, Alexandra, spent one birthday grooving in the palace where Rasputin was murdered. The birthday girl and her assembled throng gorged themselves on caviar. The next day the laws changed due to a global shortage of the black stuff. I don't *think* there's a link. (Actually they were probably aware of the pending law change and making the most of it, but I prefer to believe regulations were tightened after Richards and co basically just ate all the caviar in the world.)

The Osbournes treated their daughters, Aimee and Kelly, to a circus-themed bash one year. Never mind clowns (of which there was an entire team), Ozzy and Sharon managed to procure a live elephant for the proceedings. Calico Cooper admits she would loudly express disappointed bemusement when she realised the Teenage Mutant Ninja Turtles weren't going to perform at her less-wealthy friends' parties. "It was around then I realised how spoilt I actually was," she admits.

"But I liked the attention, I'd be lying if I said it's not a good feeling, but at that age you don't know how to process it too well. I remember being at the soundboard when Dad was doing the *Trash* tour. Dad was up on stage and people were taking pictures of me, so I started mugging to the cameras and I was shouting at the top of my voice, 'Go Dad! Yay Dad!' and my mum pulled me aside and said, 'Don't do that if you don't want to look like a tool. You don't have to point yourself out like that. Just be aware it can look like you're spoilt and stupid. Is it really that important that everybody knows?'

"But I was proud of him and I wanted to be a part of that, and when I saw him on stage, I thought, 'That's what I want to do.' And I've seen and lived the possibility of what I'm shooting for. It's not a very low bar! I want that success but I want to earn it. I want command of a crowd that big. I still get goose bumps when I raise my hand and the entire crowd starts yelling. Maybe I was a dictator in a past life!"

One of the standout advantages of Calico's life on the road with the Cooper Show is that she and her dad have golden opportunities to satirise the figures in American pop culture that are ripe for ridicule. They famously 'executed' Britney Spears. They rather indelicately 'deconstructed' Paris Hilton, the characters always played by Calico. It's pure, if rather bloody, pantomime.

"On the *Brutally Live* tour it was Britney, and the next year we did Paris. Everybody loves to see the big star take a pie to the face or get knocked on her ass, so it's funny that *I* do it. I do have opinions on people being down on these girls, and then I play a character that takes the piss out of them. They're all lovely, I've met Paris and Britney, they're really nice. I think they get the joke…

"The Britney thing was when she'd been doing the Pepsi ads, so I would come down the stairs in a Pepsi top, Pepsi skirt, all Pepsi'd out. I hand Alice a can of Pepsi, and he'd open it, drink it and then spit the entire can in my face. He'd chase me off stage and then come back onto the riser with my head on a stake, everyone loves it.

"And when we did Paris, I came out with my chihuahua and purse, paparazzi following me, and I'm mugging for the cameras. Then the dog attacks me and bites a huge hole in my throat, and blood just covers the audience, my weave falls out, we're basically deconstructing this perfect character, make-up everywhere, and then you see the 'real Paris' having a temper tantrum and she ends up kicking the paparazzi's ass, she's no longer pretty and composed and she's throwing right hooks and kicking them in the crotch.

"We did a show in Vegas one time when Paris was in the audience and everyone was like, 'Oh, are you going to offend her?' and I said, 'Absolutely not, I think she gets it.' It has no bearing on anything, it's just my dad's genre poking fun at their genre."

A sense of humour, strong principles and a continued grip on reality seem to be the qualities that always pull children back from the brink of becoming high maintenance super-brats looking towards a future of insufferable diva-dom, and ultimate disappointment when they don't get away with their demands to the same extent (because they're not a cute seven-year-old any more, for example).

But if the parent is every bit as indulged as the favourite child, then their own sense of reality goes out of the window. Elvis Presley was extraordinarily generous to his daughter, Lisa Marie, nothing was too much for her and his gestures of affection became more and more grandiose – one day he presented her with a pony, which she was allowed to ride through the house (until it relieved itself impressively outside Presley's formidable grandmother's room).

After Lisa Marie told Elvis she wanted a puppy, he woke up the entire household at 3am and they drove in a convoy to the local pet shop. Before you get your hopes up, it was not a 24-hour pet emporium (although there really should be such a thing – we can get petrol and white loaves in the middle of the night, so why not hamsters?) so the owner had to be woken and told to open up.

Elvis bought puppies for each of the 20 members of the Graceland household who had driven out with them that night. Priscilla remembers Elvis renting the Memphian Movie Theater for his family and watching four movies back to back, hiring the skating rink just for them or closing a fairground just so the Presleys could play on the rides until the break of dawn. Anything might happen at any time.

Presley adored being a father but he couldn't bear to shout at Lisa Marie when she was naughty, which was most of the time. Why would his daughter expect the world to treat her any differently from this, if this was how she was brought up? It must have been a culture shock to realise that this was not reflective of the real world in any way. But while she was still at Graceland, this *was* the real world, and she was allowed to run wild.

"I don't think anyone really had any control over me," remembers Lisa Marie in *Elvis By The Presleys*. "They all tried but no one succeeded. My father slept in in the mornings, which meant I could do whatever I wanted. I'd see guys in my father's entourage with women on their laps who were not their wives. I'd threaten to fire them or tell their wives if they didn't do whatever I said."

It is the glamorous upper echelons of privileged rock star children that many of us are enviously fascinated/irritated by. I was interested to discover the roots from which this media obsession sprang, especially as much of the editorial is far from celebratory in some cases. *OK!* magazine reporter Elizabeth Curran, who also writes for *Uncut* and *NME*, admits that from her perspective, as a Rolling Stones fanatic, her interest in their daughters came from the fact they were of a similar age but were a world away through no effort of their own, living an exciting life she wished she was living herself.

"There was jealousy there," she says. "They were the same age as us, they dressed like we did, but their parents weren't secretaries or nurses, their parents were really cool, they had amazing jobs. I personally felt I had a hard, long journey, I grew up in a house where there was no music, I had to fight to find music, hunt it down. When I was a teenager the internet hadn't exploded like it has now, so to hear about music and hear original versions of songs was really difficult.

"We all felt these kids had everything handed to them on a plate, they were so lucky to be brought up listening to the blues, influenced by glamour – all of the Jagger children had mums like Marsha Hunt, Bianca, Jerry Hall. And they were brought up having backstage passes. When I was at university I had a summer job at a vintage clothing shop. Leah Wood's summer job was singing backing vocals for the Stones. I got paid

£25 a day and it took me three days' work to pay for one Stones ticket, and there she was. She was doing exactly what I wanted to do."

It is, but it isn't, just like hanging out with dad at the office; the perks are a little more thrilling than just being allowed to try all the different types of scalding hot beverages in the vending machine or unlock the stationery cupboard and stare at different coloured paper clips. (Author's own experience. Word to the wise, don't try the oxtail soup. I'm referring to the vending machine example of course. *Definitely* don't try any oxtail soup you might find in the stationery cupboard.)

One of the main differences is that even if you're impatiently kicking your heels waiting for your parent to finish up and take you to Forbidden Planet, if you happen to stand in the right place, you'll end up in the spotlight too and maybe accidentally become an integral part of an iconic album cover, as in Baxter Dury's case.

Ian and Baxter Dury were traversing the metropolis with new wave photographer Chris Gabrin, who had been granted the mission of providing images for the artwork of Dury's 1977 release *New Boots and Panties!!*. They were looking for the ideal location for the cover image when Ian caught sight of an odd little shop in Victoria with a curious window display of Doc Martens and ladies' underwear. (Courtney Love would have adored it.)

According to Jim Drury's *Ian Dury & The Blockheads: Song By Song* book, Ian "secured the permission of the shop's owner, who told them 'I didn't see ya, and I didn't 'ear ya,'" (not sure why if it was his shop anyway) and as Gabrin was taking pictures of Dury leaning up against the window, Baxter, five years old and increasingly weary of watching his dad pose in front of an incongruous mix of accoutrements, wandered up next to him, hands in pockets, and slouched against the window too. "It was the perfect shot," said Gabrin. So perfect, in fact, that Baxter gets asked to stand in front of lingerie shops with *his* son to this day...

Baxter Dury's sulky visage ensured he would become a part of rock history, but in a way, he always would be, regardless of whether he appeared on a record sleeve or not. His father is the kind of character that fans take to their hearts with a mixture of affection and awe, and, when this deference is transferred to Baxter by default, it becomes an irresistible opportunity for a bit of Dury-style mischief-making.

159

"People laugh at your jokes more when they realise your parentage," says Baxter. "I toy with it, I find it funny. I'd hate to be ignorant to the way people exaggerate their reactions.

"Any false relationships based on that stuff, ever since the age zero, I've been aware of. If people do it they're kind of idiots and I'll take the mick out of it. For instance, filming, I could sit in the room with a producer and an actor and I can say possibly the worst racist joke you could ever do, on purpose. Just to test the water. They'd all sit around laughing for weeks."

Baxter was treated like visiting royalty, understandably, whenever he was on the set of *Sex & Drugs & Rock & Roll*. He also found himself being taken out for a lot of lunches courtesy of the press, who all wanted a piece of his personal take on a very personal film. Baxter is proud of the movie – who wouldn't be excited to see their own childhood brought to life in glorious Technicolor?

"This film… really it's the best therapy that we as a family have ever had," he says. "Imagine how privileged we are. How many people get to see their whole lives done so beautifully on the screen? And to see little wild me in it, doing drugs and throwing things out the window…

"I'm quite broad-minded, I wasn't going to be shocked by anything, although they made a play recently (*Hit Me! The Life and Rhymes of Ian Dury*). That was a bit of a nightmare. I didn't like that at all. I thought it was a bit crude. This has taken a different route. First, as you'd expect, it was a bit *Only Fools And Horses*, slightly crude cockney fest of idiots. We're not cockney really, there's about one per cent cockney DNA. You never know what a film is going to be like, there are so many random variables, but he's (director Mat Whitecross) been striving to make it right.

"They rebuilt our whole lives, it's like going through Jurassic Park, 'Oh, there's a mum, there's a me…' And they've changed me completely, like I'm a brilliant skateboarder, really handsome… my Bax-agerrations on 20-foot of celluloid. It's a strange experience that I've adapted to very quickly. Quality people. They're a bunch of nerds who are trying to be a bit like dad. No one's like dad at all but they're lovely.

"Then a few days after I saw it I thought, 'Fuck, the floodlights are going to turn on.' There's going to be a lot of attention, I have to not become a disciple of this, because you could. Seeing it was like having a séance, it was emotional and raw, but then it left me also feeling slightly cynical, which I didn't see coming. 'That's my life up there, warts and all, my dysfunctional upbringing is now someone else's entertainment.'"

Obviously neither Baxter nor Jemima could ever have been described as your typical celebrity kids with a father like the tough, unpredictable Dury. However, their (much) younger siblings, Billy and Albert, would have the opposite treatment. By the time Dury's sons with his second wife, the artist Sophy Tilson, were born during the mid-Nineties, Dury had been diagnosed with colon cancer, and by all accounts underwent a significant personality change. He was softer, more philosophical and he doted on his children, cooing to journalists about how lovely they smelled (coconut and chocolate, apparently) and generally behaving in a manner that was the polar opposite to how the children from his first marriage – or indeed anyone in his life – were used to being treated.

Yes, the man who once tore a Rastafarian's dreadlocks out in a lift during a tussle and famously won a shiner from an angry Omar Sharif had mellowed. The fact time was running out can't not have had an effect, and he was making sure he milked every second he could with his family. He even told his writing partner Chaz Jankel, "One thing I've learned is you should spoil your kids rotten."

Being spoilt, lucky, rich or living a life deemed simply more interesting than other people's can turn an embarrassment of riches and benefits into just plain embarrassment. Add to that the fact that you are, to a varying extent, on show and you can turn the shade of red up to vermilion. And add to *that* the fact that, like all mums and dads, the rock 'n' roll parent can be as, if not more, embarrassing as the next well-meaning mater or pater (particularly given some rock stars' predilection for being as weird as possible), the blush factor goes off the scale.

For example, imagine you have a very outspoken mother who has no sensitivity to how self-conscious you might feel as a teenager. Then imagine that woman is incredibly famous, as are you, and muse on how you might feel if you heard Mother Dearest say this, publicly, about you: "She never cared about her appearance. She pooped in her pants or pissed herself and kept right on going." Thanks mum. That was Sharon Osbourne on Kelly in case you didn't recognise her by the description.

As you may have deduced, the next chapter uncovers the embarrassing, the awkward, the silly, the mildly shameful and the downright mortifying. It's time for a vicarious cringe-fest. Sweaty palms and bitten knuckles are provided, blusher not required.

CHAPTER 10

Embarrassment

"The rate at which a person can mature is directly proportional to the embarrassment he can tolerate."

Douglas Engelbart, inventor

As Philip Larkin wrote: 'They fuck you up, your mum and dad, they may not mean to, but they do'. It was a matter of time until this cropped up. The 'they may not mean to' line is the most poignant of the poem, for my money. The 'fucking up' might be down to archetypical rock antics, or they might be the sort of issues experienced by any family, but either way they will be exacerbated by the extra focus they receive should your clan be a well-known one. (This depends on how careful your parents are. If they ensure your face is always pixellated in photos, you should be OK. For the time being.)

Embarrassments suffered by rock offspring range from the blushes caused by unwanted attention or having better stuff than your mates to the wince-inducing horror of your dad appearing on TV in Day-Glo leggings that leave nothing to the imagination. (From Liv Tyler to the Jaggers, they've all put their dad's choice of pantaloons on the top of the shudder list.) It could be the things your parent says. Like this, from

Frank Zappa, about his wife and the mother of his children: "Gail was a groupie, and an excellent groupie too." Oh good.

As we know, away from the direct glare of the public eye, at school or in the community, celebrity kids go through their fair share of everyday finger-pointing. Resentment or lack of understanding can come even from those who have known possibly greater riches than they, the sole difference being that their family's wealth was not harvested from creative areas. In a bid to be accepted as a teenager, Dylan Howe admits he, and others of a similar background, overcompensated by briefly taking on the lifestyle of one rather less privileged than himself. The shining joys of childhood had started to oxidise with the dawning of adolescent self-consciousness.

"When I started to forge my own identity in my teens, I was embarrassed to feel like I came from an affluent background. You can feel good if it's something you have personally done, but if it's your parents you can feel separated and stigmatised.

"It was important to break out of that Hampstead cocoon. I did start to hang out with people that were small-time crooks for a time. I didn't like being known as 'the rich kid', I was kind of showing that and I think a lot of people think that in that situation, they can go a bit extreme the other way. When you're existing in a kind of aristocratic world, it's only when you get a bit older that you see things through a darker glass."

Considering you're likely to be targeted at school if you wear the wrong socks or you have ginger hair, one ushers in over a decade of potential embarrassment in sending these kids to a 'normal' school, say, where they are inevitably singled out because they have no hope of being 'normal'. They have to cope with their flashing neon sign of a name being read out in the register, or being picked up in a nice car while the rest of their compadres trudge to the bus stop. They cringe silently on parent's evenings, walking yards ahead of, say, patchouli-scented mum and dad drifting along in their kaftans, for example, while everyone else's parents wear suits. And trying to constantly downplay who you are on a day-to-day basis just so you don't get alienated or used can lead to feelings of guilt and even shame regarding your parents' success and talent, which is truly sad.

"The attention does make you embarrassed of your dad's success, which is terrible," says Callum Adamson. "'I'm sorry we can afford stuff, it's not my fucking fault he's good at what he does.' I never really got to experience my dad when I wasn't feeling that."

Callum was mercilessly victimised as a result of his father's pop success. Brought up in a small town near Dunfermline, Scotland, Callum would start drinking and smoking at the age of 11 in a bid to be accepted, only to be punished by his dad as a result. "I was like, 'Dad, you sent me to the local fucking school...'

"Because my dad was such a socialist bastard, he wouldn't ever let it be seen that he was raising his son any differently from any other child. I got into so many fucking fights every single day. I was just like: 'Dad, can we just not go in that car...?' But this is why he was a dick – he was a socialist, yet he bought stupid cars then sent his son to a normal school.

"If he'd sent me to a decent school I'd have been fine because I'd have been with all the other spoilt brats. There was a resentment right up until I left Scotland when I was 12. You don't realise it until you go back over it. 'Wow, everyone had a lot of issues with me being around!' 'Your dad was on *Top Of The Pops*, what a dickhead! You think you're better than everyone else?' Great..."

Charlotte Gainsbourg, daughter of Gallic legend Serge Gainsbourg and British actress Jane Birkin, had a similar experience after her father notoriously broke the law in France and shocked the nation when he burned a 500-franc note on TV to show how much he had left after he'd paid his taxes. For all of Gainsbourg's provocative indiscretions (including the time he told Whitney Houston he wanted to "fuck her" on live TV) this was the moment that caused Charlotte the greatest embarrassment. "After he burned the money on TV, I was doing my homework the next day and big bullies came, took my work and burned it," she lamented to *Vanity Fair.*

During Harleymoon Kemp's school years, the kids were not the problem – it was the teachers, thanks to her father, Martin's, New Romantic pin-up status. They'd all gazed at his poster in their teens, drooled over him on *Top Of The Pops*, and this ensured that any parental visit to Harleymoon's school would be packed with incident.

"The worst bit is when you're 13 and you do school shows, and you're like, 'Please don't come!' because you know everyone's going to stare," explains Harleymoon, cringing as memories of Kempmania come charging back. "When I did a talent show, Dad came and everyone *literally* started chasing him! He got chased by the teachers. One of them was trying to hug him and go, 'Come this way, get away students! Get away…' I was like, 'Run Dad! Run!' It's funny… now! That made it so awkward the next day. After that I was like, 'Never come back to the school!'"

Teenagers are perfectly capable of embarrassing themselves without any parental input, of course. After Charlie Harris' parents, 'Whispering' Bob and Jackie Harris, split up, another musically minded mentor entered her life in the role of stepfather – the radio DJ Richard Skinner, who also presented the *Whistle Test* in the early Eighties. Skinner sometimes took Charlie to recordings during the 'second Summer of Love' in the early Nineties. His influence undoubtedly informed her eclectic musical taste; she had no shortage of promo CDs to rifle through or gigs to attend, and with her baggy idols literally beating a path to her door (to see Richard, admittedly), the era of the floppy fringe was a memorable one for this teenager – if nothing else because she inevitably met her heroes when she wasn't at her most alluring…

"I remember the front doorbell ringing, I was in some really awful pyjamas and I opened the door and it was the Soup Dragons who'd come to be interviewed by Richard." Not too bad, is it? It gets worse though.

"Then Richard took me to *Top Of The Pops*. I was wearing a black Stone Roses T-shirt and just before we walked into the BBC a pigeon pooped on it. I was mortified, and because I was Richard's daughter they put me right next to him when he was on the mic. Teenage Mutant Ninja Turtles were on the show so there's me with a Turtle on either side of me, poo on my T-shirt and the Soup Dragons were on there as well, it couldn't have got worse. Everyone was great though." I guess pigeon excrement is a bit of an icebreaker. Literally, depending on how much roughage they've been consuming. But we are digressing.

Any of the joys of growing up in an exciting, bohemian atmosphere can often be cruelly punctured around the turbulent time of puberty. Publicly, in the case of these young adults. This struck Calico Cooper when her teenage attempt at looking glamorous was guffawed at heartily by the British tabloids. We all commit the odd fashion faux pas as a teenager (unless you're surrounded by a pack of stylists at all times) but we non-famous plebeians at least are allowed to make those mistakes without there being any kind of global reaction. "I was just a kid, maybe 14 years old, really before you learn how to do your make-up," remembers Calico. "I was getting out of a car somewhere and the paparazzi were there, and I felt all special and neat having my picture taken.

"A couple of weeks later a friend sent me this clipping saying, 'Alice Cooper's daughter has obviously adopted her father's love of make-up…!' and I looked at it, and I do have too much make-up on, but I'm 14 and going to a TV show, I was just trying to be cute."

Normal pubescent changes are photographed, stared at and, excruciatingly, ridiculed and archived for the rest of time with this lot. Madonna's daughter Lourdes is barely in her teens at the time of writing, but already there are pictures of her on the internet with comments galore about her 'unibrow' and facial hair. But she's in the first throes of puberty and she's of Latin descent – this is normal. Were the people choosing to criticise these kids perfect all the time, even when negotiating adolescence? I doubt it.

"Whenever stuff like this comes up, I feel like saying, 'Think about yourself when you were 14,'" says Calico. "Think about the horrible outfits you wore and the social faux pas you made and the dopey dudes you dated, all the times you got caught drinking or whatever, that's humiliating enough. Now imagine having an entire country in on it."

It's hard enough for kids to grow up wondering when the next picture of them looking stupid is going to crop up for all to see, but the embarrassment is all the more paralysing when their interviews are edited in such a way that, even if their own answers were perfectly reasonable, they end up looking like, as Cooper says, "a tool".

"People always say, 'What's it like to be a rock star's daughter?' And I was asked that on TV," she says. "It ended up being one of the biggest faux pas I ever pulled in my life. I got edited, and they made me sound like the world's biggest ass… my full answer, because I answer it all the time, was, 'Well, when I was growing up, I didn't know anything else. My dad wasn't a bus driver, my dad wasn't a librarian, my dad wasn't a janitor. That's the only reality I ever knew.' But all they put on was me saying, 'Well, it's not like my dad was a janitor…' and then they cut it. I was like, 'Oh no!"

"That's what is entertaining about those shows. I think they kind of want us to be stuck up and clueless because it's funny. But to edit me like that, I was like, 'Come on!' But I can only take it with a grain of salt, because what are you going to do?"

The belief appears to be that if someone is famous (even by proxy), they are therefore impervious to criticism, regardless of age, and probably deserve being taken down a peg or two with a dose of public humiliation.

It is perhaps fortunate that Jack Bruce and his family, like the Coopers, share a wry sense of humour, and this is crucial once the editorial fangs sink into the juicy fact that one's parent has, or had, an alcohol or drug problem, for example. He or she might have been clean for a decade but that just means the words preceding their name in the headlines change from 'Junkie rocker' to 'Ex junkie rocker…' Bruce was also known for having a large family. Sex *and* drugs. A double whammy as far as the press was concerned.

Bruce's daughter Natascha Eleanore: "When my little brother Corin was born, Paul and Linda McCartney had an art exhibition opening, and my parents were invited and they took the baby with them. This picture of them all got into the newspaper and the first line is like, 'Ex Junkie Cream Star Spreads His Seed Again!' Horrible!" Jack and Margrit thought it was hilarious, framing the cutting and hanging it on the wall. (The slightly distasteful 'seed' reference might come from the line in 'Sunshine Of Your Love' – 'I'll be with you 'til my seed has all dried up'. Either way, a lovely clipping for Corin to treasure…)

Joking aside, it is reductive and limiting when musicians like Bruce are written about in this tone. There is so much to write about that is perhaps less directly sensational, but far more inspiring. Bruce is a transcendent character from working-class Glaswegian roots who became one of the world's most respected bass players with a gift for radical composition. Bruce is also credited for pioneering jazz–rock.

"But it's the drugs people want to read about," muses Natascha. "He came from nothing and managed to become a classically trained musician and changed the face of rock music – that to me would be something that would be inspirational to people who maybe feel threatened by the arts or classical music. But it's what sells newspapers and what catches people's interest."

Teenage rock heirs suffer the same discomforts as any other adolescent. When you're a certain age, it doesn't matter who you are, parents are just embarrassing. Whether it is wilful or well meaning, whether they are a god-like stallion with tumbling locks and an army of worshippers or a newsagent with a comb-over who attracts nary a glance from the old ladies when they come in for their Typhoo, it sometimes seems as if their very raison d'etre is to ruin your cool, cramp your style, or just engage in the kind of wanton exhibitionism that no teenager wants to witness.

For Duncan Jones, even the idea of watching his father in *The Man Who Fell To Earth* brought him out in hives. "Too grown up... I was embarrassed." For those of you who haven't seen the cult Nic Roeg film, here is a quote from an online movie forum that I think sums up why Jones might have blanched at the idea of sitting through it: "So, *The Man Who Fell to Earth* is a film, starring David Bowie as an alien, that involves such scenes as a girl speaking into a young Rip Torn's penis, and several kinky alien sex scenes that, at one point, involve erotic gunplay? Sign me up!"

Rod Stewart made his daughter Kimberly blush at the *GQ* Awards in 2006. No, not by turning around and wiggling his posterior while onstage, as he is often wont to do, but by being publicly rather daddyish in front of quite a lot of people. Russell Brand earlier in the evening had quipped on the mic that Stewart had criticised Brand for being a womaniser (bit rich, I know), and that he'd "had a go on his daughter". Brand jokes like this all the time, but Rod took it very seriously. Naturally no father wants to hear that their daughter has been defiled by the sort of man who could give Warren Beatty a run for his money. When Stewart stepped up later in the evening, he commanded Brand to stand up and admit he hadn't even touched Kimberly. Stewart responded, "Fucking right you didn't. You mustn't come up here and boast. I speak as a father." Kimberly once chose to send her old breast implants to Jack Osbourne. She can probably look after herself.

Cosmo Landesman admits his instant inauguration to the "embarrassment elite" was in part thanks to his razzle-dazzle parents' determination for recognition, and their ultimate achievement of it.

During the Seventies the Landesmans chose to broadcast to the nation that they were in an open marriage, and quite an active one at that. They were interviewed about their groundbreaking relationship, in which they blithely revealed their breakfast table would often be surrounded not just by the family, but Mr and Mrs L's various lovers too, presumably making awkward small talk as they passed around the granary toast. The young Cosmo was not happy.

Surely an honorary membership to this 'elite' should be granted to Julian Lennon. Yes, even 'cool' famous dads can give cause for recoil from time to time. Bad jumpers? Dad dancing? A stupid car? In his dreams. In 1969, Julian was six. But at an age when most children are being filmed making their first snowman, or being cute in a paddling pool, John Lennon preferred to turn the camera on himself, making and publicly exhibiting a film of his penis achieving erection. You might blanche when your family digs out the old home movies, but that should put things in perspective. Most people would place cuddly, gaffe-prone Paul McCartney higher on the cringe-ometer than arty Lennon, but I'd take repeated viewings of 'The Frog Chorus' over 'Dad's hard-on (do not tape over)' any day.

When friends came round to play at the Zappas' house, they were impressed by the unorthodox behaviour that was permitted. Yes, life at the Zappas' was free... too free, as far as the kids were concerned. They needed boundaries, they didn't want to be treated as smaller versions of their parents, although it was easier for Gail and Frank that way.

But Zappa's determination to be liberal had an eye-poppingly uncomfortable side, including Gail's insistence that, according to Barry Miles' Zappa biography, the children "shower with their overnight guests to conserve water". They'd also watch porn with their parents. For those of us who squirm when two people kiss on *Coronation Street* if our parents are on the sofa next to us, this is a painful thought. Apart from the obvious concerns, it could be argued that along with a slower, more organic evolution into adulthood, the Zappas denied their teenagers the right to rebel, at least in the general sense. "Nothing had a charge on it," said Moon.

Moon, a writer and actress who has appeared in the HBO comedy series *Curb Your Enthusiasm,* admits this liberal stance had the opposite effect on her, making her want to cover up her body and retreat, and she even nursed ambitions to be a nun. This may also have been in order to create a sense of self away from her parents. Most of us experience this but in reverse – we seek to be wilder than those that went before us. Either way, a rebellion is often a necessary part of working out who you are in your own right as you grow and change.

If your parent has reached a certain level of notoriety, there will be no escaping his or her embarrassing antics, especially in this age of mass communication. It's all there to be Googled, and if you don't do it, someone else invariably will, and maybe even send you a printout. "If you were the child of a rock star, would you Google your parents? You'd try not to," says *OK!* magazine reporter Elizabeth Curran. "I mean, Led Zeppelin… gee whiz, there are so many disgusting stories about that band, as much as they are celebrated. Imagine hearing those stories about your father?!

"When you're 12, you might look them up or think, 'I'll read this book about my parents…' you can't escape it. Paula Yates was so famous, I remember there were always lots of very explicit stories about her. It must be a burden – maybe if you get a *Vogue* cover or a Chanel contract, that's some kind of pay-off!"

Adolescence is often a paranoid time during which not many of us would welcome extra attention (like staring or pointing), so if your parents are instantly recognisable, you have to get used to becoming recognisable too. Not fun if you are trying to hide behind a strategically cut fringe and high-necked jumper combo in a bid to conceal, say, volcanic teenage skin, braces and a greasy mono-brow. Alice Cooper and his dancer wife, Sheryl Goddard, could never resist the opportunity to perform for the gawping masses however…

"As an adult, it's pretty hard to embarrass people in a showbiz family," says Calico. "But when I was going through that awkward teenage phase where you're desperately trying to be cool, I'd be walking through the mall with mum and dad – it's bad enough you're at the mall with your parents, you don't give a crap if he's a rock star or she's the most beautiful woman in the world. Everyone's staring at us anyway, but this was the period in my life where I didn't want to be stared at.

"Suddenly my parents would break into this magnificent ballroom dancing sequence, singing, my mum would sing at the top of her voice all these Disney songs. Everyone's staring at them, and in my teenage brain, I was like, 'Arrrrgh! Everyone's looking at me!'"

Harleymoon Kemp has had to put up with confused passers-by shrieking 'murderer!' at her benign father, Martin, thanks to his villainous *EastEnders* role, but she managed to avoid having to go out in public with him during his New Romantic make-up-wearing era – which she feared would make a return when she learned that he was reuniting Spandau Ballet in 2009.

"The first thing we (she and her brother Roman) said: 'Don't wear make-up. What are you going to wear? No joke, if you're going to wear something stupid you can't go, you will ruin our lives! Just wear suits. Respect your age. Just a black suit, Dad, please.'

"I'm very excited about seeing Spandau, I just can't imagine my dad playing on stage. I'm a bit embarrassed! My friends are like, 'Yeah! Are we going backstage for the after-party?' and I'm like, 'What for?! They're all about 45...' There'll be lots of ladies of a certain age in the audience though, oh yes.

"I've seen so many pictures of my dad wearing loads of make-up, and my mum (Wham! singer Shirlie Holliman) hardly wore any at all. She remembers when she first met him he had mascara on... My brother and I don't think that's cool. I remember the big hair, hairspray everywhere, stinking out the house. You'd hear it in the bathroom. 'Shhhhhhhhh. Shhhhhhhhhhhhhhhhh ... Shhhhhhhhh' Going on forever..."

Clothes, hair and make-up, generally when sported by men, can be the source of much hilarity – the wizard hats and capes of the insouciant Rick Wakeman, the Bacofoil romper suits of Benny and Bjorn, the ladies' dresses sported by David Bowie on TV, the pearly lipstick of Nick Rhodes (especially amusing when teamed with the 'Problem with that?' expression)...

At least Natascha Eleanore never had to worry about her father primping himself to the point that he could rival one of *Dynasty*'s leading ladies. At least not publicly anyway. Cool as many of us perceive Jack Bruce to be, he still managed to cramp her teenage style, appearing out of the darkness like a mad wanderer in the middle of one of her all-night parties. "My sister and I grew up in the country, and we had some mad parties in the fields around our house, like raves!" she remembers. "My dad's not a huge fan of drum and bass, garage, the stuff we were into at the time. We were having this party and he'd got a bit drunk. I thought he and mum had gone to bed. It was about 4am and he came out wheeling this wheelbarrow... we had a bonfire going and he was just being helpful and bringing stuff for the bonfire. He had this funny hat on and a huge mac and he was saying, 'This isn't music! This isn't fucking music!' And I was like, 'Dad! Just... go away!' It was really random. We had to turn the music down. It's quite funny to be told by your rock star dad to turn the music down!"

Most parents would never deliberately show up their kids. However, Loudon Wainwright III, who thought nothing of putting his family down through the medium of song (and announcing who the songs were about in live performances), didn't realise he had not only met but spawned his own match when it came to vengeful songwriting. His daughter Martha was furious at the apparent ease with which Loudon had left his family behind, not to mention how he'd regularly embarrass them so acutely in song, even as children. "A shitty thing to do," Martha complained to *The Guardian* in 2005. "He always makes himself come across as funny and charming while the rest of us seem like whining victims, and we can't tell our side of the story." Two can play that game... although it's far from a game: you don't write a song like 'Bloody Mother Fucking Asshole', which Martha did about Loudon, lightly. Forget commercial suicide, this was commercial patricide.

The sheer ubiquity of one's parents' material can also cause awkwardness: film-maker Anna Gabriel, daughter of Peter Gabriel (who used to dress up as a giant sunflower on stage with Genesis, also quite embarrassing) has admitted that she once accidentally indulged in some heavy petting as a teenager to the unfortunate radio accompaniment of her dad's rather romantic song 'In Your Eyes'. "I had to stop," she said. "It was like he was in the room!"

When it comes to being embarrassed by famous parents, I was really hoping to be able to include the mortifying mother of them all – Sting and Trudie Styler's supposedly incessant Tantric sex sessions, and the fact the world knows all about them. Most of us have trouble viewing our parents as sexual beings at all, but Sting's children have had to live through constant chortling reports that their folks can do 'the nasty' for hours on end. Disappointingly, Sting's daughter Coco has dismissed this as a lie put out there by a certain Irish mischief-monger.

"Bob Geldof made up this thing and it stuck and it's an international joke," Coco complained to *Love* magazine. "It's embarrassing when people bring it up but I don't really have anything to do with my parents' sex life. They love each other, so what?" What a killjoy.

True or nay, any blushing caused by rumours of parental sex marathons is obliterated well and truly by the fact that, in 2006, Trudie Styler decided to blow the dust off the notoriously graphic video of her giving birth to her son Jake and screen it in front of all of his friends at his 21st birthday party at the exclusive London members club Drone.* Unlike Calico's shopping mall incident, this was not a case of "Argh! Everyone's staring at me!" but "Argh! Everyone's trying *not* to stare at my mother's expanding vagina on the big screen." That would definitely put you off your vol-au-vents.

Traumatised guests spoke of their shock and how nobody knew where to look, but according to Sting fan site 'Sting Us', Trudie said: "Jake's a film producer now so I thought it would be an idea to show his first film role. Afterwards he groaned but secretly he was probably quite proud of it all and chuffed we made the effort. I honestly don't think he was that embarrassed. I think it was all quite sweet."

I wasn't there, but from the description of this incident, sweet isn't the word I would use. It's sweet that when Paul McCartney was inducted into the Rock'n'Roll Hall of Fame as a solo artist in 1999 daughter Stella wore a T-shirt with the words 'About Fucking Time!' on the front. A year later, Paul presented Stella with a *Vogue* award, and made her giggle bashfully when he then revealed a T-shirt bearing the words, 'About Flippin' Time', clearly a more appropriate wording for a *Vogue*-sponsored ceremony.)

That is the kind of slight 'Oh dad' embarrassment that might be described as sweet. Not the sort that ensures you never refer to 'that birthday' again.

---

* This gruesome sequence had been also featured in Michael Apted's 1985 Sting documentary, *Bring On The Night*.

It would be awful, wouldn't it, if one of your most embarrassing incidents ends up becoming one of the crowning moments of an internationally adored movie? Unofficially, but almost certainly, this is what happened to a young Dylan Howe while he was staying in the Malibu Colony in the Seventies.

"I woke up in the morning and had decided just to slip on my trousers without underpants to go to the loo. Everything was fine but afterwards I zipped up my trousers and slightly misjudged things and the zip stopped halfway up. I then realised a horror that no man should ever know, having lodged the end of my chap in the zip. I couldn't move the zip even a millimetre for the pain. After abject panic had taken over, I hopped upstairs to where my parents were sleeping and threw open the door and yowled.

"My mum and dad woke up and immediately understood this was an emergency. To make things even more embarrassing, my dad's approach was to start squeezing my legs really hard to divert the pain while my mum dialled 911.

"What happened next is a little blurry and hard to completely understand but within minutes I heard sirens outside, the front door opened and some very heavy steps coming up to the bedroom. While lying on the bed, crying in pain with my dad squeezing my legs, I was then greeted by six of the biggest firemen I had ever seen all trying to fit through the small doorway.

"Almost no words were spoken, the head fireman just said to my mum, 'Where's your fridge?' I was a bit confused at this point but then he appeared again with a handful of ice cubes, which were immediately plunged onto my nether regions, which at this point had shrunk drastically, and after a minute or so, I *heard* the sound of a zip going down but felt nothing. It was only years later when I watched *There's Something About Mary* – it seems that word of this incident had spread to Ben Stiller…"

Mortified? Good. Because we're now going to take that mortification and run with it straight down Freaky Street, peering through our fingers into those oddly enticing windows…

CHAPTER 11

'I can't look...'

"All strange and terrible events are welcome..."

Cleopatra

I hope you're wearing flippers. For this is where we dip our toes into freakier waters before plunging in without a care to what weirdness lies beneath.

Naturally there is always plenty of mildly odd driftwood floating in the glittering ocean of fame. For example, there's the time Ronnie Wood picked up a pair of knickers that had been thrown at him onstage, and noticed a note written inside: 'Dad, I love you, your daughter Leah.' Pretty strange, although no surprise that 'appropriateness' isn't in the Wood gene pool...

There's the fabled 'Osbourne Curse' (some would venture there are less esoteric reasons why Ozzy occasionally falls off things or his jewel-crammed mansion is sometimes a target for burglars). There's Yoko Ono's refrigerated fur-coat room (not quite enough peace and love to go round when it came to minks), and 50 Cent's six-year-old son, Marquise's, tiny bulletproof vest. Kurt Cobain would record his track 'Rape Me' while little Frances bounced on his knee. It's not exactly 'The Wheels On The Bus'... A gift for apparently guileless provocation is clearly in the DNA:

the teenage Frances gave photographers a start in 2006 when she turned up for an *Elle* shoot in her deceased father's cardigan and the pyjamas he got married in. The concept *was* 'celebrity offspring in their famous parent's clothes' though.

Some bizarre elements come from outside forces, thanks to the more warped effects of fame: like the time George Harrison and his family came home one evening in 1998 to find a strange woman cooking pizza and doing the laundry, claiming to have a psychic connection with George. Harleymoon Kemp would frequently open the door to take delivery of yet another obsessed fan's worshipful offerings. ("Big cakes with my dad's face on it!")

We are diving deep into the substrata of strangeness, however, where we will meet masked children, babies getting daily exercise drills, and we shall hide behind the chaise longue when Charles Manson makes a home visit. And beyond that… well, we don't have to worry about that *just* yet.

There are not many of us who could say that we had worked with the outrageous gay artist Leigh Bowery before we'd even started school. In fact I would imagine most children would be actively shielded from even knowing about Bowery, known for his fetishistic outfits and boundary-smashing, sexualised performances. But model Daisy Lowe not only appeared on one of his record sleeves at two years old, she had one of her favourite dolls mock-asphyxiated by him. Which is nice.

Bowery had a group called Minty during the early Nineties – a band that was proclaimed to be 'the sickest in the world' according to *The Sun*, which no doubt Bowery took as a compliment. Daisy was already a child model and was granted what some might see as the dubious honour of being photographed for the artwork of Minty's release 'Plastic Bag'. Her singer mother, Pearl, not exactly known for being a prude, has the single framed on her wall.

"I brought my doll to the shoot and they made me put her head in a plastic bag," Daisy told *The Times*. "I didn't realise what it meant. Looking back, that was quite sinister."

Sonny and Cher's only child, Chastity Bono, has had a roller coaster journey, not least because 'groovy' hippy mum Cher appeared to be rather more conservative than one might have thought. Chastity, an

Blanket, Paris and Prince Jackson attend the 52nd Annual Grammy Awards, 2010. (KEVIN MAZUR/WIREIMAGE)

Madonna and her daughter Lourdes, 2006.
(KEVIN MAZUR/WIREIMAGE)

Peaches (L) and Pixie Geldof.
(GARETH CATTERMOLE/GETTY IMAGES)

Private Eye's 'Celeb': the cartoon that pastiches celebrity baby names chosen by the likes of Bob Geldof and Paula Yates, in turn inspiring the Geldofs to humorously name their third daughter 'Pixie'.
Veteran rock star Gary Bloke, his wife, ex-model Debs and his children, Pixie Frou-Frou, Rose-Drop Bunny-Petal and Troy all appear in the 'Celeb' cartoon strip.

Jack Bruce (R) of Cream with his daughter Natascha Elinore during the Rock 'n' Roll Fantasy Camp's 10th anniversary Campalooza concert at the House of Blues, 2007, Las Vegas. (ETHAN MILLER/GETTY IMAGES)

Baxter Dury with his dad Ian Dury in the cover photo for *New Boots And Panties!!* 1977.

Yes guitarist Steve Howe and his son, jazz drummer Dylan Howe, 2010. (ZOË STREET HOWE)

Dhani Harrison of thenewno2, 2009. (JOHN SHEARER/WIREIMAGE)

Zak Starkey performing with The Who 2007. (DIMITIS LEGAKIS/REX FEATURES)

Ben and James Taylor. (CLIVE BRUNSKILL/GETTY IMAGES)

Van Halen – featuring Eddie's son Woldgang.
(KEVIN MAZUR/WIREIMAGE)

Dweezil Zappa performs Zappa Plays Zappa, 2010.
(LARRY MARANO/GETTY IMAGES)

Coco Sumner, daughter of Sting, of I Blame Coco
at the Haiti Earthquake Fundraiser at the Roundhouse,
London in 2010. (SAMIR HUSSEIN/WIREIMAGE)

Steve Tyler with his daughter, Liv, at her high school graduation.
(RICHARD CORKERY/NY DAILY NEWS ARCHIVE VIA GETTY IMAGES)

Jerry Hall with her daughter Georgia Jagger and son James Jagger after Led Zeppelin's performance at the
Tribute To Ahmet Ertegun Concert, at the O2 Arena on December 10, 2007. (JON FURNISS/WIREIMAGE)

Duncan Jones, son of David Bowie, poses with his
Outstanding Debut BAFTA for *Moon* in 2010.
(GETTY IMAGES FOR ORANGE)

Louden and Rufus Wainwright.
(EBET ROBERTS/GETTY IMAGES)

Scarlet Page and Jimmy Page.
(RICHARD YOUNG/REX FEATURES)

Jethro Cave, son of Nick.
(VITTORIO ZUNINO CELOTTO/GETTY IMAGES)

Alice Cooper and daughter Calico Cooper. (FRAZER HARRISON/GETTY IMAGES)

author based in West Hollywood and now known as Chaz, was named after *Chastity Sun Bono*, Cher's first feature film, which premiered just before her child's birth in 1969, and in which, interestingly, Cher played a bisexual woman.

Always a tomboy, as a child during the Seventies Chastity more often than not dressed like Sonny rather than Cher when she appeared on *The Sonny & Cher Comedy Hour*. But when she came out as a lesbian publicly in 1995, Cher was reported to be horrified, ordering her to go into therapy. Cher also openly expressed concern over her daughter's weight problems (Chaz at least did what any vaguely well-known person with a few extra pounds should do – she appeared in the US version of *Celebrity Fit Club* in 2008, losing two stone, by the way).

However, the ageless queen of the sequined bodysuit had another bombshell heading her way. In 2009, Chaz's spokesman Howard Bragman announced that his client, "After many years of consideration, has made the courageous decision to honor his true identity." Yes, Chaz Bono decided to undergo a sex change and is now happier than ever, wishing only that he'd undergone a gender reassignment sooner. Transgender rights campaigners applauded, America's bloggers went crazy, and Cher released a statement admitting she didn't get it, but she was still going to try to support her child. "I respect the courage it takes to go through this transition in the glare of public scrutiny, and although I may not understand, I will strive to be understanding." What *is* slightly confusing is where this now leaves Chaz's relationship with his lesbian girlfriend, Jennifer Elia. Chaz is now a man, Jennifer's still a lesbian... Oh well. Hooray for Hollywood!

Out of the unholy trinity of sex, drugs and rock 'n' roll, it is generally the sex and drugs (not in that order) that lead to some of the most bizarre experiences that the kids would either witness or, rather more worryingly, be involved with.

Brian Wilson was already going rather strange before his daughters came along, behaving like a power-crazed child. He insisted visiting record executives held meetings with him in the sandpit he'd had built into his living room. This also meant not only would their suits get immersed in sand, but they would also invariably be covered in dog excrement, as the family pets used the sandpit as a handy toilet. (You can only really do this when you are confident you are a certified legend.)

Everything's relative however, and some years later, when his daughter Carnie was just a few months old, a very unusual man whom even Wilson would describe with repulsion as "dirty and disrespectful" came to visit with his 'family'. Brian's wayward brother Dennis had fallen in with Charles Manson, gifting him numerous gold discs belonging to The Beach Boys, and assuring him he would help him get a record deal, telling him they could record a song at Brian's. With Dennis, Manson and his followers turned up unannounced at Brian Wilson's family home, ransacked the kitchen and all but trashed the place.

"The idea of this wizard filling my house with bad vibrations freaked me out," said Brian. Nonetheless he allowed the recording session to take place, although no track would be released. The Beach Boys would later record and release a Manson song in 1968, however: the worryingly prescient (for some) track 'Cease To Exist', reworked as the more amiable-sounding 'Never Learn Not To Love', with Dennis on lead vocals. The track would be released as the B-side to 'Bluebirds Over The Mountain'.

The following summer, days after the horrific Tate-LaBianca murders carried out by the Manson Family, the crazed, charismatic cult leader himself would visit Dennis, claiming he'd been 'to the moon'. "Dennis wanted to distance himself from this strange man who'd become a nuisance, but it was difficult," wrote Brian. Manson would drop by again, this time with a pistol. Dennis was on tour. Manson unloaded a bullet, handed it to Dennis' friend who had answered the door and said, "When you see Dennis, tell him this is for him." The Wilsons would thankfully never see Manson again, but the idea that he and his Family had been in Brian's house in the presence of baby Carnie is frightening.

Another cult known originally as The Family and The Children Of God, now known as Family International, attracted founding Fleetwood Mac member and guitarist Jeremy Spencer, and he is still a member to this day. Seven of his eight children managed to escape the cult, which practiced the dubious teachings of leader David Berg. They have recently renounsed former practices, which involved underage sex and basically child abuse. Sex would also be used to try to lure potential converts, 'flirty fishing', as it was known.

The story goes that one afternoon before a Fleetwood Mac gig in Los Angeles in 1971, Spencer popped out to visit a bookshop, and subsequently went missing. Five days later, he was found in a warehouse, shaven-headed and answering to the name of Jonathan, supposedly having been reprogrammed by the Children of God. Spencer has recently dismissed this story as an exaggerated myth, but his former bandmates recall events unfolding exactly like that, and Spencer's daughter Tally insists he was definitely brainwashed. "That's exactly what they did. David Berg himself called it brainwashing – he said people have dirty minds that need to be cleaned."

Four of Spencer's brood – Jez, Ben, Nat and Tally – now live in north London and have formed their own rock band, the rather inauspiciously titled Jynxt. Growing up, however, they were banned from listening to any music other than hymns strummed and warbled by a fellow member. There was no radio, television or books other than those linked with the sect. Many of their fans now are former cult members who managed to extricate themselves. Jynxt has created a kind of healthy focus for those that got away.

Jez, now a bus driver, was three when his father signed up to become a Child of God, and is the only sibling who can recall pre-cult life. He told journalist Tim Cooper, "I remember sitting backstage at dad's Fleetwood Mac gigs, leaning against the speakers. When we started our new lives, I resisted at first. I had not made a choice and I didn't know what everyone was so happy about." At 16, Jez would be locked up and deprived of food when an attempt to escape was foiled.

He finally got out and moved back to the UK, soon to be joined by his brother Ben. Ben was, understandably, socially inept when he left the cult – his contact with the outside world was restricted to proselytizing missions, during which he generally just sang and smiled. All he could do once he'd escaped was try and hold conversations with people about Armageddon, a fixation of the Children of God. It took a while for the Spencers to adapt, but they found that daily visits to the cinema helped to give them a crash course in general social interaction. (Then they could hold conversations about the movie *Armageddon* instead.)

Apparently Jynxt don't know what their father thinks of their music, although it probably isn't on the Family International iPod playlist. By the early Seventies Spencer senior had renounced his former love of rock and blues anyway. "He said that music was like a demon, that the blues was Satan's music," said Ben. "Although that sounds like LSD to me."

In contrast to these terrifying experiences, it's a relief to know that some 'seekers' within the rock community of the Sixties and Seventies had a rather more fulfilling, positive experience. Pete Townshend took his family to California to see the Sufism-inspired spiritual guru Meher Baba, a teacher Townshend follows to this day. Pete's daughter Emma: "As far as spiritual indoctrination went, we went to yoga classes, learnt about reincarnation, went camping in the mountains and drank out of streams; it was very, very gentle. You'd be hard-pressed to see it as anything cultish; it was less *My Life In Orange* and rather more *The Big Lebowski*." The kids would also slope off with their new-found American friends and mischievously sneak into each other's houses "through the cat flaps." (Emma admits these cat flaps must have been built for super-size American moggies.)

Cults or no cults, it doesn't get much stranger than when the supposedly natural order of things gets skewed, particularly when it comes to choosing lovers. In the world of rock 'n' roll, the young try to grow up too fast, and the old want to stay nubile forever, often proving their virility and youth to themselves by acting like hormonal adolescents and taking much younger partners, younger, often than their own kids. Which straddles both 'embarrassing' and 'freaky' camps. Then you have the insidious projections of the media, revelling in sniggeringly prurient slow-news-day inferences that James Jagger dated a 'Jerry Hall lookalike' (Alice Dellal) just because she had long hair tumbling over one shoulder, or that Paul McCartney's girlfriend, Nancy Shevell, looks like his daughter Mary. (They're not dissimilar, but is it tasteful to do this?)

Love indeed moves in mysterious ways, lust less mysteriously so: *OK!* magazine has already expressed concern that Madonna is getting "jealous" of her beautiful young daughter Lourdes, particularly because they believe toyboy-tastic Madonna and Lourdes will both be gunning for the same men.

"To have a smart and pretty daughter like Lola (Lourdes) coming up behind her, frankly I don't know how she's going to deal with it,"

Madonna's brother Christopher Ciccone told the *Daily Mail*. "She can't fire her like she does everyone else who threatens or disagrees with her."

In 1989, the oldest Rolling Stone, Bill Wyman, took things a bit far when he married Essex girl Mandy Smith (who funnily enough had her eye on a pop career with Stock, Aitken & Waterman). Even if Bill's then 30-year-old son, Stephen, had gone out with Mandy he'd have been accused of being a bit of a cradle-snatcher.

Bill was 56, Mandy was 18 – and they had been dating for five years. Which made Mandy 13, and Bill 51, when they first got together. Which is… sort of illegal? Not in the lawless land of rock. *Hello!* magazine, I seem to recall, thought the whole thing was great fun, and printed pictures of their 'fairytale wedding'. (No coincidence that Mandy then left Bill weeks later. The old *Hello!* curse strikes again.)

This whole affair must have made Stephen feel a bit odd, surely? Well, apparently not: he was too busy whispering sweet nothings into the ear of … Mandy's 46-year-old mother, Patsy, whom he later married. Funnily enough, this made *Bill* feel deeply uncomfortable, and he banned Stephen from his wedding.

San Francisco Chronicle journalist Phil Bolsta observed at the time that should both romantic partnerships have succeeded, "Bill Wyman would become his son's son-in-law, because he would be married to his son's stepdaughter. Mandy Smith would become Stephen Wyman's mother because she would be his father's wife. By virtue of his marriage to Mandy's mother, then Stephen Wyman would be both Mandy's son and father. Likewise, Patsy Smith would be Mandy's daughter as well as her mother.

"Things get interesting if both couples have children. If Patsy Smith has a son, the child would be Bill Wyman's brother-in-law and Stephen Wyman's uncle because he would be the brother of his stepmother, Mandy Smith. If Mandy has a son, the child would be Stephen Wyman's brother as well as his grandchild because the baby would be the son of his daughter.

"It then follows that Patsy Smith would be her husband's grandmother because she was his mother's mother. Stephen Wyman would be both his wife's husband and grandchild. And since the husband of a person's grandmother is his grandfather, Stephen Wyman would be his own grandfather."

His own grandfather. He'd have had to offer himself Werther's Originals. Natural order would have gone out of the window. It's just a few steps from sheep raining down from the sky and people eating each other.

Unlike Bill Wyman, weird as it is, at least his fellow Stone Mick Jagger kept his todger away from Mackenzie Phillips until she was 18. Although I find it creepy that once his opportunity to pounce arose, he told her he'd "been waiting for this since you were 10 years old". Creepier still that Mackenzie, when relating this story in her autobiography, *doesn't* find this line creepy. She was as predatory as him. "I was proud of my conquest. I knew a golden opportunity when I saw it."

Yes, the man she sat next to as a little girl at her father's wedding to model Genevieve Waite (in a Chinese restaurant with a one-legged Buddhist priest) had been biding his time – the fact he was married to Jerry Hall was immaterial of course – and they had sex in his and Jerry's bed during a party in their New York apartment, Mackenzie's father John Phillips banging on the door outside. "We ignored him," she shrugs.

When I spoke to a therapist whose clients include some high-profile offspring, the word that kept coming back was 'boundaries'. Boundaries getting confused, boundaries being broken, boundaries being disrespected. In music, breaking boundaries is generally hailed as a good thing. In families, it's rather different. Which brings us to a truly dark incident endured but eventually, perhaps inadvertently, embraced by Mackenzie Phillips. She still uses protective language regarding the damaging pattern that would ensue, a classic trait of the abused. "He was not a man with boundaries," she writes. "He was full of love and sick with drugs."

In 1978, Mackenzie, just 18, was preparing to wed Jeff Sessler, then a member of The Rolling Stones' entourage. Nobody approved of the match, and for once John Phillips showed up to try to dissuade Mackenzie. On the eve of the wedding, Phillips travelled to their hotel, booking a room just doors up from Mackenzie's. It wasn't long before father and daughter were taking downers in her room, and Mackenzie soon lost consciousness completely. There is little that can prepare one for what happens next, so I'll leave it to Mackenzie to tell the story:

"I woke up from a blackout to find myself having sex with my own father. There is only a vague memory of the middle, of waking up to a confusion and horror that I was unable to stop." The marriage to Sessler went ahead as planned, although the couple would split in 1981.

This would not be the last time this would take place, always after spiralling together into heavy sedation. By the time Mackenzie was 20, herself touring with the 'new' Mamas and Papas, the incest became consensual. In later years, when Mackenzie became pregnant, she was unaware whether the baby was her father's or her then husband, Shane Fontayne's. John Phillips paid to have the child aborted. It was at this point that Mackenzie put a stop to their relationship.

After the first time, however, Mackenzie told her mother and Phillips' sister Rosie, and they elected to 'let it go' rather than taint the family name. When she decided to approach the subject with him, she said: "Dad, we have to talk about how you raped me." He said, "Raped you? You mean when we made love?" Mackenzie was utterly on her own, and completely controlled. Her father was responsible for her income and her drug supply – and that kept her chained to his side. He would later confuse and disturb her by allegedly suggesting they run away together and live in Fiji, raising Bijou and Tam (Mackenzie's half-siblings) as their children. It was at the point he "tried to make it romantic" that Mackenzie was jolted into lucidity. "No," she shuddered. "We're going to hell for this."

Phillips only revealed the truth about her sexual relationship – which would last for 10 years – with her father in 2009, causing ructions within the clan: Michelle Phillips refuses to believe it, claiming Mackenzie is 'mentally ill' but Chynna Phillips insists her sister is telling the truth. Tam, meanwhile, made a YouTube video while in drug recovery to express, wild-eyed, that he thinks the whole debacle is a 'bowl of dog urine' next to the spiritual enlightenment he has recently found through his guru Nityananda. Tam's video also includes a link on which one can click to give money to him. (He claims he has given most of his money to his guru.)

Mackenzie has faced criticism for bringing this up after her father died, when he can't defend himself, but she countered this by explaining that she "waited until he died to talk about this because I didn't want to put him through it. I have profound love and respect for him. My first instinct is to preserve his great legacy. He wasn't a good father but he was a musical genius, (but) the desire to preserve his legacy is not reason enough for silence."

In 1985, allegations of incest between the French singer-songwriter Serge Gainsbourg and his daughter, Charlotte, now an actress in her thirties, were rubbished by Serge, who insisted that whoever could think that must have a "dirty mind" themselves. Either that or their suspicions had simply been raised by the fact that Gainsbourg and daughter had released a deliberately provocative song called 'Lemon Incest' – a play on the French pronunciation of lemon zest: 'un zeste de citron' became 'Inceste de Citron'.

The song referred to "the love that we will never make", and the sleeve featured Gainsbourg shirtless on a bed, with his 12-year-old daughter reclining on his chest wearing only a shirt and panties. Fortunately Charlotte was in boarding school by the time the record was released, and unaware of the scandal it had caused. (Scandal and provocation are themes that follow this family around to this day, however – in 2009, Charlotte starred with Willem Dafoe in the Lars Von Trier movie *Anti christ,* which featured scenes of violent sex and genital mutilation, perpetrated by Charlotte's character. "It was fun," she told traumatised film journalists.)

The Family Gainsbourg tried to fob the world off by insisting the song expressed the "purity of paternal love" but no one was fooled, and Charlotte has since admitted that was never what it was about. She knew what she was doing, but, she told *Vanity Fair,* "I look at it now and I see how uncomfortable I look in the video, like a robot."

Gainsbourg senior insisted the song was at least never autobiographical despite the impression given to the contrary, but there was obviously an intense bond between the pair. Jane Birkin recalled that, just before he died he told her, "(Charlotte) wants to live with me. She said I was the man she'd been looking for all her life."

Gainsbourg's daughter was so attached to her father that she couldn't bear to let him go, even after death, sitting with the corpse in the bedroom for days. "I knew people you could contact who would preserve the body," said Birkin. "I got to my friend who rang up the people so they could preserve Serge and not have to bury him right away, because Charlotte didn't want him to be buried, she wanted to keep him."

Charlotte keeps her father's house in Paris, in which he had lived since the Seventies, as a shrine-like museum. Everything has been kept exactly as it was since Serge died, aged 62, in 1991. It is a home in stasis and a perfect time capsule – right down to the dried flowers by his bedside, the black felt on the walls (Serge insisted it should be the same specific type of felt policemen's trousers are made from, naturellement) and the cans of Nineties food in the cupboard, some of which did finally explode. The desired effect is a feeling that Serge could walk in at any moment.

Trevor Horn and his family are used to strange presences lurking in Sarm Studios, especially Studio 2. The building in Basing Street, in London's Notting Hill, was formerly Island Studios and the offices of Island Records, and most of the illustrious artists signed to the label recorded there at one time or another. Also, famously, Jimmy Page recorded his guitar solo for Led Zep's 'Stairway To Heaven' there in 1972.

Recording studios seem to magnetise energy in a very particular way, holding onto sounds long after the source has gone, attracting unexplained vibrations. When Aaron Horn mixes in Studio 2 late at night, for various reasons, he never feels quite alone. "It's insane the history there. And if you get properly stoned, I swear all the people show up, everyone... You're playing music, completely fucked after a long session and you have this feeling, it feels like the room is full of people who have been in there before. You hear things that weren't there. After a day in Studio 2 you feel like someone's been sucking energy out of you, like there are people behind you when you're mixing. It's cool though."

"Studio 2's an old crypt, allegedly," continues Aaron. "It used to be a church. They say energy never really dissipates, so it's not like any of the sounds ever technically leave the space. You feel when you're playing there, you're adding on to something quite big."

The Horns' former country home and luxurious residential studio, Hook End in Oxfordshire (previously owned by David Gilmour), was also filled with spectral guests – Aaron admitted his father could never be in the studio alone without his dogs.

Aaron: "Hook End was super fucking haunted. People genuinely saw

187

ghosts in that studio. That spot was really old. It was an old natural spring, people had obviously been there for a long time. I'd always think there was this woman in the other room and suddenly I'd come back from the mix and think, 'Woah, she's there,' and the dog would run towards the door… And there are certain songs you'd listen to, and you'd hear a woman singing along."

The family no longer own Hook End, but the main reason for this is the tragedy that occurred in June 2006. Aaron, 22 at the time, was playing with an air rifle in the garden when a pellet accidentally hit Jill, then 55, in an artery in her neck. She is still in a coma. To go through this, and to see it replayed in the press, must have been unimaginably difficult. But Aaron is courageous in bringing the subject up, displaying how strong and supportive a family they must be to survive such a heartbreaking incident. He is now embarking on a Nordoff-Robbins music therapy course, and it is no coincidence that he is keen to explore the possibilities of music as a tool for healing.

"We had to sell Hook End, that's where the shit went on with mum; we had to let it go. It was too much. Dad had spent too much time with her there and it was too painful. I supposed I'd gone a bit mad after all that shit happened with my mum, but I accept (the spiritual side) a lot more. I even feel it more.

"Music speeds up a kind of energy – you go and sit in a river and it really pushes. I am really interested in the physical effects it has. We see it as a cultural thing most of the time but I think it has another effect on you, cognitive and physical. It's definitely good for your health.

"Music therapy takes all the things that are interesting to me about anthropology and sharing experience, helping people and interacting with them. It's such an otherworldly thing, it's powerful. After what happened with my mum, I definitely found a lot of solace in music. I was still at uni when it happened, I was still getting my head together as far as what I was going to do. After that happened, I just … just did a lot of music. Escapism I suppose, sort of cathartic as well."

To close this curious chapter, we are going to meet the most curious of them all, a troubled soul who died during the writing of this book in almost as mysterious a way as he had lived. Michael Jackson died of a cardiac arrest in June 2009 aged 50 amid swirling questions, speculation suspicion, just before he was due to perform a demanding string of live dates in London, his "final curtain call", as he said.

Michael Jackson is often associated with children, and not always his own. The thought of Jackson as a parent still seems to be an odd concept; if his self-styled Peter Pan persona is anything to go by, he was forever a child himself.

In 1994, at the age of 36, Jackson married 26-year-old Lisa Marie Presley whom he had first met when she was a little girl at one of his concerts. They shared a passionate relationship, according to Presley, which was not a sham despite media claims to the contrary. When the marriage foundered, however, Presley made it clear she was not interested in having children with him, despite his almost desperate wish for a family. Presley felt her husband was too in need of parenting himself.

One day over breakfast, Jackson said he didn't even mind if they didn't have sex, he just wanted babies. "My friend Debbie said she'll have my baby. If you won't do it, she will. How about that?"

According to Jackson's biographer J Randy Taraborrelli, Lisa Marie agreed. Whether it was as a sarcastic retort or not was irrelevant, because before she could turn around, everything was organised. Debbie Rowe, whom Lisa Marie had dismissed as a crazy super-fan, was a nurse Michael had met during the Eighties, when he was diagnosed with the skin-lightening disease vitiligo.* She had become a supportive friend to the pop star and, it is said, they both became rather fixated on each other. Presley and Jackson divorced on January 18, 1996, and the attempts to make mini-Jackos began (artificially of course).

The pair married that same year – Jackson's mother didn't want an illegitimate grandchild (I'd have thought the Jackson family had long since given up worrying what the neighbours might think, but there we are) – but the union apparently remained unconsummated. Rowe was happy just to "do him a favour", and Neverland staff said it appeared almost as if the children didn't even have a mother. She was never a presence there, and was kept very separate.

Even when the first child, Prince Michael Jackson (now known as Prince Michael I), was born in 1997, Rowe barely had a chance to look

---

* Jackson would reportedly undergo complete depigmentation as a result.

at him before he was rushed back to Neverland by Michael. Similarly, when daughter Paris was born in April 1998, Michael admitted in his infamous interview with Martin Bashir, he was "so anxious to get her home after cutting the cord, I hate to say this, I snatched her and just went home with all the placenta and everything all over her. I just got her in a towel and ran." The 'Wacko Jacko Kidnaps Baby' headlines were inevitable. Both children had started their unique childhood in typically bizarre Jackson fashion.

Jackson, not known for his devout Catholicism, had his people contact the Vatican about the possibility of the Pope christening his babies. Mystifyingly, they saw it as a publicity stunt. "The Vatican had been down this same road with Madonna a few years earlier when she attempted to have the Pope baptise her first child, Lourdes," writes J Randy Tarborelli. (Madonna's 'Jewish' now. That showed them.)

The children would be assigned teams of day and night nannies, reading and singing to them at just three weeks old, building them up with "exercise drills" when they were still babies, and, purportedly, every utensil or toy was disposed of after a single use. (Although on clips of Jackson's rather orchestrated 'home movies', showing the singer and his children playing with a jigsaw, the lid of the box looked used and collapsed... who knows what to take as truth? With a figure as unusual as Jackson anything could be said and potentially believed.)

Prince Michael II, born in 2002, was known as Blanket. Why? "It's an expression I use with my family and my employees," explained Jackson. "I say, 'You should blanket me or you should blanket her...' meaning like a blanket is a blessing. It's a way of showing love and caring." It was Blanket who was, as a nine-month-old baby, dangled over a balcony in Germany. Jackson later apologised publicly but also believed he was giving the public what they wanted, a glimpse of his baby. Who, by the way, had a cloth over his face. And so we broach the subject of those masks and veils the Jackson children were rarely seen without in public.

Sometimes they were Hallowe'en masks, all the more startling when not worn at Hallowe'en. Other times they were silk scarves or veils. Was Jackson protecting them from the press? Shielding them from possible kidnap attempts? Debbie Rowe has insisted the masks were her idea, to hide the children's identity. Either way, the paranoia at the root of this decision could have far-reaching effects on the children's psychological development, social worker Dr Dorian Traube told Tarborelli in his book *Michael Jackson, The Magic And The Madness*.

"The masks could send the message to the children that they need to be fearful of people," said Traube. "They could end up feeling there is something wrong with them and that nobody can see them." Jackson surrounded himself and his children with staff, but did anyone have the audacity to challenge his parenting? Outlandish his actions may have been, an eccentric, confused prescription drug addict and own worst enemy he certainly was, but he was doing his best.

"What if they grow older and resent me, and how my choices impacted their youth?" Jackson asked rhetorically during the speech he made at Oxford University Student Union in 2001. "'Why weren't we given a normal childhood like all the other kids?' they might ask. And at that moment I pray that my children will give me the benefit of the doubt, that they will say to themselves, 'Our daddy did the best he could, given the unique circumstances he faced…' We all have been someone's child and we know that despite the very best of plans and efforts, mistakes will always occur, that's just being human."

CHAPTER 12

Following In The Footsteps

"I'm very proud of my father, Julio. But when you read Billboard now, you see my name…"

Enrique Iglesias

If the average child of a musician had a pound for every time they heard the words 'footsteps' (as in 'following in the…') or 'shadow' (as in 'living in the…'), they'd end up nearly as wealthy as we assume them to be already.

There are those who do continue in the family business, insisting there was never anything else they wanted to do. Then there are those who come back to it after experimenting in other fields, satisfied they've at least arrived at the decision themselves. Some become, whether through accident or design, a 'mark II' of their folks, and are expected to replicate their parent somehow, particularly if the original model has died, or just doesn't fancy doing the gigs any more. Rick Wakeman's son Oliver has taken this route, taking his father's place in both Yes and The Strawbs. He even has the same hairdo. Dweezil Zappa also successfully tours a show called 'Zappa Plays Zappa', honouring his father's work.

They might collaborate with their parents musically, or join their band should the vacancy arise, like Tom Waits' son Casey, who plays drums in his father's band, or the ambitiously named young bass player Wolfgang Van Halen (named after Mozart) who started appearing on stage with his father, Eddie, when he was just 15 in 2004, and is now officially in Van Halen himself. His actress mother, Valerie Bertinelli (who co-starred with Mackenzie Phillips in *One Day At A Time)*, has said when he finds himself in too adult a situation he rings her up and says, "Mum, I'm not comfortable here…" He must have been thrilled when she shared that with the world. Rock 'n' roll!

"This is only different to someone following their dad into the plumbing business because people care more," says Callum Adamson. "I spent every day of my life with my dad in TV studios and on tour buses and standing at the side of the stage. Music is a massive part of my life and I chose to make it stay a huge part of my life.

"Maybe some people get a distaste for what their parents do and go in the opposite direction. But as long as you're not doing it for the wrong reasons, like, 'I've got to be my dad, I have to be onstage and have hookers and coke, this is going to be awesome…' then I don't think that should bother you, it's like you're compelled to do it."

For many, the presumption that they are obviously going to follow their parent's lead is irritating and reductive of their own uniqueness, however those who do 'work in the family store', to quote a Rufus Wainwright lyric, are not allowed to get away that easily either. There is the suspicion of a lack of authenticity, despite the fact they have naturally absorbed and loved music from a very early age, and have probably been writing songs and playing instruments since childhood. This is all symptomatic of a culture that wants to see an individual break through solely as a result of their own efforts, and having any association with someone who has already 'made it' causes confusion and scepticism.

"People assume when you break onto the scene you are suddenly doing it, when in fact you've been beavering away for years," explains singer-songwriter Holly Williams, daughter of country icon Hank Williams Jr. "I've had people say, 'Why did you suddenly decide at 28 to make an album?' And I'm like, 'No, I've been doing this a long time.' Once they see that, they're OK.

"But a lot of radio people have said, 'She's Hank's daughter and we don't want to support something that is just kind of made up.'"

Lovella Ellis, daughter of the late reggae singer Alton Ellis, has experienced a similar prejudice, particularly since her father passed away in 2008. Many of Alton's children are singers in their own right, however Lovella and her brother Christopher's decision respectively to concentrate on celebrating their father's work while also writing their own material is a brave one, which could see them forever linked to Alton. But to Lovella, making sure Alton Ellis' music is forever remembered, loved, sung along to and danced to is more important.

"The strongest thing I come up against is that people think I've all of a sudden just come out of the woodwork now Daddy's gone. The line is 'riding on the back'… but that's not really the case," she explains. "I know some people are going to be thinking that but I take it with a pinch of salt.

"My brother Christopher is in Jamaica doing what he's been doing for years: writing stuff and singing Dad's songs in his own way to keep them alive. Like him I'm keeping my dad's stuff alive too. My dad moulded us into a certain mindset, he sang about peace and love and so do I. I'd like to spread the message all over the world. It's not just about singing and being on stage.

"I promised my dad at the hospital, just a day or two before he passed, I'm going to carry on the music. Seeing his face light up even though he couldn't talk was nice.

"I'm not out there as Alton Ellis' daughter," she insists. "I'm out there as Lovella, Daughter of a Legend… Whoever knows, knows. Whoever doesn't, it doesn't matter. I don't want my dad to be forgotten."

Natascha Eleanore's own affinity with Caribbean music is very apparent in her material with Aruba Red, and she believes there is a reason why it seems to be more accepted in Jamaica to continue the music of a relative. "In more traditional cultures, like in Jamaica or Cuba, the heritage is very important: if you've got Bob Marley's kids doing a show they will perform their dad's songs, but it's not done in a cheesy way. It's a very honest offering of his message and tradition, carrying it forward. Damian Marley, he's got remixes of his father's songs on his records. It would be seen differently if I was to start performing Cream songs though."

Ginger Baker's son Kofi, however, does exactly that with 'A Tribute

To Cream'. This is bound to have renegade rock offspring shaking their heads, but Kofi insists that while the group play the music of Cream and also Baker and Clapton's supergroup Blind Faith, they are not a 'tribute band' and, true to the spirit of the originals, improvisation is at the heart of their shows.

"We don't dress up like Cream. We don't sound like Cream. We just do Cream songs," Kofi said. "I'm not going to tell the bass player, 'No, that's not what Jack plays.'"

In all fairness to Kofi, he didn't really stand a chance with a father like Ginger – what else was he going to be? As we know, Kofi was practically bullied into playing the drums with the fierce discipline and focus of a professional from the age of five. At the age of six, Kofi was having a play on his father's kit on the set of *The Old Grey Whistle Test*. The production team thought initially it was Ginger himself.

While his talent is obvious, what is also clear is the monstrous shadow of Ginger Baker within which he lives. Kofi, who teaches his father's technique to eager Californians in Orange County, often advertises his lessons under the title 'The Ginger Baker Jr. Drum School.' It's an understandable marketing ploy of course, but indicative of one who has long since swallowed his pride and admitted that even if he was christened Kofi, he will forever be Ginger II.

As Baxter Dury observed, identity crises can haunt the son or daughter of such a respected figure. As you develop, you go from "dealing with it without knowing how to deal with it, then thinking about what it means, what value *you* are in relation to how valuable they're considered to be."

"I literally didn't want to go into music production at first," says Aaron Horn. "I just felt like it would be walking in someone else's shoes. I was annoyed with myself as I was getting into it, it was definitely an issue. I never really realised what he'd done, it was just: he was busy, there was music, there was Mum shouting at *Top Of The Pops,* we'd know people… but it never clicked when I was young."

Trev Lukather bravely took on the same instrument as his father, Toto guitarist Steve, but thanks to the less imaginative side of the music industry, he has had to fight against allowing himself to be pigeonholed in a similar way. "I'll write a song, and believe it to be really good, but then I'm told by people, A&R, producers, 'Oh you need to do a song like a modern 'Rosanna', or a modern 'Hold The Line'...' songs my dad did with *his* band. They think I need to write a song like what my dad did – I'm not my dad! Let me be myself, let me do my own thing! If I come out sounding like a newer version of my dad that's going to be worse! People are going to be like, 'He's trying to be like his dad.' I just want to be me."

Passed down from parent to child is not only the talent or the inclination to embrace music, but a savviness, an ability to hear in a different way, a belief, a work ethic and, of course, access to a fine record collection. It might surprise some to learn that despite the great prog/punk wars of the Seventies (waged largely by *NME* because they hated rival paper *Melody Maker* on principle, and whatever *Melody Maker* liked, such as prog, *NME* thus derided), Yes guitarist Steve Howe was genuinely intrigued by The Sex Pistols and punk rock, music that would inspire its fans to cut their hair and strip things back to three-chord simplicity after years of 20-minute solos and complex arrangements by rock bands. On Howe's shelves, *Never Mind The Bollocks* sat happily next to Kenny Burrell, Big Bill Broonzy, Bob Dylan and Stravinsky.

"I take his as the template," says Dylan Howe of his father's behemoth collection. "It has everything and there aren't any taboo areas, he's not a snob. I remember seeing *Never Mind The Bollocks* in there, it was very striking, and of course the 'God Save The Queen' image, it was the first subverted image of royalty I had ever seen. It was propped up on the shelf, 'Here's the latest album I've got' kind of thing. I was only eight or nine. There was everything in there though, and that's what you need to have to be a complete musician.

"In a musical sense I think there were other musics that were more shocking, but what punk stood for, an anarchic stance, is always good. A lot of them loved Yes anyway, secretly!" Public Image Limited guitar and keyboard pioneer Keith Levene adored Yes, Howe in particular, and travelled with the band as a roadie throughout the Seventies until Rick Wakeman told him to go away and do his own thing (and stop messing around on his keyboards when he was supposed to be setting them up).

Journalist Emma Townshend's "first job" was to put her father, Pete's, equally diverse and fulsome record collection into alphabetical order *and* categories. (This admittedly sounds like the best job in the world.) "The blues records were all to stay together, and the same went for the heavy operas... I was about eight: not equipped with much useful knowledge for the job.

"Doing it, I learned about who went where, and began to tell something useful from the covers. I got the enormous sum of £10 for the whole job, which whiled away a few weekends. Over the course of the next few years, some of these names became real musical presences for me. Talking Heads, Joni Mitchell, Ray Charles. I began to identify the sound of whole record labels: Motown, Atlantic records, East Memphis."

Jack Gahan remembers his father, Dave's, very considered choices of CDs to pass on to his son in order to educate him in 'good music'. "Led Zeppelin, Miles Davis, John Coltrane, *Dark Side Of The Moon*," remembers Jack. And Johnny Cash similarly insisted on providing his daughter Rosanne with a grounding in the essentials of what he felt was music that would not only be important to her, but that was also a part of his own identity and, in turn, hers. In 1973, he sat down with his 18-year-old daughter and wrote a comprehensive list of 100 "essential country songs" for her to listen to.

"We were in the tour bus talking about songs, and he mentioned a song, and I said, 'I don't know that one.' He mentioned another, and I said, 'I don't know that one either.' Then he started to get alarmed, so he spent the rest of the day making a list on a legal pad, and at the top he put '100 Essential Country Songs.' And he handed it to me and he said, 'This is your education.'

"I think he was alarmed I might miss something essential about who he was and who I was. He had a deeply intuitive understanding and overview of every critical juncture in Southern music – Appalachian songs, early folk songs, Delta blues, Southern gospel, right up to modern country music.

"I looked to that list as a standard of excellence, and to remind myself of the tradition from which I come."

Thirty-six years on, and this definitive 'top 100' according to Johnny Cash finally inspired Rosanne to record an album of her favourites from this inventory, including Bob Dylan's 'Girl From The North Country', Patsy Cline's 'She's Got You' and 'Silver Wings', on which Rosanne is joined by Rufus Wainwright. The album is called, naturally, *The List*, and is produced by Cash's husband, John Leventhal, closing, significantly, with the Carter Family's 'Bury Me Under The Weeping Willow'.

"That song had a lot of emotional resonance for me because of them, and June (Rosanne's stepmother)," explains Cash. "This album enables me to validate the connection to my heritage rather than run away from it, and to tie all the threads together: past and future, legacy and youth."

Johnny Cash had slipped a couple of his own songs onto the list, including 'Sea Of Heartbreak' and 'I'm Movin' On', and as Rosanne observed, this distinguished roll-call of classic country songs was as much to shine a light on her father's own character and the influences that shaped him, as to simply provide a fuller appreciation of country.

Listening to a parent's own records and hearing their thoughts transmit through music, whether they are ambiguous and elliptical or starkly direct, can unlock another level of understanding one's parent, especially if, through absence, they have become something of a mystery figure. Galen Ayers listened to her father, Kevin's, records in order to get closer to her dad during long periods of time apart when she was in boarding school, and she makes the interesting point that she feels she was "parented" by those records; he was there in his way and she absorbed his words, voice and presence straight from the vinyl.

Galen: "I go deeply into the psychology side (of songwriting) I think because I missed my dad terribly for years and years, so I listened to his records all the time, he definitely parented me through his music. And I remember stealing his lines to send to boyfriends…"

The idea of being 'parented' by records provokes an interesting thought for the rest of us depending on the artists we loved during childhood, and how intensely we focused on them. It's different from the point of view that we weren't so much listening to these records with the express intention to feel closer to the artist, of course, but we still listen intently to the words, learn and absorb concepts that might have been otherwise new to us and we are shaped in part according to this influence. For instance, for years as a child I listened frequently and closely to Pete Townshend's albums, inhaling his words and sounds and hyperawareness. (Townshend, incidentally, is another example of an artist born into music: his father, Cliff, was saxophonist in RAF dance band The Squadronaires and his mother, Betty, was a singer.) I might venture that the darker, more introspective, analytical elements of my own character may be due to his records partly 'parenting' me, informing my development and thinking.

Some might suggest it isn't such a great idea for a little girl to listen almost daily to the musings of a (then) alcoholic former heroin addict from a choleric group that described itself as a collection of the most "horrible geezers" you could wish to meet, the troubled maverick who birthed the disturbing rock opera *Tommy* ... but I think I'm OK with it. (And Townshend is a dad himself after all. Pained lyrics and guitar-smashing aside, he is still the man who would carefully make "very thin toast" when his daughter Emma was unwell, or take her to the British Museum and sit for hours, bored to the point he started hallucinating while his little girl happily drew Egyptian mummies.)

It is arguable that this concept of 'parenting' through music goes some way to explain why fans might be keen to connect personally with the star and his or her family. If the listener feels moulded and guided by those records, and thus, the artist, they may almost feel as if there is a familial bond and respect, especially if they were listening to those records in their youth to emotionally escape their own situation. It's a thought...

Music aside, something that is instrumental in informing the lives of children, whether they decide to take the same route or not, is approach. One could 'follow in the footsteps' of a famous father or mother not simply by taking on the same occupation, but by inheriting a mindset. Christian Davies shares an interest in spirituality, yoga and, more unusually, UFOs with his father, Dave, which in turn he feels solidified his decision to become a reiki practitioner and trance DJ. Versatility, 'thinking big' and the ability to draw easily on a variety of skills were ways in which Quincy Jones' producer son, QD3, felt he was most influenced by his father. And in the case of many musicians' kids, workaholism would also invariably be in the DNA.

Dylan Howe remembers the point at which he realised he was not going to get away with staying in his room listening to David Bowie albums throughout his summer holidays... "I flunked my 'O' levels and I thought I had the whole of my holidays to stay in bed until three and then go out at night like all of my other school pals.

"Second day in, the door is opened at 8am, the covers are pulled off, 'Get a job, now.' I'm really glad, there's nothing like having your own money. And I started to understand that no one gives a shit who your dad is outside this cocoon, you've just got to get on with it. I had to clean car showroom toilets and be a sales assistant, clean windows. But I wanted to stand on my own, and I'd seen that in my dad. Just because you work hard and establish some security for your family doesn't mean that when your kids are old enough they shouldn't understand that you've got to do it on your own now. It really instilled a proper work ethic in me that I still have.

"A lot of people have a generalised view of musicians, even now. 'When are you going to get a real job? I suppose you've only just got up… It must be a real laugh…' For most musicians it's their profession, you want to take care of business and to do that you have to focus and be professional… a lot of people find that hard to grasp.

"Yes were also pioneering in how they ate, they were into vegetarianism, they were aware of how the environment was being damaged 35 years ago, and at that time it was like, 'What are you talking about?' It wasn't just the music. If you're able to do what you want to do and have success and security from it, you can adopt it as a way of life."

"The workaholism, that rubbed off on me," says Aaron Horn. Trevor Horn and uber-tough label boss and studio manager Jill Sinclair were nothing if not serious workers, and they passed on that ethos to their children. There would be no resting on laurels for this family. "You get used to accepting every single job that comes, working hard. People don't always get it.

"I think the 'being good at' stuff just comes with time. Anyone can be good if they put the time in, but lots of people can't be bothered, or moan, 'Oh, that person's related to that person, so of course, everyone's going to hook him up.' I used to care at the beginning…

"When you look at what your father genetically codes for you, technically it's just your testes and hypothalamus gland in your brain. I don't look like my dad. I've got a lot of the genes from my mum. But I think the hypothalamus makes a big difference to the style in which you grow. The road I end up taking seems to be similar to my dad's, my decision-making processes or the way I assess certain situations, not just in music.

"The forcefulness (of Jill) had an inverted effect as well, you get used to someone fighting your battles for you... I think that's how it was a bit for me," he explains. "She was so business-minded and strong. I always felt a bit bad for the people she was rinsing when I was around, watching it all happen.

"The way I've developed as a person is sort of knowing that I can't challenge my dad. I've taken different avenues. He never had time to get certain pieces of paper, so for me, doing an MA is one-upmanship basically! (laughs) No it's not, he's been given a few free ones..."

Plenty of musicians were hopeful that their bright young children would shun the limelight themselves and turn to management or the business side of the music industry, possibly with the ulterior motive that they'd have free legal advice on tap, or a tough representative who could fight their corner. This would be the only time one could emotionally blackmail a manager with wistful memories of how you bought them that special Barbie even though they'd been naughty, or how you introduced them to New Kids On The Block when they were 12 despite risking your own credibility. And delicious it would be.

Most of the time, such plans to shoehorn children into a life of sorting out contracts and phonecalls come to nothing (come on, they've seen the other side of the fence – it looks a lot more fun than an Excel document of your expenses). But they might pick up a few skills along the way, which in turn makes their own path in whatever they choose easier and safer.

"I've got that savviness because of mum's experiences," says Celeste Bell, daughter of punk star Poly Styrene. "It's not a fantasy for me, I know the dark sides of it. I know most people involved are in it just to make money. That's fine, but I can separate music from life. Sometimes it's hard and you get absorbed and make it your life."

Maria Gallagher, daughter of Blockhead Mickey, remembers having her telephone manner commented on and critiqued by her father, keen to ensure she wouldn't have to be beholden to other people, possibly even hoping to enrol her in a managerial sense (and Maria did work in music management temporarily). The Blockheads, like many bands, had certainly been conned enough times to warrant a 'keep it in the family' approach.

"I was encouraged to do the business side of things, I guess dad just wanted his kids to have a better handle on things like that. I was never musical anyway. It's probably from being a product of that kind of family. My dad's notoriously been ripped off. What did they get for 'Relax'? A £250 session fee, and it's one of the best-selling records... that felt quite sinful."*

"I saw a programme about number ones," continues Maria, "and they were talking about 'Relax'... You know how the business works, if it's a session then it's a session and that's what you get paid for. I admire the Blockheads because it's water under the bridge to them, it can be frustrating but it's also very valuable. Enough people are in it for the wrong reasons. It's nice to be around their sort of energy."

The children of Jack Bruce severally inherited his musical talent. All are artistic, but even more important, his daughter Natascha insists, was his political, ethical influence on their developing minds. "The rebelliousness," she says. "My dad got me into the more political side of things, he took me on my first march in the Eighties, during the time of the Gulf War. I made a placard at home!

"He'd encourage us to read papers and watch the news, giving us insights into things that maybe as kids you wouldn't always have. When Mandela was released, for example, Dad sat down and explained apartheid, he would tell us certain brands from South Africa we shouldn't buy because they supported apartheid. He showed us there are different ways of changing things, and sometimes economically the best way to impact on a government is to not support certain companies they endorse or get money from."

For Calico Cooper, comedy, with a sting of provocation, is a gift presented to her by her genes, and it's also constantly by her side as she continues to tour the world with her father, Alice. Add to that the fact she can ballet dance, stage fight, sing and act and be thrown around by her 'shock rock' father in a way that often befuddles and unnerves an audience of hard-bitten bikers and you have a courageous one-woman

---

* In 1984 The Blockheads were recruited by Trevor Horn to play on Frankie Goes To Hollywood's 'Relax' and 'Two Tribes', the bass-lines of which were dreamed up by Blockheads bassist Norman Watt Roy.

variety show within a variety show. Even Groucho Marx hailed the Cooper show as "the last hope for vaudeville". Fact.

"I knew my niche was in comedy," Calico says. "Doing the Cooper show, I'd fall down stairs or take a pie in the face or whatever. It's crazy, people have nightmares about being on stage in front of 50,000 people in their underpants – I do it for a living! I love it.

"We definitely had our share of backlash, the Miley Cyrus syndrome.* It's like, 'Is that really appropriate to be doing this with your daughter?' and I'm like, 'Look, dude, I'm 27 years old. I'm not getting hurt, it's not weird.' I'm not playing a love interest. People misunderstand, but there's always been blood, guts, incest... When Shakespeare did it, it was like, 'He's a genius!' but when Alice Cooper does it, it's like, 'That's gross!'"

What of the sons and daughters of our late heroes who are expected to carry the torch of a parent's legacy generally because their physical resemblance says so? What about their own path? Baxter Dury's music is defiantly different to his father's in its comparative introversion, although he occasionally utilises the same thoughtful 'sprechgesang' technique. However, Ian Dury's formidable aura simply as a character and a force is a difficult one to escape. Having chosen to be a singer as well, Baxter gets his fair share of people expecting him to simply ape Ian, but taking a different route stylistically was his way of protecting himself from being determined by his father.

"If you get a singer father, I mean, pop music itself is not usually defined by someone's ability as a musician, it's their rare point of view, their rare character that applied to music makes them unique," he says, "It's about their characteristics, how big Jagger's lips are, how weird this or that is. That thing can't be passed down."

Indeed, while the child might be fortunate enough to be taught certain skills because their gifted father or mother is on hand, it is something indefinable that has made that person a 'star' or a 'hero', and we can't measure their children against them. "When I was little," says Emma Townshend, "My dad, Pete Townshend, spent hours of his precious free

---

* Country singer Billy Ray and his singer/actress daughter were lambasted after they were photographed 'inappropriately' draped over each other in *Vanity Fair* in 2008 by that splendid troublemaker Annie Leibovitz.

time when not playing with The Who photocopying chord symbols to make a left-handed instruction book for his awkwardly gifted daughter. But although I can play the guitar, I'm no guitarist."

Pete's insistence that his children had the options around them should they wish to embrace music themselves is in direct contrast to his own upbringing. "(My parents) did not have a piano, or a good record player. We were musicians, it seemed strange to me. They encouraged me to draw and to write, but not to make music. I tried to provide the resources my kids needed, whatever they were. If certain teenage enthusiasms hit a cul-de-sac, so be it." His father did, however, take him to see Bill Haley's *Rock Around The Clock* in 1956 – a formative moment. "My father's implicit 'OK' mattered to me," he told me. "He said the Haley band had 'swing'."

"Most 'sons of' or 'daughters of' are awful," continues Baxter. "Dylan (Howe, Charley Charles' replacement in the Blockheads) is very different because he's chosen a different route and now he's probably considered one of the best drummers in the country.

"There's a selfless aspect to being the 'son of' too. Working round someone's ego, and the fact that that ego is part of their livelihood. The other sons and daughters I've met, sons mainly, I've become automatically good friends with, we understand each other's plight. Ronnie Wood's son (Jesse) is a good friend of mine... that sounds really insincere doesn't it? That's what rock star sons are like!

"He's sort of a model but he doesn't really want to be. He always ends up modelling plastic spoons and butter, rubbish things. He's the sweetest guy. He's got it a thousand times worse than I have because his dad's a proper nutter. As a result that's made him really understanding of everyone, he's a real humanitarian." Ronnie's younger son Jamie, a former tearaway, whom Keith Richards suggested might be better off "at sea", has become a successful businessman who managed to save Ronnie and Jo's finances after they were ripped off and abused by one too many takers.

After Ian Dury's demise from cancer in 2000, Baxter would sing his father's song 'My Old Man', backed by the Blockheads at Dury's wake at the Town and Country Club (now The Forum) in Kentish Town, north London. Dylan Howe, on drums, recalls, "People were quite stunned by it, everybody was very moved. Initially he didn't want to do it, but we were having a jam on stage, Norman (Watt Roy) started to play the bass-line and he joined us." Despite the obvious physical and vocal resemblance to his father, perhaps the fact Baxter would soon set his own, very different, music in motion prevented him from being expected to stand in for his father too often (and punning headlines such as 'Chip off the old Blockhead' could thankfully be avoided).

After the death of his father, Stuart, in 2001, Callum Adamson would also endure a period in which he was compared almost continually to his late father, which can't have made his own process of grieving any easier. "It was the weirdest thing, after my dad died, everyone looked at me when I walked into a room, even my own family, like, 'Shit, you look like Stuart.' So I had to do the memorial concert, I had to be the one to speak and play... once you've done that you can pretty much do anything. Yeah, I'm fine now.

"It was a strange time, it must have been a kind of defence mechanism but there are things in print I apparently said that I cannot remember saying or doing, but I kept it together somehow. We had a service where the fucking Carnegie Hall wasn't big enough to fit everyone in, we had to move speakers outside and I later found out that there were another thousand people outside listening."

"We did a gig at the Barrowlands and they wanted to do it four nights running. We did it ticketed for charity, and they sold out in minutes. I thought it would be nice to print a run of memorial T-shirts, with the guitar on which he wrote 'In A Big Country' on the front, I thought 500 would be enough. They were gone within five minutes of the doors opening. Then you've got David Bowie getting in touch to say, 'Really sorry, Stuart was a great guy,' Nils Lofgren, Noel Gallagher, crazy. It's nice."

Keith Moon's daughter Mandy felt her father was largely a stranger to her, and has few memories of him, so it is nature as opposed to nurture that saw her inherit not just his estate* but also some of her dad's addictive streak, the madness for which he became celebrated, not to

---

* As it happened Keith, being Keith, had spent the fortune he made from The Who by the time he died but once the dust had settled and debts been paid, Mandy would receive substantial annual royalty payments from the ongoing sales of his recordings with The Who.

mention an aptitude for the drums. She played in a number of bands but, according to Tony Fletcher's book *Dear Boy*, spent her twenties battling a drink problem and coping with turbulent relationships. "By the age of 30, she appeared to have finally come to terms with being the child of such a complex and famous man, had settled into her third marriage, and was running a boutique in Los Angeles, where she had remained living since her mother and stepfather (Ian McLagan) moved her there in 1978 (after Keith Moon's death)."

In 1990, Mandy Moon represented her father when The Who were inducted into the Rock'n'Roll Hall Of Fame. The ceremony was held at New York's Waldorf Astoria Hotel, which seemed amusing given the trouble Moon himself had caused there back in 1968. Mandy said she was proud to accept the honour on his behalf, adding, "even though I know my father was banned from this hotel".

It wasn't going to be long until we discussed Julian and Sean Lennon in this chapter. As we know, after John Lennon's death in 1980, Julian's subsequent career in music was easier *and* harder because of his father's vast profile – Julian, vocally and facially, was so similar to John that he would often be employed as the next best thing.

This hits home on the Chuck Berry film *Hail Hail Rock And Roll*, where Berry performs with an array of stars in a concert musically directed by Keith Richards. Berry makes it clear he would have invited John Lennon, who was a big fan of Berry's, to play. Instead, Julian was invited to sing. He gave a brilliant performance, grinning through the inevitable cries of 'Doesn't he look like his Pa?' from Berry, but there is a terrible moment at the end of the number when Berry shouts, 'John... I mean, Julian Lennon!' It's a shock for the viewer let alone anyone else, and the young Lennon looks momentarily crushed. Understandable, but painful...

Julian eventually left music behind for more than a decade, leaving England for Italy. In 2009, however, he revealed he had started writing again because he "still had things to say". Sean Lennon's path has been a little smoother, although he is practically playing John Lennon himself in the revived Plastic Ono Band with his mother, Yoko. His guitar and piano playing, not to mention his aesthetic, are pure John. It is hard to imagine how strange it must be to be expected to almost *be* his father, not to mention the fact that, in a way, he has also put himself in that position. As a result, when he opens his mouth to speak between numbers during a Plastic Ono gig, you are taken aback when it turns out he has an American accent. It is very easy to get lost in the John-ness of it all.

Away from the Plastic Ono Band, he continues to work on his own projects with various beautiful people from the New York scene. In fact, John Lennon's shadow aside, he seems to be quite happy to remain in the vast shadow of tiny Yoko, "the oldest teenager in the business" at 77. Sean has an influence on his mother too, of course, introducing her to the Japanese multi-instrumentalist Yuka Honda (formerly his girlfriend) and her band, Cibo Matto, who still collaborate with Ono to this day.

Sean seems happy just being Ono Lennon Jr. He's already admitted he's a 'living tribute', but believes he exerts his rebelliousness, a quality he claims he inherited from dad, in not feeling he has to talk about him in interviews. Fair enough, but, with respect it's easy to 'rebel' when you are in an almost untouchable position of privilege and don't really need anyone on your side – you don't need that magazine to champion your latest effort, you don't need to play the game. And in sporadically refusing to talk about John, is he not rebelling against the people who made it possible for him to rebel in the first place: the many people who bought his father's catalogue in every new format, and supported The Beatles, and continue to do so 40 years after they split?

It's complicated, extreme and confusing, there's no doubt about that. But you can unknit that brow and put away your painkillers, we're going to face that 'shadow' straight on and discover what constitutes a successful, but respectful, escape from it. To get ourselves in the right frame of mind, I think Jakob Dylan's approach conjures an effective mental picture: "Arms up, head down, and just blow through it..."

CHAPTER 13

Emerging From 'The Shadow'

"Where there is much light, the shadow is deep."

Goethe

Ominous references to 'the shadow' are always rife, for these particular sons and daughters. It is undoubtedly hard to avoid being pigeonholed; it takes energy not to become resigned. But regardless of the direction you take, it is possible to transmute this syndrome into a healthy, warm glow of mutual admiration and support.

Duncan Jones is a man hailed for his down-to-earth demeanour in the face of an unusual childhood with single parent David Bowie. His father did his best to protect him from the darker aspects of his world, and friends from that time observed that Bowie's efforts to keep life sane for his child ensured that he stayed on the right track himself.

It is possible that glimpsing the traumatic side of his dad's life steered Duncan safely away from, he says, even being interested in music at all. Jones has admitted his choice to become a film director as opposed to a musician was his "big rebellion... but I was on set on a lot of the films he was on, and that had a huge impact".

Jones is now forging his own path with success: he directed the critically acclaimed 2009 psychological thriller *Moon*, space and identity being themes to which both father and son are clearly drawn (cue lots of 'Space Oddity' quips and headlines like this one, from the *New Yorker*: 'Son of Major Tom at Ground Control'. "It'll change one day…" sighs Jones.)

Trudie Styler produced the film, but is quick to assure us that, as with Guy Ritchie and *Lock, Stock And Two Smoking Barrels*, she agreed to back the film because she was convinced of the director's abilities. *Moon* was a low-budget film, and before you carp that Jones must surely be using gold bars as doorstops, sleeping on a bed of £50 notes and bathing in Krug before breakfast, it might interest you to know that Duncan has up to now been house-sharing (in Chelsea, admittedly) and hopes that since his successful debut with *Moon* he can move out and live on his own.

Duncan Jones shares his father's affection for Berlin, as he is also working on another sci-fi movie, *Mute,* set in the German city, a "love letter to *Blade Runner*". Lest we forget, Jones also once caused a furore with an advert he directed for high-street brand French Connection, which featured two women fighting and then kissing. Complaints flooded in. His mother, Angie, would surely have been proud.

It is difficult, however, to anticipate what Angie Bowie would feel about anything, particularly as this was her response to *Moon*: "I felt only one overriding emotion and that was grief. My son is messed up. The film is about one man's isolation and confusion and I now realise, through Zowie's art, what a mistake I made leaving him."

Jones responded to this quote by adding: "I think she also said it was about her, which figures… Whatever."

While understandably every article about *Moon* mentions Jones' parentage, he did succeed in making a name for himself without having to be accused of 'playing on' his father's famous surname. Duncan, born in 1971, was, as we know, originally called Zowie Bowie, a name selected by Angie because she liked the meaning of the name Zoë – 'life' – but couldn't call their baby boy a girl's name. That would be too weird even for them. So she added a 'W' and made it visually rhyme with 'Bowie', which naturally made it perfectly sensible. Not as sensible as Duncan Jones though.

"I'm fond of (Zowie)," says Duncan, "and it's the most obvious reminder of my background that I have, but if I was a director called

Zowie Bowie the name brings so much baggage. It allows people to feel, 'Oh, he's got where he is by using his name.'"

David had chosen 'Duncan' as his son's name in the first place before Angie stepped in with her suggestion. Jones is Bowie's real surname. Voila! His folks didn't even need to get offended.

However, it is clear that the sort of parent who dreams up a smirksome moniker such as the following clearly isn't too worried about offending the child on the receiving end: Diva Thin Muffin Pigeen Zappa, Rolan Bolan, Apple Martin, the various Julian Joneses (all sons of deceased Rolling Stone Brian), Blanket Jackson and of course, Bono's bundle of joy, Elijah Bob Patricius Guggi Q Hewson. Ozzy Osbourne's daughter from his first marriage experienced a near miss: the doting dad called his daughter Jessica Starshine (because he saw a big, bright star in the sky when she was born), but he admits he considered changing her name to – wait for it – 'Burt Reynolds'. Why? Because he's a big star too…

Many consider changing their surname, whether to be judged as a separate entity, or just to be left alone by overeager fans, despite the complex feelings about identity and parental rejection it might spark. Toto's Steve Lukather however actually suggested his son Trev drop his last name, just to give him a fighting chance. Singer Jakob Dylan also considered changing his surname, but realised he would be in part denying how proud he is of his father by doing so – not to mention the fact it would appear as if he was trying to run away from his heritage.

I was long intrigued as to why concern was expressed for Dylan Jr and Rolan Bolan having to labour under their parents' famous names, when Dylan and Bolan were not even their fathers' real names anyway. I later learned that Bob Dylan did have his name legally changed from Zimmerman, but Rolan's surname on his birth certificate is Feld, his father's real name. Arguably, Rolan could have done himself a favour by simply using 'Feld' for his professional work if he truly wanted to be seen as an artist in his own right, but he decided to stick with Bolan, a name invented for his father by his record company, Decca. Still 'Rolan Bolan' does trip nicely off the tongue. It is possible, of course, that he feels by keeping Bolan in his name he is paying tribute to his late father.

For better or worse, and in part as a direct result of keeping the Bolan moniker, Rolan remains anchored to Marc's legacy and profile.

However, the fact that his pedigree is mentioned before anything else in the information section on his Myspace Music page indicates that this doesn't bother him too much. His biography on the page leaves us in absolutely no doubt as to his bloodline, starting thus: "Growing up the scion of rock stars could make for a childhood sprinkled with stardust. However Rolan Bolan - son of T. Rex glam-rock icon Marc Bolan and Gloria Jones, the Motown songstress who wrote 'Tainted Love' - found the situation to be as normal as milk'n'cookies. 'I just thought it was the same for every other kid,' says Bolan. 'You know, 'My mom's in the studio and my dad's a rock star.' What's suprising (sic) is that Bolan definitely inherited his parent's talent genes and - maybe added a few more…"

A by-product of this approach is that there is a well-intentioned 'Rolan Bolan support site', set up by fans of Marc Bolan, urging the world to get behind this talented young singer-songwriter. It is only when you continue reading that it becomes clear that these fans really just want the legend of the feather boa-wearing one to live on, in their words, a "new age of Bolan". It has little to do with Rolan's uniqueness as an artist at all. The plea reads: 'Can you imagine Rolan Bolan on *Top Of The Pops* or being courted by MTV? The older Marc Bolan fans amongst us want Rolan to succeed so that they can witness a new age of Bolan. Younger fans want a Bolan that they can connect with…'

The Grammy-winning singer-songwriter Jakob Dylan, who released his first solo album, *Seeing Things,* in 2008, previously chose to perform and write under the name of his group The Wallflowers, refusing to gratuitously flag up his name if he could help it (no mention of Bob in his Myspace biography), and this has paid off. Initial attempts by the press to steer every interview resolutely dad-wards have at least died down somewhat, as he has proved to be an enduring talent himself. And his early wariness to face the subject of his father eventually softened. He even chose to touch on his heritage in his 2000 album *Breach*, after several years of agonising as to whether he could bring himself to write about his own life, and his complex relationship with Dylan Snr. In the end, as he told journalist Elizabeth Weitzman, "It was more difficult not to. It's everyone's right as an artist to draw from their own environment. Before, I didn't want to attract any more attention to the subject... But when I got to this record, I didn't think it was fair to purposefully censor who I was.

"I have more confidence in myself now. I don't think people are going to buy the record because they heard I'm speaking about (family). But before, I didn't want some sixty-year-old bearded guy in a Grateful Dead shirt looking for clues on a record."

Joe Strummer's daughter Jazz has dropped her last name altogether (Mellor, Strummer's real surname), but she admits that having an unusual first name tends to raise suspicions. "I just use my first names, Jazz Domino Holly. I was even thinking about changing it by deed poll but my sister got really upset and was like, 'No you can't do that!'

"But my dad was a massive inventor of names, he changed his name loads of times, and he was really into that, 'You are who you want to be'. He hated his last name as well. It wasn't very rock'n'roll, 'Mellor'… it reminds me of that disgraced labour MP David Mellor… I have bad associations with the name because I remember reading about that when I was a kid!"

Dylan Howe chose a different instrument to his guitarist father, Steve, and finds it hard to imagine how challenging it would have been had he decided otherwise. "It would just be too much of a straight line of comparison," he says. Interestingly, none of Steve's children play guitar – his younger son Virgil initially played keyboards before following Dylan's lead and becoming a drummer, and also a DJ and producer, while Georgia works in advertising and Stephanie is studying anthropology. Even so, Dylan is occasionally questioned by fans on why he is "hiding behind his name", because they only associate the name with his father.

"On my YouTube profile description I'd said what I was doing, all my own stuff, and at the end I said, 'Son of Yes guitarist Steve Howe' simply because I get a whole load of people saying, 'Are you the son of…?' So I was like, 'Look… yes. I'm going to put it here so you can stop asking me and everything's fine.'

"Then I get this comment from someone saying, 'You don't have to hide behind his name…' That just shows you everybody's individual vantage point…

"At one point I did wonder whether I ought to change my name to be seen as a musician in my own right, but what an insult. People will find out anyway, and then they're going to ask, 'Why did you change your name?'. It is part of who I am. I'm not ashamed of it, I'm very proud of my dad. But the first time it stung was in school and Asia (Steve Howe's Eighties supergroup) were playing Wembley Arena and suddenly all these people were being nice to me just because they wanted to get on the guest list. I had a bit of a moment about that."

Crosby Loggins knows what it's like to be the owner of an unmistakable surname. How many other Logginses can you name? One? Kenny? Precisely. "It's amazing what a complicated issue it is," he says.

"I performed a handful of shows in my late teens using my middle name, Sullivan, instead. In the end that felt insincere. I was trying to emote and sing about things that mattered to me, and one of those things has always been coming to terms with my parentage, so the act of performing under a fictitious name felt counterproductive.

"But that doesn't mean I felt comfortable with my name as soon as I resigned myself to using it. To be honest, I still shudder a little every time I hear it. I don't know what that is. It's not that I'm embarrassed of my father's success, but I am a very private and sensitive person, and every time I hear my surname some part of me is reminded of how my life will never really be private.

"There is also the obvious fact that I've been pursuing music professionally for over 10 years now and that inevitably puts me in competition with him, a competition that, at the moment, I'm still officially losing by a significant margin! We would only laugh about that, and we are very close, but nonetheless the competition exists whether we engage in it or not."

Dhani Harrison, who has his own group, thenewno2 (pronounced 'new number two') with collaborator Oliver Hecks, has expressed that while his own music is "not The Beatles", he can't not have absorbed their influence – you don't have to be related to be touched by the Beatles effect. But while pop aspirations were never for Dhani, he sees no reason why he should stifle his own natural métier for the sake of avoiding comparisons.

"I don't really plan to be a pop star; I just want to be able to make music without the whole My Dad thing hanging over me, which everyone in my position goes through," he told *Guardian* journalist Will Hodgkinson.

"It's a tricky one. You can't help being a musician because you've grown up with music, yet being one means being compared to your dad and being slated for it."

Part of the solution, for Dhani, is to avoid spotlighting his name at all, making thenewno2 a democratic group so that, as Harrison says, "I could send anyone to a meeting, and when they were asked who they were, they could simply say, "The New No 2.

"I wanted it to be a faceless entity, because I didn't want to be Dhani Harrison & The Uncles or whatever. There was too much flak around the name 'Harrison'."

As a result thenewno2 have been credited for creating the artwork for *Concert For George* (Hecks was also stills photographer), *The Dark Horse Years* box set and the menu design for the DVD of *Concert For Bangladesh* as well as George Harrison's final album, *Brainwashed*, of which Dhani completed production with the producer Laurie Latham the year after George passed away. The posthumous release features George and Dhani chanting together. "We talked about putting a chant at the end," explains Dhani. "A really nice vibration to leave you in a good place. He never liked sad stuff, and this is a light-hearted record, a joyous thing."

It was up to Dhani to ensure his father's songs were completed in the way he would have wanted. Who better to finish the record than one of the closest people to Harrison, a man who was part of him and shared his spirituality and approach? (When George was alive, he apparently was more interested in working in his garden than finishing off the record.) But despite Dhani's sensitive, attuned production, some critics had their own ideas about how it should have sounded.

"I've been criticised for making them sound too posh," explained Dhani. "One interviewer asked me: 'How do you feel that you've betrayed your father?' That wasn't really very cool."

The problem with the members of a band as universally loved as The Beatles is that everyone thinks they know them, and know what they would have wanted, because their ubiquity in our culture has been such that we feel almost related to them ourselves. This reminds me of when I read a preview of this book at a Beatles-themed spoken word (Talking Musical Revolution) event organised by Gavin Martin and John Robb. I explained I would be reading about 'The Beatles as parents', and Robb, semi-joking, asked whether I meant I would be speculating on the idea of The Beatles as *my* parents, *everyone's* parents, simply because to us they have always been omnipresent, their songs etched into the fabric of our everyday lives whether we always register consciously or not.

Baxter Dury is happy to leave his father's musical legacy to the Blockheads, ("It's their thing now"), which also prevents any similar overprotective and rather unreasonable vitriol being levelled at him. He is the first to admit he has, on occasion in the past, enjoyed reflecting some of the rays beaming off the Dury name when it suited him, or at least when dinner party conversations started running dry.

Baxter's advice on preventing a dad-tinged cast colouring everything you do is to almost seal off your own ambitions to prevent the lines becoming blurred, especially if your parent is rooted in popular culture, continually celebrated almost regardless of how he may have been as an individual.

"I can't deny Dad's presence, his influence, Dad this, Dad that, but there's a point where you have to stop and say, 'Fuck everything, I know what I liked about my dad, I know what I didn't like, he was also a fucking arsehole.'

"Sometimes you've just got to stop and get your dignity back. Not that anyone's trying to take your dignity away, but it's for yourself. You've got to shut yourself away a bit sometimes. Like at the moment, I can see this big wave coming (because of the Ian Dury biopic) and I will be sort of resigned to... you know.

"It's really easy in an awkward moment to just go, 'My dad's Ian Dury!' He's the housewives' choice, the cabbies love him, it's a get-out clause, and fuck me, I've used it a billion times. I also think I'm bright and talented, and your talent doesn't mean anything unless you totally close it off. You have to accept it as a thing in its own right. But I've got people saying, 'Why don't you put your album out at the same time as the film?'

"It's been interesting looking at Dad-related things. It's not even like I become sad talking about it, it's such a common subject, I see it on the TV... I tried to go to sleep last night by listening to a radio play and suddenly it goes, 'And now, starring Ian Dury...' and I was like... I couldn't escape from him. It was sort of nice, but it was like he was in my sleep. It's his birthday today as well (May 12 2009). That's quite weird."

Pete Townshend found that, while he loved his father, Cliff's, music – predominantly swing – he would become an intrinsic part of the prediction Cliff made for the future of popular music: that bands of four or five people with amplifiers would take over from big bands. "I loved the music of my father's era. Even when I was first listening to jazz, rock'n'roll, skiffle and early country blues (before I discovered R&B). My favourite singers "were Frank and Ella. I understood the function of the music my father played. It was to inspire romantic vision and hope for the post-war future. What happened was that like so many of my generation, although I loved the music I failed to be inspired. I needed my own music."

Dylan Howe agrees that maintaining an initial separateness is the only way to go. After a few years, if you feel you've paid your dues and established your own identity, then it might be an option to appear professionally alongside that famous name that happens to be your parent. But not before. "I distanced myself and spent the Nineties doing every gig I was offered, earning a living, trying to improve all the time," he says. "I remember my dad saying he had this gig in New York and would I like to play with him?

"I remember saying, 'If that's the first time I'm going to play in America, then I don't know if it should be with you.' Maybe that was the wrong way to go but I did feel that. But whenever I am in America it's always going to be 'You're Steve Howe's son' anyway."

Dylan also chose to turn down a lucrative modelling job along with other 'sons of', including Rolan Bolan and Zak Starkey, for the American designer Tommy Hilfiger some years ago, preferring to tough it out on £20 a night playing Soho jazz gigs. (And yes, daytime TV fans will remember him from the anarchic house band of Mel and Sue's cult magazine show *Light Lunch*. He appeared daily on national TV dressed in a number of guises, including a Native American, a woman, and in one instance, not dressed at all.)

Harry Waters didn't make a conscious rebellion against his father, Roger, and Pink Floyd when he chose jazz over rock, and piano over guitar, but it's clear that the choice has helped him peel away from his father's weighty reputation and start building his own.

"If I was up there with a guitar and trying to sing, there'd be far more obvious comparisons. I'd definitely experience more of the focus on the 'dad' thing if I'd continued as a rock musician. People can't really compare now because what I'm doing is very different. It wasn't a big deal to me not to go into rock music. And I can't write lyrics for one.

"(Ex Deaf School saxophonist) Ian Ritchie and I are the only two jazzers in Dad's solo band; there's a sort of joke if anyone plays any jazz we have to put a quid in a pot. Whatever city we're in we find out where the jam sessions are and go along. We went to one in Vermont and got up and played. At that point I'd already done a recording session at Eastcote studios with Neville Malcolm and Seb Rochford and Ian, playing standards.

"Some guy came up to me after this jam session and said, 'Are you Harry? Oh I'm such a big fan...' and I'm like, 'Thanks...' so used to it, and then he said, 'When you played that standard...' and then I realised, 'Hang on, he's actually a fan of me! Wait! You're a fan of me?' I don't think he even knew about my dad, I don't know. My first assumption is of course that it's going to be about Dad, they all come up, 'Oh my God, I'm such a fan of your dad's music,' 'Yes... thank you...' So that was really nice."

From an early age, Rufus Wainwright was veering steadily away from his parents and the music they brought him up on, rejecting even the pop music his sister Martha would listen to, preferring to immerse himself in classical music, Verdi in particular. The melodrama, fierce, sweeping emotion and histrionic theatricality of opera resonated with his own intense sense of drama and romance, much to his mother, Kate's, concern. She believed the music was too "escapist" and dark, according to the writer Kirk Lake, unlike the raw, real folk music she continued to try plying her son with. Rufus dismissed it as "poor people's music" and turned Verdi up to 11.

Rufus also identified with the rusting retro glitz of Hollywood, refracting it through his own early song-writing. George Gershwin, Cole Porter, writers who could combine humour, romance and a lightness of touch poetically but potently with obsession, passion and rejected affections were studied closely by Rufus, who was well-acquainted with the themes and feelings that fuelled them.

It was Rufus' sensational Judy Garland tribute concert in 2006 at Carnegie Hall, costumed by Viktor & Rolf whom Rufus had met through the gay magazine *Butt*, that would truly throw a spotlight on the renegade Wainwright's camp two-fingered salute to Loudon's growling machismo and chilly incomprehension of his son's sexuality.

Loudon believed the *Rufus Does Judy* show was "a terrible idea, (and) Kate claimed to not even know what he was talking about." This was, in no uncertain terms, Rufus Wainwright standing on the shoulder of giants – but the giants were not his parents, they were the tragic, beloved Judy Garland and the proud, defiant strength he was projecting by being himself, and doing what he wanted to do.*

Choosing a completely different route musically can certainly help to loosen the glue that fixes your reputation to that of your parents, but depending on the level of fame and success you are associated with, you still have to be on your guard for inverted snobbery or foundationless assumptions that you are a trustafarian. "Don't ever be fooled that that ever goes away," warns Dylan Howe. "Even if you get to a point where you're not thinking about it very much and you're working with people who you think also aren't, the stereotypical preconceptions are definitely there.

"When I was putting together my quintet, I heard that generally a lot of people thought I was getting sponsored by my dad and that it was just a kind of play thing. The fact I had a Mercedes estate – quite an old one, I bought it after a succession of cheaper cars that broke down (and he's still paying for it) – meant people still thought that I was getting handouts from my dad and always had that security net, which I never had. I've earned my own money since I was 17, have never received handouts and am glad about that. It's made me work as hard as I do.

"Even aside from the 'rock star dad' thing, starting my own jazz group, because of my session credentials if you like, I was often reviewed as 'rock drummer dabbling in his hobby'… Jazz was always what I wanted to do, I just started to get offered work in other genres and you've got to pay the rent. So in another way, I had another kind of ceiling to break through, which did frustrate me quite a bit at the time."

For Callum Adamson, the 'shadow' issue is a state of mind. "With

* While working on this particular passage, the news came on the radio that Kate McGarrigle had sadly died after a long battle with cancer. 19.1.10.

music everybody always asks me, 'What's it like living in your dad's shadow?' But I never set out to be like Dad anyway. I only ever set out to be a songwriter. We [he and his Ahab bandmate Dave Burn] write for other people too.

"I never wanted to be a rock star, I just wanted to be a writer. My dad's heroes were guitar players, my heroes are lyricists."

Jason Bonham made a brave decision in choosing exactly the same instrument as his father, late Led Zeppelin drummer John. He will forever be compared to his dad, particularly because he also plays in the same way – he hasn't chosen to concentrate on a different genre in a bid to separate himself. His playing is so close to his father's that he has since played in John Bonham's stead with Jimmy Page, Robert Plant and John Paul Jones, most recently when they reformed Led Zeppelin in 2007 for a one-off show at London's O2. He first sat behind the Led Zeppelin drum kit during an afternoon soundcheck at Knebworth in August 1978 as a favour to his dad who wanted to hear what the group sounded like from the front – he'd only ever heard them from the back.

Jason's key to shrugging off the shadow is simply to stop fighting it. Jason, who was just 14 when his father died in 1980, had this epiphany during a period in which he was striving to go against his natural playing style after years of being criticised for 'trying to sound like John Bonham'. He soon learned that many of his own drum heroes were simply trying to sound like his father anyway.

"I don't remember being taught," Bonham said in an interview with the fan website *Old Buckeye*. "I only remember one incident where he put on the jukebox 'Turn It On Again' by Genesis; it has a little time skip in it. He kept saying, 'Play this, play this.'

"Some people say I'm trying to sound like him – I'm not trying to do anything like that, I just end up playing like that.

"I tried hard at one point to steer away, (but) every time I spoke to the people I was getting into, people like Jeff Porcaro (Toto, Steely Dan), and all these other guys, they all said, 'Well, I got that from your father.' So I went, 'Oh fuck it, I'll just carry on doing exactly what I'm doing!'"

So, a fine selection of useful insights from those that know. To conclude this chapter, I've compiled a top five chart of handy hints should you be in a position to need them, an emergency kit for the progeny gasping for air in the sometimes suffocating atmosphere that surrounds that superstar parent.

1.) The obvious one. If things get out of hand, at the possible risk of upsetting your folks, try dropping the name that glues you to your universally recognised parent for a while. Then leave the country just to be on the safe side.

2) Choose a different field of endeavour. Your parent is a musician, so become a hedgehog breeder, a pylon designer, a burlesque welder. I'd like to see them try and suggest your folks pulled strings for you at the hedgehog farm.

3) If accused in an interview of succeeding as a result of your parents, just agree, and then say something strange and oblique. The more nonsensical the better. *Then* you'll become famous for you.

4) Try to somehow spread the word that while "the door might have been opened for you, it's up to you to walk through it", so says Dylan Howe. Perhaps by subliminal messaging on TV and radio (ask your dad to put you in touch with someone. Only joking). Or just drive around town bellowing it through a loudhailer until people get really irritated and never mention 'nepotism' again. (Make sure the megaphone isn't too snazzy, people will assume you got it free because the shop assistant was a huge Yes/Stones/Duran Duran fan).

5) Become more famous than your parent (hard but effective). Start getting them gigs and conduct lots of sympathetic interviews in which you discuss that he/she is "really coming on" and while they're going to have to stand on their own two feet at some point, you "think he/she understands that".

Even if the suggestions above prove effective, you'd still better be prepared to answer the question, 'How's your dad?' fairly frequently whenever well-meaning but excitable fans have a chance to corner you. They don't know you, they don't know your dad, but it's a chummy, inadvertently presumptuous opener that makes them feel as if they do.

It's about time we visited that place where whatever you do, whatever you don't do, your status as a rock 'n' roll souvenir is assured... A word to the wise, a pithy, deliberately point-missing retort like, "Fine thanks, how's yours?" can buy you a bit of time to run away to the backstage area. What else are AAA passes for?

CHAPTER 14

'So, How's Your Dad?'

"I've never felt it comes from a spiteful place, although it can sound rather like: 'It's all very well that crap you just did, but your dad, he's the real deal, how's HE doing?'"

Dylan Howe

We are now ready, after having been through the trials, the tribulations, the joys and the freak-outs, to discover the true significance of the titular question, *How's Your Dad?* It might not sound like such an unreasonable thing to ask, you might think. But it's what this choice of words, when asked by the complete stranger or slightly obsessed super-fan, often unintentionally stands for: an inevitable passing over of the person on the receiving end.

I'm not suggesting the offspring or associates of your heroes aren't happy to talk at all, or indeed that they don't want to discuss their famous loved one. They're used to it, and are generally proud.

The devil, as they say, is in the detail. It's the specific wording that's the problem. The question isn't: 'What's your dad up to these days?' Or, 'What projects has your dad got lined up?' (Both would be OK, better still if you use his actual name.)

Rather, it's: 'So how is the old rascal then?' (You don't know him.)

It's: 'Has he got over that cold he caught last year then? The one he mentioned onstage on the December 17th 2009 at the Hammersmith Odeon?' (Please just go away.) It's also, basically: 'I took no notice of whatever you were doing on stage there, I just came because of the association with the person I *really* like, and as you're related to him, here I am!'

The timing of the approach is also crucial. Right before the son/daughter is about to go on stage to strut their *own* stuff? Wrong. Just after they have staggered offstage after a blistering gig, before they've even had a drink of water? Absolutely do not do it. Unless you enjoy being stared at witheringly and have little regard for other people's feelings, or, depending on the respondent's temperament, your face. At the merchandise table while they're signing programmes or CDs and saying to themselves, 'At last! People are interested in me – for me!'? Only after having congratulated them – no, not on their fine choice of parents, but on whatever it is of note they just did.

Finally, only use the words, 'How's your dad?' if you *know* their dad. And by that I do not mean if you've had your forehead signed by him, you've shown him the tattoo of his face you've got on both kneecaps, you've bought his records and *feel* like you know him or you've seen him in court when he was taking out that restraining order against you.

"It's become a joke now, the 'HYD?' thing, but I do appreciate where they're coming from. There was a time when I was sensitive about it in my late teens," explains Dylan Howe, the man whose 'How's your dad?' experiences, witnessed by the author, inspired this very book. "The more you start to mature as a person, the less sensitive you are about it. To come offstage and have a stranger ask you in a very familiar way, 'How's your dad?' as if he's friends with him... it does stun you a bit at first, and then you think, 'Are you only talking to me because of this? Or did you think I was shit and is this all you can possibly think of in the many choices of an opening line to a stranger after their gig, and you choose to say that to me? How am I supposed to feel about that?'

"There are a lot of people who are just really into the music, and are also interested in what I'm doing as well and I'm very thankful for that: 'Through your dad, I've found you and now I'm into this...' That's such a nice thing, I have done that with other people as well. But when it becomes more polarised and the heat goes up a bit then the ones that do say, 'How's your dad?', and it's the first thing they say, or you can feel it coming in the conversation… it's a bit different.

"It's the familiarity," continues Dylan. "Like trying to prove they know your dad a bit. What they want me to do is talk about him to them, and maybe get something they don't know, or… they're just showing they like him. It would be interesting to think if I met Miles Davis' son, I might have the same feeling if Miles was still alive."

There is the possibility that the 'How's your dad?' approach makes the asker feel they are somehow proving they maybe don't *know* your parent, but they damn well know more than the other average fan… 'I'm not like those crazy other ones!' Also, in many cases with older bands, and older fans, they feel they've seen the child of their hero grow up, they know about them because of their obsession with the band, hence a kind of sense of ownership and misplaced familiarity. This familiarity only dissolves when you try to engage in a regular exchange of social niceties with them – in many cases the super-fan doesn't even want to have a really normal conversation, besides the initial thrill of approaching you in such a chummy way, they still want to worship, they don't want the spell to be broken.

"There is a sense of possession through commerce," adds Dylan. "They've bought into the thing, and I'm more approachable than my father, they're not going to dry up on me. But then if you try and ask them how they are, the very devout fans, it's not like you can have a conversation in the normal sense. Those are the extreme cases.

"It also comes from the association that famous musicians are synonymous with a kind of idolisation, they have done something rare, they're very talented, but they also work their arses off. But there is a lot associated with it, a kind of mystical nano-world they're in.

"If you're obsessive about someone, it's like religion I suppose. You've found an idol, he or she fills in all the gaps you feel you might have, especially if they've got into these people at a very impressionable age."

Jack Osbourne, the approachable face of the Osbourne family, was a magnet for Ozzy fanatics whenever the yearly Ozzfest swung around. And, he says with some pride, he became quite skilled at working out who might potentially be a problem. "You learn to recognise the look in the eyes, the tone of the voice, just something that tells you it would be a good idea to keep your conversation short.

"You know they're going to get round to asking the inevitable question, 'Can I meet your dad?' so you also learn to let them down politely but firmly. That said, I would do my best to accommodate the fans if I could. At times I used to feel I was a bit of a slave to these people."

Crosby Loggins: "People are naturally aware of the fact that one of the best ways to gain emotional access to someone is through their children. As a result my brother and I were constant targets. We were everyone's best friend, and could do no wrong. On or off the road people said hello to us, offered us stuff, tried to give us a leg up. I remember asking my dad when I was about eight why everyone gave us everything for free when we were rich? We didn't need it! Why didn't they give the free stuff to the guy living in the cardboard box out front? I was always deeply troubled by that reality – one that persists in Hollywood through copious 'swag bags' to this day."

"The 'How's your dad?' thing? I can always tell when someone's going to do that," laughs Jack Gahan. "I can almost pre-empt it! But I'm aware that it would be there. Maybe there are expectations from other people, I suppose you could think, 'Maybe they want to work with me, or hang out because they know who my dad is and they might think that would give them a leg up in some way,' but I'd hope that I'd be able to tell. The fans are really nice, I like it really."

There is always the option of taking out HYD insurance. Someone who went to enjoy a performance at London's magical Union Chapel by the musician Ben Taylor (because they really did like Ben Taylor, they assured me) observed that Taylor chose to openly face the fact most people were there because of their admiration of James Taylor and Carly Simon, rolling out stories about them during the show.

"Half of the people there were of an age group that was double his, they were blatantly there because of who his parents are. All he could do was go with it and do loads of anecdotes about his mum and dad, and he delighted the audience. He obviously knows and understands." The pre-emptive strike. It saves time and ensures you aren't too beholden to hanging around by the bar being given a benevolent but determined dose of the third degree. 'Hold it right there with your enquiries about my parents! I've already filled you in. So there.'

The collector mentality is, I think, an interesting factor to be considered, and it is particularly relevant in this digital age because it has become so easy to 'add' your favourite stars to your own network, electronically at least. Speaking from my own experience, on Myspace and Facebook, Yes fans will not only add all of the band members and their children, but in many cases their children's partners. I'm all for making new pals; I'm one of those naïve souls that believes a stranger is just a friend you haven't met yet. But in a majority of cases, this e-connection is not going to turn into a two-way communication in which you learn anything about each other as individuals (other than the fact they have learned how to play the solo from 'Roundabout'). They have 'added' you as a 'friend' despite having little to no interest in you. They are, rather, collecting Howes, Squires, Andersons...

Not that I mind in the slightest, but as a twist on the 'How's your Dad?' opening gambit, I quite often get, 'How's your husband?' and, intriguingly, before "How are you?" 'Is he still playing the drums?' accompanied with a fast drumming mime, as if a) I don't know what drums are and b) he might have suddenly stopped. I can't imagine people saying: "Is he still a doctor then? How's your wife, still a greengrocer?' and then miming the writing of a prescription or the weighing of an aubergine. The difference must be largely to do with the fact that creative professions involving art, music, sport even are equated by many people with 'hobbies' that don't demand any particular commitment or lifelong dedication. It will be good when that perception changes.

There is another refrain that crops up with well-meant regularity. But woe betide you if you say it to Will Hunt, the frontman of electro band Dansette Junior. "I get this more from my friends' parents. They're your dad's 'biggest fan'...'Your dad was in ELO! Oh my God, I've got all their records.' Everyone always says they've got all their records.

"I've never met anyone who's actually got ALL their records. 'I've got all your dad's records!' 'Let's see 'em then... you've got one! The Best Of!" You'd better watch it before you come out with that particular cliché if Will's about – he will *not* let you get away with it.

Geography seems to make a difference to how often, and how ardently, one is approached. Almost everyone I spoke to about this told me that they are far more likely to be approached in America, although I wonder whether it is genre-specific too: there are plenty of British classic rock fans who are practically card-carrying 'how's-your-dadders'. Maybe in the UK, those who ask *that question* are probably going to be your die-hard fans, otherwise they'd be too shy generally to approach at all. They might have been working themselves up to a state in which they can muster up the confidence to even come up to you for several years. (NB: different rules may apply up north, where people are less scared of… well, other people.) In the friendly, more fame-focused US, on the other hand, if the person knows you, fan or not, they're impressed by your lineage and, bless their hearts, they're going to let you know about it.

"The English aren't really so bad at that," says pianist Harry Waters. "They're so polite, I get it a lot more in America. It's not that Americans are rude, but they just don't realise that it might be irritating to come up and go, 'I love your old man! He's awesome! How is he?' and I'm like, 'Yeah… thank you, I know he's all those things, and he's fine…'"

Crosby Loggins: "Touring Europe recently was a real eye opener for me. My father's career never transitioned to Europe. Asia, South America, even some of Eastern Europe, sure, but Western Europe has hardly ever heard of him. He can't get arrested in the EU and the UK couldn't care less. This made for a touring climate unlike any I had ever experienced before. Folks would actually start conversations with me that didn't include *Footloose* references."

While all this attention by proxy can start to pall, it's worth remembering that beyond the adoration lies the murkier side of obsession. That's never good. In this case, maybe too much acid was dropped in the Summer of Love and a belief that there is subliminal messaging in Soft Machine records has spiralled into full-blown mania. Who knows? All we do know is that it's at times like these that one might *long* for someone to cheerily ask after your father's well-being – stranger or not. "I've had negative stuff at gigs," says Galen Ayers. "Like some guy who went, 'I've fucked your mother and I'm going to kill your father.' You get weirdoes…" You don't say. Luckily these sort of chaps are in the tiny minority.

Steve Howe's eldest daughter, Georgia, isn't a musician, and so maybe doesn't feel the same trepidation when she is pounced on by a good-natured fan, and has a little more patience when it comes to breaking the fourth wall of fame and giving fans what they want in terms of insights and attention. "Fans just want a little sense of being closer to the star," she says. "You are a conduit in a way, and I am fine with that, I have my own stuff going on and appreciate people's interest in him. Hopefully they'll buy some music or a ticket, and then somewhere down the line I might get a nice Christmas present – it's all karma, man…"

But she too remembers some of her odder experiences with fans expressing an intense interest in her and her siblings occurring in America, New York to be specific. Georgia, who lives and works in New York now herself, says: "Some guys at the show wanted pictures with me and (sister) Steph and queued up by our seats for it – so awkward! They're relatively harmless though.

"Random people have said things to me like, 'Can I just touch you?', and held my hand, and messaged me on Facebook. That's where it gets annoying, but generally it's a nice response. Dad's particular about keeping family very separate, like if he gets recognised when out and about he never lets it get into a big conversation, which is good, even for the sake of being basically rude to the ecstatic fan!"

Georgia makes the interesting point that, in her position, she has a responsibility that comes with her outwardly glamorous pedigree. She sees herself as an ambassador for Steve Howe and Yes, a representative of sorts. "You kind of do a PR job as a musician's kid sometimes, if people don't know much about the band or the music you promote it very naturally. You need to make it relevant to people: 'Oh, they used their music in X film', or 'remember X song?', wheeling out the Eighties chart hit example for accessibility. It's in your interest to spread the word, and it helps you not really talk about yourself to a stranger.

"You're at the coalface of fan-management it feels like, sometimes. They ask you huge vague questions like, 'What's it like?' or geekily specific questions like what type of plectrum he used at some gig or what strings on some song, something I'd never know!

"They really want the stereotypes to be true, sometimes the easiest answers are what pleases them: "Yes, he has a recording studio in the English countryside, buys a plane seat for his favourite guitar and meditates before going onstage…"

Callum Adamson is questioned even more about his late father presumably because he is no longer here to face the adulation himself. "Everyone asks about my dad and wants to know about the rock star, but to me he was just my dad in a kilt," he says.

"Every artist has that, that's why *Spitting Image* is such a success because that's how people see them. They see the *Spitting Image* character. Sometimes it becomes almost like a religion to them. People have flown over from Germany to see me play acoustic gigs, and you feel really bad because you're like, 'I only meant to turn up here for half an hour and then I'm going to go for dinner… this wasn't a big deal for me. I'm so happy you came over and thank you very much, I'm sure my dad would have loved that you came over, but please stop.' Also, you know, if I'm shit then I'm quite happy to be shit on my own, without being shit next to that name…

"I grew up with this: 'Always be nice, don't tell anyone anything.' The first time I was able to go into town and buy a magazine, immediately, 'How's your dad?' 'Fine thanks,' 'Going on tour soon?' 'Oh, I'm not sure…' You get good at avoiding the point."

When the attention basically comes from a place of love, respect and guileless enthusiasm, well, it's difficult to get *really* grumpy. But when it appears to stem from a sense of ownership that overrides your own feelings, it can be harder to bear. When an icon dies, the grief can be felt universally, by people who never knew their hero but felt a strong sense of kinship. This shared expression of mourning might be a comfort and source of strength to the loved ones of the deceased. But it can also be easy to forget, for the more passionate fan at least, that someone else's anguish might be greater than yours.

Rosanne Cash, who lost her father, Johnny, in September 2003, four months after the death of his wife June Carter-Cash (Rosanne's stepmother), felt the inadvertently somewhat selfish advances of various fans to be inappropriate. "People took his death very personally. And although I appreciated that people felt so deeply about it, sometimes it was profoundly intrusive.

"People I didn't know at all would come up to me in a store and begin to cry about my father's death and not bother to say, 'I'm sorry you lost your dad.' They would just go on and on about their experience of Johnny Cash."

"I never resent my dad for being famous, but it's weird having to deal with those things," adds Callum Adamson, who had to face the reality of being practically under siege from the press after his father died in 2001. He had to put his own grieving on hold for the sake of putting on a brave face for the cameras.

"He was sober for the entire length of my life almost up until he died, and then he started drinking again and became this tragic rock star... now he is dead, he's fucking revered again, it's the weirdest thing to go through, three different stages of public perception.

"It's just strange because of the public attention – Dad dies and there are photographers outside your door, you don't get to have any quiet time, it's like 'smile zone', or stand there and be sombre and say things ... but what are you going to say? My dad died and I haven't come to terms with it yet? You can't say that."

Just like Georgia's 'PR ambassador' analogy, when a parent dies your job continues, becoming more intense as you are expected to speak for them all the more. While sometimes that involves defending them, most of the time you will simply be listening to other people talk about how fantastic he or she was, which, depending on your own relationship with your lost parent, can be frustrating and restrictive for you.

Julian Lennon has said that people approaching him in order to gush about how much they loved his father, who, in his eyes, was less than perfect, was something that always elicited "mixed feelings" for him. Now, however, he is feeling strong after what he describes as a "tough few decades", and his own sense of compassion and forgiveness towards John Lennon eclipses any bitterness he used to feel.

The main thing that irritates him now is "there's a lot of misinformation. Even now, in this day and age with technology, Sean and I get mistaken all the time, even though we're very different. People just don't research and don't follow through. That's something that at least along the way through interviews I've done in the past, I just try to tell the truth." 'How's your dad?' is all very well, but there's almost definitely a book to be written called, 'How's your brother?'"

John Lennon has long been seen as the ultimate star, and because of this Sean Lennon suffered the ultimate example of 'Never mind you, what about your dad?' And it was during his most important appearance:

he was basically just trying to be born. It was a difficult birth, in John's words: "because of a screw-up in the hospital and the price of fame. Somebody had made a transfusion of the wrong blood type into Yoko, she started to shake and go rigid. I ran up to this nurse and said, 'Get a doctor!' He walks in, hardly notices Yoko, goes straight for me, shakes my hand and says, 'I've always wanted to meet you, Mr Lennon, I always enjoyed your music...'"

To a lesser degree part of this might be seen as an unconscious passing over of the then not especially popular Yoko. There was an inherent possessiveness people felt about The Beatles when they got married: Yoko being the obvious example, but Cynthia went through it, as did Linda, as did Maureen – it wasn't easy to be a Beatles wife. In the case of seriously big stars like this, everybody is in their shadow, not just the children.

As Baxter Dury expressed in the last chapter, it often happens that those of a similar parentage come together and bond, the only people able to understand each other's very particular situation. "It is like a secret club," agrees Dylan Howe. "Even if you don't know each other very well, you appreciate something of what the other person has grown up with."

Sean Lennon and Rufus Wainwright became close friends, and they would often perform together in New York. They were fascinated by the symbiotic reaction they both had when they listened to each other's parents' work. They would listen to the records together, Rufus playing Loudon and Kate's records to Sean, and Sean playing John's to Rufus, and both would feel they were almost hearing something that was vicariously part of them.

In Ladbroke Grove, west London, there is something of a community of musicians' children including TV presenter Miquita Oliver (daughter of Andi Oliver of post-punk group Rip Rig and Panic's), Jet Letts (son of Don), Phoebe Oliver (daughter of The Slits' Tessa Pollitt and Rip Rig and Panic's Sean Oliver – she is Miquita's cousin), Maria Gallagher (Mickey's daughter), Baxter Dury, Hollie Cook (daughter of Sex Pistols' Paul), Lauren Jones (daughter of The Clash's Mick) and Joe Strummer's daughters Lola and Jazz, who find they are treated as curios far less because the people around them when they go out, or in their day-to-day lives, are just like them.

As Jazz maintains, the children of punkier stars such as The Clash or The Slits are more likely to hold the cards that point to their pedigrees close to their chests. The Ladbroke Grove set would often go to Gaz's Rockin' Blues at the St Moritz in Soho, a club night run by Gaz Mayall, son of Bluesbreakers' John (this was one place their parentage would never be a novelty), where they would often bump into fellow west Londoner (and famous-dad owner) Lily Allen, and Jazz would often run into her dad there too.

"I think all those children are well-adjusted because that's just what the bands were like," said Jazz. "We never grew up with notions of going partying, going out to be seen, it's not how we are. It may be because of the kind of parents we have, they were down to earth. It was more dirty and realistic. None of the punk kids are really doing that whole Peaches Geldof thing. Unless you class the Boomtown Rats as punk, ha ha ha!"

The parents' relationship with the press and their own visibility inevitably has an effect on whether the second generation court attention, hide from it or just ignore it. Aaron Horn's parents, Trevor Horn and Jill Sinclair, might have presided over the pop world in the Eighties but it was always work to them, and continues to be so for Aaron. "I'd rather work than go out. Dad's always been like that, he's never enjoyed going out. We'd come back from awards and mum would be like, 'I wouldn't do that if I didn't have to, I hate those things!' So whenever I've had opportunities to go to the Brit Awards, I'll go there if I have to; if I don't then I'm not going!

"There is a weird part of me that always wanted to go and do all those things, be cool and go to Bungalow or whatever the twat it is… there's the arrogant Jewish north London part of me that wants to do that, but maybe what it wants to do is sit here and think it wants to do that.

"When I find myself in those situations I usually last about half an hour. I do the same thing my dad does as well: 'Oh my God, it sounds horrific in here, I have to go!' I use my ears a lot, and when you get that thing, a nasty sound, then it's, 'Bye, I'm going,' it's painful.

"A lot of people do use (their status), and maybe if they're in *Heat* they feel they're pleasing their parents somehow, like it's the only way they can live up to them."

Jazz: "We're (herself and her sister Lola) not very commercial people. We like doing things that are a bit subculturey and independent. We find Peaches Geldof and that lot quite strange the way they kind of go to all the parties – what do they actually do? I guess they're just IT girls, aren't they?

"They're building their profiles and they get given huge amounts of money to do silly things. I remember me and Lola worked at this party for Hendricks Gin for people we knew from Las Vegas whom we'd met at Glastonbury. They asked us to do the tea and serve cakes, and provide atmosphere. (Jazz and Lola used to run the cult London tea-dance club night Viva Cake.)

"We went along and it was all fine, and then we heard Peaches Geldof was being paid ten grand to come and DJ. We were like, 'That is ridiculous!' It is clearly beneficial to go to these parties and be seen out. I think there is a big business side to it, very clever in a way."

Peaches' mother, Paula Yates, certainly did dance an almost daily pas de deux with the press, although most of the time they'd trip over each other's feet and crash down together in a salacious heap. She tantalised photographers with her 'Little Miss Trouble' T-shirt just as the papers were aflame with reports of her illicit romance with INXS frontman Michael Hutchence.

Hutchence, on the other hand, hated being a target for the press, and would often end up in violent scuffles with paparazzi, thus resulting in ever more coverage in the papers. But I was surprised when a friend of Fifi Geldof's told me of an occasion when Sir Bob Geldof was planning to wear a particularly provocative t-shirt himself "in order to get papped. That was the first time I'd ever heard anyone say anything like that, like you're actually courting the paparazzi by trying to be outlandish."

In a similar way to Princess Diana, it is fair to say that Yates in particular had a love-hate relationship with the newspapers. She tempted them towards her, but would be horror-stricken by their fervour, which, invariably, could be forceful, amoral and animalistic. It was like a coquette flashing at a sex offender and then being outraged when he tries to ravage her. She loved the attention, enjoyed scandalising middle England... but maybe she just didn't account for how the situation could turn, or indeed how any of it would affect her children until it was too late. As

Barry the Baptist said in *Lock, Stock And Two Smoking Barrels,* "when you dance with the devil, you wait for the song to stop". Some might argue the song is still on repeat: at the time of writing Peaches Geldof has won 'substantial damages' from *The Daily Star* after they printed a fictitious story about her being a high-class prostitute.

"Fifi was chased up our street by paparazzi," Yates wrote in her autobiography. "When she fell, they'd crowd around taking pictures, which they'd print with captions such as 'Fifi cries for her parents' lost marriage.' During my pregnancy (with Peaches) I experienced the venom of the press again. One paper ran a picture with me with the caption: 'One Geldof bastard is enough,' I cried for about a week."

"I didn't read any of it," said Bob, in a later interview with ABC, about that very quote. "That's the way you deal with the press. I absolutely go along with an utterly free press. Intellectually, it must be so... you have to accept everything that goes with it, and I do. But you also have to trust that maybe they'll just be humans a little bit, and sometimes they're not, and they forget their humanity."

It cannot have escaped many people's attention that Peaches has seemingly placed herself numerous times in the hands of the press in a similar way. Plenty of stories are constructed purely from recycled bits of gristle, glitter and muck that constitute the warped imaginations of this country's less honourable journalists, but they don't seem to make up stories about people who don't put themselves out there in the first place, and as Jazz noted, the people who throw themselves into the West End party merry-go-round are far from spontaneous about it – it's quite an organised process. Indeed, the whole roller-coaster ride can become self-perpetuating on an ever-increasing spiral: the more you appear in the press, the more the public take an interest and the more papers are sold, hence the more you appear in the press...

Natascha Eleanore had her first taste of the "party clique" at the Cream reunion in 2005. Cream is very much a family affair for Natascha, so she was amazed she didn't recognise 90 per cent of the champagne-quaffing guests at the after show. "Loads of young people, real socialites, the party clique... I guess they just get put on these guest lists that are around all the time," she muses. (I for one would be very interested in hearing what their favourite Cream albums are...)

"It was just a really weird experience. The show was amazing, then they put on this after party near Buckingham Palace in the Mall, and there were all these people that knew each other, and I was like, 'I don't know anyone here – there's only three people in the band and one of them's my dad!'

"I was thinking, 'I guess this is how they live all the time.' It's cool but very different to how I grew up."

One rock star's daughter, who shall remain nameless, contacted Georgia Howe to see if she "wanted to 'get on the scene' with her, I think this involved getting tarted up and hanging around members clubs in Mayfair trying to get in tabloids. I politely declined."

There does seem to be a rather worrying gender divide: the daughters of rock royalty are photographed and praised, sometimes derided, all based on what they look like, how they dress, and how they behave on a night out. The sons tend not to be photographed quite so much (unless they lamp someone or dress in drag). But they do seem to get taken more seriously, or at least, they're left alone by the press to a greater extent, and are allowed to just get on with whatever it is they're doing. In some cases it isn't even assumed that the daughters *are* doing anything of interest, other than being girls...

"If you look at the Jaggers, or the Woods, people aren't really interested in Tyrone Wood even though he's cute," says *OK!*'s Elizabeth Curran. "James Jagger, no one is interested. But the girls, is it just because they're girls and they're pretty? I guess maybe. Men's magazines wouldn't celebrate rock star kids generally, although *Maxim* did that 'DILF' thing – 'Daughter I'd Like To Fuck' with Nick Mason's daughters... it was really gross actually."

Georgia Howe: "The most hilarious occasion was at that Prince's Trust thing at Wembley Arena a few years back, when Trevor Horn brought all those bands together (*Produced By Trevor Horn* in 2004, featuring Yes, Frankie Goes To Hollywood, Seal, Propaganda, ABC among others). The after show was at Boujis in South Ken no less – Steph and I got our pictures taken for *OK!* magazine whereas Virgil actually got to talk to the musicians about music..."

Aaron Horn spent his own childhood "getting bored" waiting for pop stars to turn up to the studio, resenting Seal for getting in the way of a family holiday and seeing celebrities "get above their station", so he is the perfect person to prime his younger sister for what may lie ahead. "My sister Gabrielle is still at school, and she is just starting to understand celebrity culture. I'm not celebrity-minded. It had the reverse effect on me. I can't chill around people, so I have this kind of inversion, I'm quite rude to celebrities I don't like.

"They'd fuck me over, it'd be like, Grace Jones would show up late for dinner and everyone's pissed off, or some pop star and him (Trevor) would have a moody one, so it would be summer holiday ruined, 'We're going back to London.' 'Fucking dick…' It would impact on me directly. So that was why I didn't really want to get into it in the beginning, because it was full of wankers. I saw them for who they were.

"I've tried to imprint that approach on my siblings a bit, but then they've had a different experience, there have been more tickets to things, more 'celebrities' eating at our house. The Teenage Mutant Ninja Turtles weren't eating at my house when I was my sister's age but if they had have been, *I* would probably be different! But they don't abuse it.

"People have illusions that other people have something better in life, but no, life is tough, it's not easier if you're 'famous', it's just different."

Paula Yates understandably spent plenty of time cogitating on how people are treated as a result of exposure and status within the public eye. The following quote, from her autobiography, bears a message that, whatever you thought of her, has a significance for everyone featured within these pages, whether they are well known themselves or not.

"Many things happen as we get older. We acquire more compassion… suddenly you realise nothing is black and white. It becomes impossible to be truly judgmental of people because you realise how little you ever know about what goes on in people's homes and how they live together."

This book isn't just a bid to appreciate the progeny of notable figures as individuals in their own right, but to look beyond what we see on the surface in this era of the snap judgement and the short attention span … and maybe, if we get the opportunity, ask what *they* are up to, before we venture into the territory of asking about anyone else.

"It's only by going through all of this that I've started to consider what it really means," says Dylan Howe. "In a way, it's disassembled the star-making machinery – it's just people who love doing what they're doing. Maybe we didn't have a lot of the blocks that are put onto people creatively or intellectually in our early years.

"It's about authenticity. To be a credible person you don't have to come from nothing and ascend in this sort of arc and become the hero. Who is the real thing? What is the real deal? We're fooled a lot by how that is portrayed and how we feel we're supposed to see things. It's about doing what is natural to you, something you love to do. If you are steeped in something from being a child and that's second nature, then that's what it is.

"Anyway, I've decided I'm going to get some T-shirts for myself and a few choice family and friends, and print on the front, 'He's fine thanks'…"

Who's Who?
... And What They Do

Callum Adamson
(Born 1983) Singer-songwriter, founding member of indie band Ahab. Son of Big Country and Skids frontman Stuart Adamson and his wife, Sandra.
www.myspace.com/ahabmyspace

Galen Ayers
Singer-songwriter, one half of the folk-pop duo Siskin with Kirsty Newton. Also a graduate with an MA in Buddhism. She has collaborated with Talking Heads' Chris Frantz and Tina Weymouth.
www.myspace.com/siskinmusic

Kofi Baker
(Born 1969) Drummer and drum teacher based in California. Also leads a band called Tribute To Cream. Son of Ginger Baker and his first wife, Elizabeth.
www.myspace.com/tributetocream
www.kofibaker.com/

Celeste Bell
(Born 1981) Singer-songwriter, former English teacher and frontwoman

239

of punk-soul band Debutant Disco, and is based in Madrid, Spain. Daughter of X Ray Spex singer Poly Styrene.
www.myspace.com/debutantdisco

Rolan Bolan

(Born 1975) Recording artist and model. He released his latest single, 'Fire In The City', in October 2009. Son of Marc Bolan and Gloria Jones.
www.rolanbolan.com

Chaz Bono

Born in 1969 as Chastity Sun Bono. Author, actor and musician, who has had a turbulent journey in the public eye, from being initially outed as a lesbian in the early Nineties by the US tabloids to undergoing a sex change in 2009. Born to Cher and Sonny Bono.

Jeff Buckley

(Born 1966) Singer-songwriter, guitarist. Beloved for his version of Leonard Cohen's 'Hallelujah', featured on his 1994 album *Grace*. Drowned in 1997 in the Wolf River in Memphis, Tennessee. Son of Tim Buckley and Mary Guibert.
www.jeffbuckley.com

Alexandra Burke

(Born 1988) Singer, winner of *The X Factor* in 2008. She became the first British female solo artist to sell a million copies of a single in the UK when sales of her version of 'Hallelujah' passed 1 million by January 9, 2009. Burke is the daughter of former Soul II Soul lead singer Melissa Bell and David Burke.
www.alexandraburkeofficial.com

Eliza Carthy

(Born 1975) Singer and fiddle-player and recording artist, mother to Florence (born in January 2009). Tours prolifically (with baby in tow). Daughter of British folk icons Norma Waterson and Martin Carthy.
www.eliza-carthy.com

Rosanne Cash

(Born 1955) Grammy-award-winning singer-songwriter and country star. She also works with various charitable organisations including PAX, an organisation dedicated to stopping gun crime and SOS Children's Villages, a charity her father and stepmother, June Carter-Cash, were regular benefactors of. Her most recent project is the album *The List*, based on a selection of 'top essential country songs' her father gave her to listen to when she was 18. Daughter of Johnny Cash and his first wife, Vivian Liberto Cash Distin.

www.rosannecash.com

Jethro Cave

(Born 1991) Model. He only met his father when he was seven or eight, but they are now close. He would also like to "throttle" anyone who thinks he's a "lucky little rich kid". Son of Nick Cave and Beau Lazenby.

Frances Bean Cobain

(Born 1992) Seventeen at the time of writing, Frances Bean Cobain has already been featured in numerous photo-shoots (including the infamous shoot for *Elle* in which she posed in her late father's pyjamas). Daughter of Kurt Cobain and Courtney Love.

Calico Cooper

(Born 1981) Actress and performer in Alice Cooper's touring 'Cooper show'. Member of the improvised theatre group the Upright Citizens Brigade. Daughter of Alice Cooper and Sheryl Goddard.

www.calicocooper.com

Natalie Curtis

(Born 1979) Photographer. Work tends to be based on Mancunian artists such as Elbow and Doves. Her photographic mentor was the Manchester music photographer Kevin Cummins. Daughter of Joy Division frontman Ian Curtis and his wife, Deborah Woodruff.

www.16apr79.com

Christian Davies

(Born 1973) Reiki practitioner, massage therapist and trance music DJ based in north London. Born to The Kinks' Dave Davies and his first wife, Lisbet.

Baxter Dury

(Born 1972) Singer and musician, signed to Rough Trade who, he has said with some relief, had little to no interest in who his father was. Son of Ian Dury and his first wife, Betty Rathmell. New album pending at the time of writing, featuring Portishead's Adrian Utley.
www.myspace.com/baxterdury

Jakob Dylan

(Born 1969) Singer-songwriter, pianist, guitarist. Erstwhile frontman of The Wallflowers. Collaborated with Dhani Harrison on the John Lennon song 'Gimme Some Truth' in 2007 for the Lennon tribute album *Instant Karma* in aid of Darfur. Son of Bob Dylan and his first wife, Sara Lownds.
www.jakobdylan.com

Natascha Eleanore

(Born 1982) Eleanore is a politically conscious reggae-influenced singer-songwriter performing under the name Aruba Red. She is the elder daughter of Cream frontman Jack Bruce and his second wife, Margrit Seyffer.
www.myspace.com/arubaredmusic

Lovella Ellis

Singer-songwriter proudly continuing her father's musical legacy since his death in 2008. Daughter of Studio One legend Alton and Sigma Ellis. (Birth year not disclosed.)
www.myspace.com/lovellaellis

Anna-Marie Gabriel

(Born 1974) Film-maker. Has directed her father's music videos including Play, which features Kate Bush. Created the now sought-after

DVD *Growing Up On Tour – A Family Portrait*. She is the daughter of Peter Gabriel and his first wife, Jill Moore.

Jack Gahan

(Born 1988) Works for LiveNation. Also a guitarist and songwriter. Son of Dave Gahan and his first wife, Joanne Fox.

Charlotte Gainsbourg

(Born 1971) Actress and singer-songwriter. Released her third solo studio album, *IRM,* produced by Beck, in 2009. Daughter of Serge Gainsbourg and Jane Birkin.
www.charlottegainsbourg.com

Maria Gallagher

(Born 1976) At the time of writing, working towards a degree in social work with a view to a career in youth justice. Also helps unofficially with the management of her daughter, Amy Grace's, band The West Borns. Daughter of Blockheads/Clash organist Mickey Gallagher.
Her brothers, Luke and Ben, were formerly in the band Little Mothers. Luke, a bass player, works with the Blockheads, sometimes deputising for Norman Watt Roy. Ben has his own group, My Second Head.
http://www.myspace.com/littlemothers
http://www.myspace.com/mysecondhead

Theresa 'Trixie' Garcia

(Born 1974) Artist. Daughter of Grateful Dead frontman Jerry Garcia and Carolyn 'Mountain Girl' Adams.

Peaches Geldof (born Peaches Honeyblossom Michelle Charlotte Angel Vanessa Geldof)

(Born 1989) TV personality, columnist, model, socialite. Most recently successfully sued the *Daily Star* for libel over claims she was a "prostitute". She also had to apologise to distraught Miley Cyrus fans in December 2009 after posting on Twitter that the American actress and daughter of country pop star Billy Ray had died, causing widespread panic. "Turns out it was a rumour…" she wrote. Second daughter of Bob Geldof and Paula Yates.

Pixie Geldof (born Little Pixie Geldof)
(Born 1990) Model, socialite. Said to be named after a character in the *Private Eye* cartoon 'Celeb', which was itself a spoof of the names the Geldofs gave their children. Third daughter of Bob Geldof and Paula Yates.

Fifi Trixibelle Geldof
(Born 1983) PR/online media consultant. The least conspicuous Geldof, and, according to Bob, the most like him. Eldest daughter of Bob Geldof and Paula Yates

Kilauren Gibb
(Born 1965) Former model. Given up for adoption soon after her birth, but reunited with her mother in recent years. Daughter of Joni Mitchell and Brad MacMath.

Charlie Harris
(Born 1977) PR manager at Music Sales Ltd, after working at MTV. Daughter of 'Whispering' Bob Harris and Jackie Harris (designer of the Sloppy Joe sweatshirt).
www.musicsales.com

Dhani Harrison
(Born 1978) Musician, has his own band, thenewno2. Made his professional debut when he produced *Brainwashed,* his father's final album in 2001. Dhani Harrison was also involved in the development of the music video game *The Beatles: Rock Band,* and is said to be instrumental in having persuaded Paul McCartney and Ringo Starr to get involved. Son of George Harrison and his second wife, Olivia Trinidad Arias.
www.absolutelydhaniharrison.com
www.thenewno2.com

Aaron Horn
(Born 1984) Producer, programmer and DJ based in north London. Has mixed for The Kooks, thecocknbullkid and Crystal Fighter. Son of ZTT bosses Trevor Horn and Jill Sinclair.
www.dogbotpublishing.com
www.myspace.com/peaceloveaudio

Dylan Howe

(Born 1969) Session drummer, jazz musician, bandleader, composer. Best known for his jazz quintet and other projects, including a 're-imagining' of David Bowie's *Low* and *'Heroes'* and an adaptation of Stravinsky for piano and drums. Joined the Blockheads in 1998 and in 2009 Wilko Johnson's trio. Eldest son of Yes guitarist Steve Howe (they have a trio together too).

www.dylanhowe.com

www.myspace.com/dylanhowe

Georgia Howe

(Born 1982) Strategist for Redscout/MDC Communications in New York. Formerly worked for advertising agency BBH. Eldest daughter of Steve and Jan Howe.

Stephanie Howe

(Born 1986) Currently studying anthropology. Youngest daughter of Steve and Jan Howe.

Virgil Howe

(Born 1975) Musician and DJ, drummer in The Dirty Feel and Meters tribute band The Killer Meters. Youngest son of Steve Howe and Jan Howe.

www.myspace.com/thedirtyfeel

Will Hunt

(Born 1981) Musician and singer-song-writer, member of electro-pop band Dansette Junior. Son of ELO/Wizzard/The Move star Bill Hunt, cousin of Wonderstuff's Miles Hunt.

www.myspace.com/dansettejunior

(Heavenly Hiraani) Tiger Lily Hutchence–Geldof

(Born 1996) Only 13 at the time of writing. Daughter of Paula Yates and Michael Hutchence, but taken in by Bob Geldof after the death of both parents.

Prince, Paris and Blanket Jackson
Still only 12, 11 and 7 respectively, they lost their father, Michael Jackson, in 2009 and at the time of writing are "in therapy", according to their aunt La Toya.

James Jagger
(Born 1985)
Model and actor. Starred as the Blockheads guitarist Johnny Turnbull in the 2010 Ian Dury biopic, *Sex & Drugs & Rock & Roll.* Eldest son of Mick Jagger and Jerry Hall.

Duncan Jones
(Born 1971) Film director, best known for directing the 2009 sci-fi movie *Moon,* which starred Sam Rockwell. He changed his name from Zowie Bowie to Duncan Jones when he was 18. He is at the time of writing directing another sci-fi movie, *Mute,* and is to direct Summit Entertainment's *Source Code,* with Jake Gyllenhaal slated to take a lead role. Son of David and Angie Bowie (Mary Angela Barnett).
twitter.com/manMadeMoon

Norah Jones
(Born 1979) Singer-songwriter of the dinner-party jazz persuasion. Had little to do with her father growing up, as she was brought up solely by her mother. Daughter of concert producer Sue Jones and sitar player Ravi Shankar (she is the half-sister of sitar-player Anoushka Shankar).
www.norahjones.com/

Quincy Delight Jones III (QD3)
(Born 1968) Composer, hip-hop producer and writer. Regarded as a pioneer of the hip-hop scene in Sweden, where he was brought up. Recorded and co-produced the Grammy-winning album *Back on the Block* with his father in 1989 and most recently produced a Lil' Wayne DVD documentary, *The Carter,* and launched the Global Innovation Tournament at the Stanford Memorial Auditorium with fellow urban artist Chamillionaire. Son of Quincy Jones II and Ulla Andersson.
www.myspace.com/qdiesel

HarleyMoon Kemp
(Born 1989) Fashion and music photographer, also a songwriter. Daughter of Martin Kemp and his wife, Shirlie Holliman.
harleymoonkemp.com

Cosmo Landesman
(Born 1958) London-based American *Sunday Times* movie reviewer and author son of counterculture pioneers Fran and Jay Landesman. Formerly married to writer Julie Burchill.

Julian Lennon
(Born 1963) Musician, singer-songwriter. Making a return to music in 2010 after over a decade away from the public eye. He put together the *White Feather* exhibition of his father's possessions and photographs, and is the founder of the humanitarian White Feather Foundation. Son of John Lennon and Cynthia (nee Powell).
www.whitefeatherfoundation.com
www.julianlennon.com

Sean Lennon
(Born 1975) Musician, artist, collaborates with his mother in the newly revived Plastic Ono Band as well as working on his own solo projects with the likes of Vincent Gallo and Petra Haden (daughter of jazz bass player Charlie). Son of John Lennon and Yoko Ono.
www.seanonolennon.com

Lourdes Ciccone Leon
(Born 1996) Just 13 at the time of writing, but has enrolled in an acting school and has appeared in her mother's music videos in recent years. Daughter of Madonna Ciccone and Carlos Leon.

Crosby Loggins
(Born 1981) Singer-songwriter. Released his debut album, *We All Go Home,* in 2007. Winner of MTV show *Rock The Cradle.* He has also been touring with fellow LA singer-songwriters Caitlin Crosby and Jay Nash. Eldest son of Kenny Loggins and his first wife, Eva Ein.
www.crosbyloggins.com

Daisy Lowe
(Born 1989) Model since the age of two. Worked with Chanel, Vivienne Westwood, Burberry, Agent Provocateur and Marc Jacobs among others. Co-hosted *Glamour's Best-Dressed* with Peaches Geldof for Channel Five. Daughter of Pearl Lowe and Gavin Rossdale.

Trev Lukather
(Born 1988) Guitarist and songwriter. Former musical director for Lindsay Lohan. Son of session supremo and Toto guitar legend Steve Lukather and actress Marie Currie.
www.myspace.com/trevlukather

Mary McCartney
(Born 1969) Photographer and passionate animal rights campaigner. Her first job was working as a photo editor for Omnibus Press, before she went on to be a photographer in her own right. She has also directed and produced music videos, and now runs the picture department at her father's company, MPL Communications. Eldest daughter of Paul McCartney and photographer Linda Eastman.
www.marymccartney.com

Stella McCartney
(Born 1971) Fashion designer and animal rights campaigner. Has designed clothes for Madonna and Annie Lennox's tours, and her work is adored by the celebrity set. Caused a stir when she appeared to make a statement on her father's misguided choice of second wife, Heather Mills, by designing a necklace with a single leg on it. Daughter of Paul McCartney and Linda Eastman.
www.stellamccartney.com

Kirsty MacColl
(Born 1959) Singer-songwriter, collaborator with The Pogues and The Smiths. Daughter of Euan MacColl and Jean Newlove. (Died 2000 in a boating accident in Mexico.)
www.justiceforkirsty.org

Jazz Domino Holly (Mellor)

(Born 1983) Founder and president of the Shoreditch Sisters Women's Institute. At the time of writing she is also writing a book about the return of domestic arts. Eldest daughter of Joe Strummer and Gaby Salter.

shoreditchsisterswi.typepad.com

Aimee Osbourne

(Born 1983) Writer and actress. Starred in the 2003 MTV movie adaptation of *Wuthering Heights* and now writes for *Nylon* magazine. Eldest child of Ozzy and Sharon Osbourne. (née Arden).

Jack Osbourne

(Born 1985) TV personality and presenter of the stunt-packed ITV series *Adrenaline Junkie*. Son of Ozzy Osbourne and Sharon Osbourne

www.myspace.com/jackosbourne

Kelly Osbourne

(Born 1984) TV personality, singer, actress. Most recently appeared in *Dancing With The Stars*, but has also appeared in the West End musical *Chicago* as Mama Morton. She wrote an autobiography, *Fierce,* which was published in 2009. Youngest daughter of Ozzy Osbourne and Sharon Osbourne.

www.kellyosbourne.com

Scarlet Page

(Born 1971) Rock photographer. She also took pictures for the animal charity PDSA calendar, entitled 'Pet Pawtraits', of celebrities and their pets. Daughter of Jimmy Page and Charlotte Martin.

www.scarletpage.com

Chynna Phillips

(Born 1968) Singer and actress, one third of the Eighties pop band Wilson Phillips with Carnie and Wendy Wilson (Brian Wilson's daughters). Now performing as a duo: Chynna & Vaughan (with singer Vaughan Penn).

Half-sister of Mackenzie Phillips. Daughter of Mamas and Papas stars John and Michelle Phillips.
www.myspace.com/chynnaandvaughan

Mackenzie Phillips
(Born 1959) TV actress and former member of the 'new' Mamas and Papas during the Eighties. Most recently made headlines after her autobiography, *High On Arrival,* hit the shelves in 2009, as it detailed, among other things, her 10-year consensual sexual relationship with her father. Daughter of John Phillips and his first wife, Susan Adams.
www.myspace.com/mackenziephillips1

Lisa Marie Presley
(Born 1968) Singer-songwriter. Lisa Marie has most recently been collaborating with the British recording artist Richard Hawley after relocating to England. Daughter of Elvis Presley and Priscilla (née Wagner).
www.lisapresley.com

Marlon Richards
(Born 1969) Artist and model. Son of Keith Richards and Anita Pallenberg.

Jez, Ben, Nat and Tally Spencer
Musicians and founding members of the alt rock band Jynxt. Siblings who escaped the Children of God cult. Sons and daughters of former Fleetwood Mac guitarist Jeremy Spencer and his then wife, Fiona.
www.last.fm/music/Jynxt

Zak Starkey
(Born 1965) Drummer, playing with The Who and previously Oasis, Paul Weller, The Lightning Seeds, Ringo Starr and his All-Starr Band, Johnny Marr & The Healers. Eldest son of Ringo Starr and Maureen Starkey (nee Cox).

Kimberly Stewart
(Born 1979) Model, fashion designer and actress. As well as appearing in *The Osbournes* and *Cribs,* she had her own reality TV show, *Living*

With Kimberly Stewart on Living TV in 2007. Describes herself on her Myspace page as 'daughter of rock'. Daughter of Rod Stewart and Alana Stewart (née Collins).
www.myspace.com/misskimberlystewart

Ruby Stewart
(Born 1987) Lingerie model for Ultimo. Daughter of Rod Stewart and Kelly Emberg.

Coco Sumner
(Born 1990) Originally Eliot Pauline Sumner, Coco is a musician, model and actress. Her 2010 debut single, 'Caesar', under her musical guise I Blame Coco, features Swedish pop star Robyn on vocals. She has also performed with Peter Doherty. Coco is the daughter of Sting and Trudie Styler.
www.iblamecoco.co.uk

Ben Taylor
(Born 1977) Musician and actor. Tours and records with The Ben Taylor Band, which features Larry Ciancia on drums. He also collaborates with his sister Sally Taylor. Ben is trained in martial arts and refers to his particular musical style as 'Kung Folk'. He is the son of Carly Simon and James Taylor.
www.bentaylormusic.com

Emma Townshend
(Born 1969) Journalist, lecturer and *Independent On Sunday* gardening columnist. Author of *Darwin's Dogs: How Darwin's Pets Helped Form A World-Changing Theory of Evolution*. Eldest daughter of Pete Townshend and his first wife, Karen Astley.
emmatownshend.independentminds.livejournal.com

Laura Tuckey
(Born 1983) Sings as a guest vocalist with her father's blues–rock band, Legend, and is the mother of a daughter, Amy. Daughter of Suzi Quatro and Len Tuckey.

Liv Tyler

(Born 1977) Model and actress since the age of 14, most recently appearing as Betty Ross in *The Incredible Hulk* (2008). She is also a UNICEF goodwill ambassador. Daughter of Aerosmith's Steve Tyler and Bebe Buell.

Wolfgang Van Halen

(Born 1991) Bass player who has been in Van Halen since 2006, replacing Michael Anthony. Often seen on stage with his shirt off… he's young. Son of Eddie Van Halen and actress Valerie Bertinelli.
www.myspace.com/wolfgangvanhalen

Oliver Wakeman

(Born 1972) Keyboard player, has taken his father's place in both Yes and The Strawbs in recent years. He appears on The Strawbs' 2009 album, *Dancing To The Devil's Beat*. Son of Rick Wakeman and first wife, Ros Woolford.
www.oliver-wakeman.co.uk

Martha Wainwright

(Born 1976) Singer-songwriter, and part of the Wainwright/McGarrigle folk dynasty alongside her brother Rufus. Her most recent project is a tribute to Edith Piaf, *Sans Fusils, Ni Souliers, A Paris*. Daughter of Loudon Wainwright and Kate McGarrigle.
www.marthawainwright.com

Rufus Wainwright

(Born 1973) Singer-songwriter from Canadian folk dynasty (although his particular genre is known as 'baroque pop'). His latest project is an album scheduled for a 2010 release: *All Days Are Nights: Songs For Lulu*. Son of Loudon Wainwright and Kate McGarrigle.
www.rufuswainwright.com

Casey Waits

(Born 1987) Drummer, plays in his father, Tom's, group, and is featured on Tom Waits' hit 2004 album, *Real Gone*.

Harry Waters
(Born 1976) Jazz pianist and Hammond organ player, also plays keyboards in his father's solo band. Son of Roger Waters and his second wife, Carolyn Christie.
www.harrywaters.co.uk

India Waters
(Born 1978) Model. Both she and her brother Harry appear on their father's 1987 solo record, *Radio Kaos*. Daughter of Roger Waters and Carolyn Christie.

Carnie Wilson
(Born 1968) Singer and TV chat-show presenter. One third of the chart-topping pop band Wilson Phillips, with her sister Wendy and friend Chynna Phillips. She launched her solo career with an album of lullabies in 2007 – *A Mother's Gift: Lullabies From The Heart* – dedicated to her baby daughter, Lola. She is the daughter of Brian Wilson and Marilyn Rovell.
www.carniewilson.com

Wendy Wilson
(Born 1969) Singer and co-founder of Wilson Phillips. She has also been writing dance tracks. Daughter of Brian Wilson and Marilyn Rovell.
www.carnieandwendywilson.com

Jesse Wood
(Born 1976) Model and guitarist with The Leah Wood Band (his sister), The Ronnie Wood Band and his own band, The Black Swan Effect. Son of Ronnie Wood and his first wife, Krissie Findlay.
www.theblackswaneffect.com

Leah Wood
(Born 1978) Model, singer and artist. Daughter of Ronnie Wood and his second wife, Jo (née Karslake).
www.leahwood.com

Ahmet Zappa

(Born 1974). Writer and actor. First children's novel, *The Monstrous Memoirs Of A Mighty McFearless*, was published in 2006, and he is writing a sequel. Disney bought the movie rights to the original book, and the film will be released in 2011. Zappa is also an executive producer of the 2011 movie version of *Fraggle Rock*. He is the son of Frank Zappa and Gail Sloatman.
www.ahmetzappa.com

Diva Zappa

(Born 1979) Describes herself as an actress and a "knitress", making hand-made knitted and crocheted garments for her own company, Hand Made Beauty. Youngest daughter of Frank Zappa and Gail Sloatman.
www.divazappa.com

Dweezil Zappa

(Born 1969) Musician, inventor and composer. Guitarist currently touring the 'Zappa Plays Zappa' show, celebrating his father's music. Eldest son of Frank Zappa and Gail Sloatman.
www.zappaplayszappa.com
www.dweezilzappa.com

Moon Zappa

(Born 1967) Actress and writer. She has famously starred in *Curb Your Enthusiasm* and *Roseanne,* and wrote the 2001 novel *America The Beautiful,* which she has recently denied has anything to do with her own experiences of a bohemian childhood. Eldest daughter of Frank Zappa and Gail Sloatman.
moonzappa.com

Bibliography, Sources

Elvis By The Presleys – Priscilla Beaulieu Presley, Lisa Marie Presley, David Ritz (Editor) (Arrow Books, 2006)

The Real Frank Zappa Book by Frank Zappa and Peter Occhiogrosso (Fireside, 1990)

Zappa by Barry Miles (Grove Press, 2004)

High On Arrival by Mackenzie Phillips (Simon Spotlight Entertainment, 2009)

Ordinary People: Our Story by Ozzy, Sharon, Aimee, Kelly and Jack Osbourne, with Todd Gold. (Simon and Schuster, 2004)

Starstruck – Fame, Failure, My Family And Me by Cosmo Landesman (Macmillan, 2008)

Here Comes The Sun: The Spiritual And Musical Journey Of George Harrison – Joshua M Greene (Wiley, 2006)

Heavier Than Heaven – A Biography Of Kurt Cobain by Charles R Cross (Hyperion, 2002)

Paula Yates – The Autobiography by Paula Yates (HarperCollins 1995)

Paula, Michael and Bob: Everything You Know Is Wrong by Gerry Agar (Michael O'Mara 2004)

Wouldn't It Be Nice? My Own Story by Brian Wilson, with Todd Gold (HarperCollins 1991)

Ringo Starr: A Life by Alan Clayson (Sanctuary 2001)

Ronnie: The Autobiography by Ronnie Wood (Macmillan 2007)

21 Years Gone: The Autobiography by Jack Osbourne (Macmillan, 2006)

John by Cynthia Lennon (Crown, 2005)

Woman: The Incredible Life Of Yoko Ono by Alan Clayson, Barb Jungr, Robb Johnson (Chrome Dreams, 2004)

There Will Be Rainbows by Kirk Lake (Orion 2009)

Michael Jackson, The Magic And The Madness by J.Randy Taraborrelli, (Hachette, updated 2009)

'411 Music Interview: Quincy Jones III (QD3)' October 25, 2007, Tony Farinella, 411Mania.com

'Suddenly the reality hit me', September 22, 2007. Natalie Curtis, *The Guardian*

'Jeff Buckley: Heir Apparent To…' 1994, Ray Rogers, *Interview Magazine*

'Forget Guitar Hero, it takes a lot to be a pro' October 3, 2008, Emma Townshend, *The Times*

'Band on the run with rock'n'roll in their blood' October 29, 2005, Tim Cooper, *The Times*

'My Daddy of Britpop by Marc Bolan's son' September 20, 2007, David Wigg, *Daily Mail*

Bob Geldof interview with Andrew Denton, April 2005, *ABC*

'Johnny Cash's Daughter No Fan of Film', January 23, 2006, Stephen M Silverman, *People*

'The name retains the fame – an interview with Jason Bonham' Bruce Deerhake and Mike Houpt, *Oldbuckeye.com*

http://rosannecash.com/thelist/

Love Magazine Fall/Winter 2009 – Coco Sumner

'Oh Madonna, why are you turning your little girl into a pouting clone?' September 3, 2009, Richard Price, *Daily Mail*

'A Family Tree With Way Too Many Tangled Branches' June 12, 2008, Phil Bolsta, http://bolstablog.wordpress.com/

'Stella McCartney: 'Fashion people are pretty heartless'', October 5, 2009, Jess Cartner-Morley, *G2*

'Enfant terrible: Charlotte Gainsbourg on *Antichrist*' July 11, 2009, Martyn Palmer, *The Times*

'The Secret World of Serge Gainsbourg' November 2007, Lisa Robinson, *Vanity Fair*

'Relative Values: Suzi Quatro and her daughter, Laura Tuckey' August 19, 2007, Danny Danziger, *Sunday Times*

'Daisy Lowe: not just another It girl' October 3, 2009, Johnny Davis, *The Times*

'They fuck you up, your mum and dad' March 18 2005, Will Hodgkinson *The Guardian* (Martha Wainwright interview)

'Dhani Harrison Talks Growing Up Around Dad's Famous Friends' June 11, 2009, Steve Baltin, *Spinnermusic.co.uk*

'A Family Affair', May 9, 2003, Will Hodgkinson, *The Guardian*

www.familyzepp.piczo.com

www.ocweekly.com (Kofi Baker interview)

'Hank Jr's daughter wants you 'Here With Me'' June 10, 2009, Michael Bialas, NoDepression.com – The Roots Music Authority